Annotated Teacher's Edition

Be A Better Reader

Level B/Seventh Edition

Contents

Printed in the United States of America

6 7 8 9 10 00 01

ISBN 0-8359-1921-8

C12

Globe Fearon Educational Publishers
A Division of Simon & Schuster
Upper Saddle River, New Jersey

A Classroom Tradition For Over Three Decades

Be A Better Reader

By Nila Banton Smith

***NEW!* The Seventh Edition of Nila Banton Smith's Classic Program**

- **Teaches the reading, comprehension, and study skills that students in grades 4-12 need**
- **Applies these skills to the content areas:**
  - Literature
  - Social Studies
  - Science
  - Mathematics
- **Lessons always begin with instruction** so that students learn successfully (and independently) before they apply a skill.
- **Focuses on one important skill in each Lesson** so that students concentrate on a skill and master it—independently.

- **Reading, comprehension, and study skills include:**

  literal comprehension

  interpretive and inferential comprehension

  critical and creative reading

  main idea

  cause and effect

  fact and opinion

  sequencing

  details

  literary concepts (such as plot and theme)

  following directions

  graphic and pictorial aids

  locating information

  reading symbols

  previewing

  outlining

  classifying

  problem solving

  reading rate

  and much more

- **Student independence** Instruction is in the student's book, so that students work and learn *independently*.

- **Each unit follows the same structure** so that students know what to expect and can work independently:

  A Lesson with a literature selection

  A Lesson with a social studies selection

  A Lesson with a science selection

  A Lesson with a mathematics selection

  Several brief "worksheet" Lessons that reinforce important phonics (in levels A–C), comprehension, and study skills

- **Vocabulary Instruction** Students learn vocabulary words *before* they read. Students also learn to use different types of *context clues* to increase vocabulary power: definitions, synonyms, antonyms, appositives, details, comparisons and contrasts, examples, and similes.

- **Easy to manage in your classroom** Use with individual students, small groups, or the entire class. *Be A Better Reader* is used successfully with students working below level, on level, and above level. (Level A—grade 4 reading level, Level B—grade 5, and so on to Level F—grade 9.)

- **Lessons may be used in any order** Correlate Lessons to your curriculum. Use them for reinforcement of specific skills or as a complete program.

- **Each Lesson ends with a Real Life Connection** that applies what students have learned to their own lives, communities, or interests.

- **Each unit ends with a brief Lesson on a practical life or school-to-work skill,** such as how to fill out a job application and order form; how to read a bus schedule, floor plan, map, and help wanted ads; and how to follow directions.

- **Assessment tests are free** in the *Annotated Teacher's Edition* (Level A—F).

First, a sample
Be A Better Reader
Lesson with

Instruction first on one comprehension or study skill, then on vocabulary

A content area reading selection

Written comprehension activities

A written activity on the Lesson skill

(See Level A, Lesson 44)

Lesson 44

1

Primary Source

Reading a Social Studies Selection

2

Background Information

The Nez Percé lived in the plateau country, an area that is now where the states of Washington, Oregon, and Idaho meet. The Nez Percé originally called themselves Nee Me Poo, which means "the Real People." French-Canadian fur trappers called them Nez Percé and the people adopted the name, pronouncing it *nez purse*.

The most famous chief of the Nez Percé was Chief Joseph, whose Indian name was Thunder Traveling to Loftier Mountain Heights. Joseph was 31 years old when he became chief after the death of his father.

In this lesson, you will read about Chief Joseph. You will also read the stirring speech that he delivered to President Hayes in Washington, D.C.

3

Skill Focus

Using a **primary source** will help you learn about past events. A primary source is a firsthand account. It is usually written by a person who took part in the event being described. Primary sources give facts about events. They also give insight into the thoughts and feelings of the people in the events. Letters, speeches, and newspaper articles, are primary sources.

Often textbooks, magazines, encyclopedias, and so on, will contain excerpts, or pieces, of primary source materials. These excerpts are usually set apart in some way from the rest of the text.

When reading a primary source, use the following two steps.

1. **Find out all you can about the primary source.** Ask yourself the following questions.
   a. What type of document is it? Is it a letter, a report, an article, or a speech?
   b. Who wrote it? Was the author part of the event?
   c. When was it written?
2. **Study the primary source to learn about a past event.** Try to distinguish facts from opinions. A fact can be proven. An opinion is a judgment that reflects a person's feelings or beliefs.
   a. What facts can I learn from this document?
   b. What was the author's opinion about what was reported?

4

Word Clues

Read the sentences below. Look for context clues that explain the underlined word.

> As the early settlers moved west, they came into conflict with the Indians who lived there. The settlers had left their homes to find new land. They wanted land for farming and for raising cattle.

If you do not know the word *settlers* in the first sentence, read the next two sentences. They give details about the settlers. The details tell more about the word so that you understand it.

Use **detail** context clues to find the meaning of the three underlined words in the selection.

5

Strategy Tip

As you read Chief Joseph's words, keep in mind the two steps for using a primary source. Reading this speech will give you insight into the thoughts and feelings of Chief Joseph and his people.

Lesson 44 *Using a primary source* 123

1

Lessons and skills are easy to find—Lessons are numbered and give the skill in the title.

2

Background Information—provides students with important content, cultural, and historical information and tells students what the selection is about.

3

Skill Focus—Instruction comes first—so that students are successful later.

4

Word Clues—Vocabulary instruction—before students read and need help.

5

Strategy Tip—gives students background and reminds them to use the Lesson skill.

Next, students read a selection.

A Great and Honorable Leader

The Gold Rush

The Nez Percé lived peacefully in their country for hundreds of years. They had experienced good relations with the white trappers and explorers. But in 1860, white prospectors illegally entered Nez Percé territory and found gold. During the gold rush, thousands of miners settled on Nez Percé reservation lands, disobeying an earlier treaty. For the first time, friction developed between whites and the Nez Percé.

In 1863, under pressure from the gold miners to remove the Nez Percé from valuable mineral sources, the U.S. government demanded that the Nez Percé cede, or give up, about 6 million acres of reservation land. The majority of Nez Percé refused. A government commissioner bribed several chiefs who sold the land and signed the treaty. The government official reported to the U.S. government that he had secured all lands demanded "at a cost not exceeding 8 cents per acre."

As a result of the land sale, the Nez Percé divided into "treaty" and "nontreaty" bands. Among those who were angry about the selling of Indian land was Tuckakas, also known as Old Joseph. By 1871, thousands of settlers had moved onto reservation land, as was allowed by the new treaty. Near his death, Old Joseph spoke to his son Young Joseph about their homeland:

6

> *My son, my body is returning to my mother earth, and my spirit is going very soon to see the Great Spirit Chief. When I am gone, think of your country. You are the chief of these people. They look to you to guide them. Always remember that your father never sold his country. You must stop your ears whenever you are asked to sign a treaty selling your home.*
>
> *. . . My son, never forget my dying words. This country holds your father's body. Never sell the bones of your father and your mother.*

Chief of Peace

Upon his father's death, Joseph became the civil, or peace, chief of his father's band. Joseph held many councils, or meetings, with civil and military officials. In 1873, Joseph convinced the government that it had not legally secured title to the reservation lands. The government ordered the whites to move out of the territory. However, the government then reversed its decision under pressure from Oregon politicians and settlers.

7

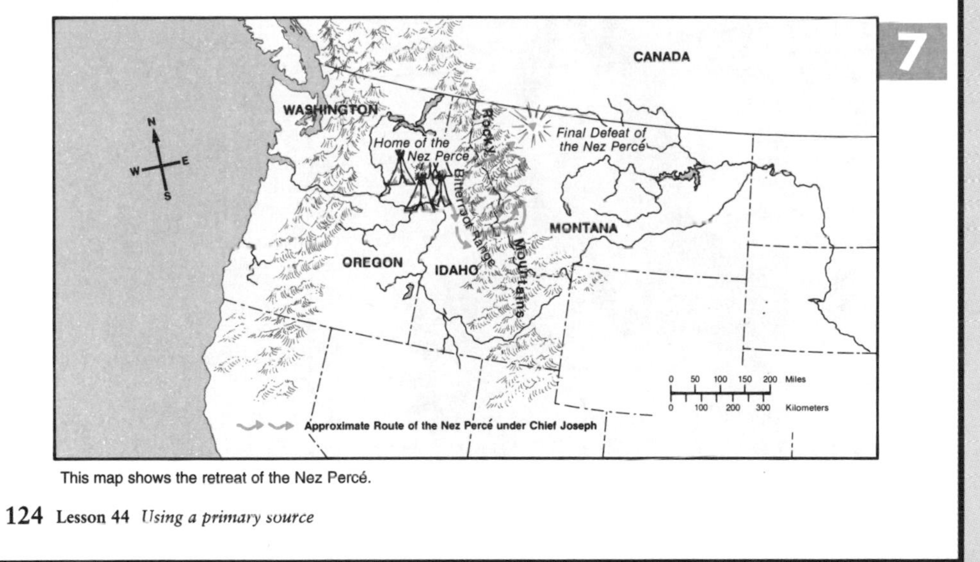

This map shows the retreat of the Nez Percé.

124 Lesson 44 *Using a primary source*

6

Primary Sources—In social studies selections, primary source materials aid comprehension, as well as provide valuable first-hand accounts of events and people.

7

Illustrations, photos, and captions increase interest and aid comprehension.

After reading, comprehension is checked.

Understanding the dilemma of the U.S. government, Joseph continued to strive for a peaceful solution to the land problem. In 1877, General Oliver O. Howard concluded that the only solution was to force all the Nez Percé off their land and onto a reservation in Washington.

Many of the "nontreaty" Nez Percé wanted to fight for their land. Chief Joseph didn't want to fight. He knew that fighting would only bring death and sadness to his people. Joseph believed that he had no other choice but to lead his people to the reservation. So in the spring of 1877, Joseph agreed to the demands of the U.S. government. Several other nontreaty bands joined Joseph's for one last gathering on their land. While there, several men decided to seek revenge on white settlers for the death of one's father and for other grievances. They killed four white settlers.

8

Knowing that General Howard would send troops after them, the bands withdrew to Whitebird Canyon. Thus began a remarkable retreat, in which the Nez Percé fought, alluded, and outwitted one military force after another for four months. With about 750 people, including sick and elderly people, women, and children, the Nez Percé circled over a thousand miles trying to reach safety in Canada.

The soldiers who fought Chief Joseph thought that he was a great and honorable man. The soldiers knew that the Nez Percé never killed without reason. They could have burned and destroyed the property of many settlers, but they did not. Joseph and his people fought only to defend themselves and their land. The white soldiers were also impressed with their ability to allude the army for so many months and over so many miles.

"I Will Fight No More, Forever"

But the end finally came. Unaware that the army under Colonel Nelson A. Miles was in close pursuit, the Nez Percé camped less than 40 miles south of the Canadian border. At the end of a five-day siege, Chief Joseph decided to surrender to Miles on October 5, 1877. He rode into the army camp alone and handed his rifle to the soldiers. He said:

> *I am tired of fighting. My people ask me for food and I have none to give. It is cold and we have no blankets, no wood. My people are starving. . . . Hear me, my chiefs. I have fought, but from where the sun now stands, Joseph will fight no more, forever.*

After Joseph's surrender, the U.S. government ordered them onto a reservation in Kansas, then to a disease-ridden reservation in Oklahoma. Many of the Nez Percé died of malaria and other sicknesses.

Chief Joseph pleaded on behalf of his people to gain permission to return to a reservation in the Northwest. In 1879, Chief Joseph traveled to Washington to plead his case to President Hayes.

Chief Joseph's Speech

If the white man wants to live in peace with the Indian, he can live in peace. There need be no trouble. Treat all men alike. Give them the same laws. Give them all an even chance to live and grow.

All men are made by the same Great Spirit Chief. They are all brothers. The earth is the mother of all people, and all people should have equal rights upon it. You might as well expect all rivers to run backward as that any man born a free man should be contented penned up and denied liberty to go where he pleases. If you tie a horse to a stake, do you expect he will grow fat? If you pen an Indian

Chief Joseph of the Nez Percé Indians.

Lesson 44 *Using a primary source* 125

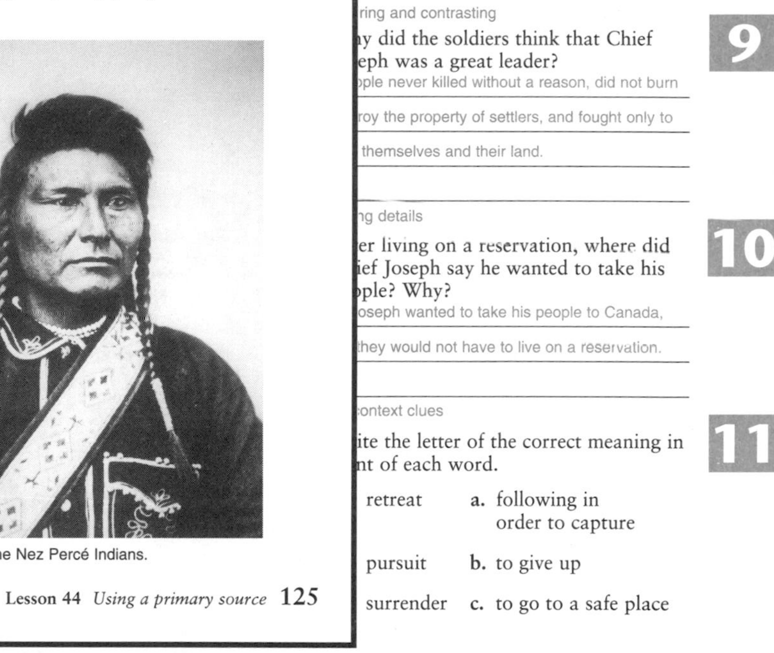

wars. We shall all be alike—brothers of ther and mother, with one sky above us one country around us and one ment for all. Then the Great Spirit who rules above will smile upon this nd send rain to wash out the bloody made by brothers' hands upon the face earth. For this time, the Indian race are g and praying. I hope no more groans unded men and women will ever go to r of the Great Spirit Chief above, and ll people may be one people.

1885, after eight years of campaigning alf of his people, Joseph and the other ercé were allowed to return to the west. Unable to join the treaty bands on aho reservation, Joseph and the others escorted to the Colville Reservation in ngton Territory. It was there that died in 1904, reportedly from a heart.

ACTS

9

ring and contrasting

y did the soldiers think that Chief eph was a great leader?

ople never killed without a reason, did not burn roy the property of settlers, and fought only to themselves and their land.

10

ng details

er living on a reservation, where did ief Joseph say he wanted to take his ple? Why?

oseph wanted to take his people to Canada, hey would not have to live on a reservation.

11

ontext clues

ite the letter of the correct meaning in nt of each word.

retreat — a. following in order to capture

pursuit — b. to give up

surrender — c. to go to a safe place

126 Lesson 44 *Using a primary source*

8

Word clues—Unfamiliar words are defined using context clues, such as synonyms, appositive phrases, comparisons, and details, to aid reading and comprehension.

9

After reading, students complete written activities.

Recalling Facts—checks students' literal comprehension of the selection. (In the *Annotated Teacher's Edition,* each question has a skill label and answer for the teacher's benefit.)

11

Vocabulary Skills—The last item in "Recalling Facts" is a vocabulary check.

The lesson ends with a skills check.

INTERPRETING FACTS

12

Identifying point of view

1. For each pair of sentences, circle t
Joseph's thoughts and opinions in
   (a.) The white man can live in peac
   same law.
   b. Because so many promises have
   man and the Indian.

   a. There will be no more wars wh
   (b.) There will be no more wars wh

Drawing conclusions

2. Decide whether Chief Joseph is a g
must look carefully at Chief Josep
are listed in order below. For each
   a. Chief Joseph first agrees to lead
   He knows that the small number of Nez Pe

   b. Chief Joseph decides to lead his
   He wants to escape the army's punishmen
   put on reservations.

   c. Chief Joseph will fight the army
   He knows that the battle will end only in de

   d. Chief Joseph leads his people o
   He is trying to avoid battle and being captu

   e. During this time, Chief Joseph
   He knows that the skills of his warriors will

   f. Chief Joseph says that he will "
   reservation.
   The army has trapped them. His people ha
   They must either surrender or die.

   g. Two years later, Chief Joseph sp
   even though he led his people t
   He believes that taking away a people's fre
   live "penned up." Yet, he has given his wor

Now answer this question: Do you think that Chief Joseph was a great and honorable leader? In your answer, first tell what you mean by the words *great* and by *honorable*. Then tell why you think Chief Joseph was or was not a great and honorable leader.

Conclusions will vary, but all answers should include the following: (a) Student's definition of *great* and *honorable* and (b) student's conclusion about Chief Joseph should be consistent with their definitions of *great* and *honorable* and should cite facts in the selection and speech that led to the conclusion.

SKILL FOCUS

13

Reread Chief Joseph's speech. Pay special attention to what it tells you about Chief Joseph's feelings and motives. Then answer the questions below.

1. *Find out all you can about the primary source.*

What type of document is this? a speech

Who wrote it? Chief Joseph

Was the author involved in the event? yes

When was it written? 1879

2. *Study the primary source to learn about a past event.*

What facts can you learn from this document? Indian lands were being overrun by white men; many Indians were dying and being treated as outlaws.

What was the author's opinion about what was reported? Chief Joseph believed that the Indians and white men could live in peace if all were subject to the same laws. He thought that his people would prosper if they could be moved back to the Pacific Northwest (Oregon).

▶ Real Life Connections Write an interesting fact or story about the history of your community. List your primary sources.

14

128 Lesson 44 *Using a primary source*

12

Interpreting Facts—checks students' comprehension on *inferential* and *critical* levels.

13

Skill Focus—checks students' understanding of the Lesson skill. In the "Skill Focus" at the beginning of the Lesson, students learned about the Lesson skill. Now students complete a written activity that applies the skill to the reading selection.

14

Real Life Connections— asks students to apply what they have read or learned to their own lives, communities, or interests.

Brief end-of-unit Lessons follow.

Lesson 40

Main Idea and Suppo

15

Many times in reading, you will l
details. Details give more informati
supporting details because they sup

Below is a paragraph about how the brakes w
the supporting details are listed.

Braking a car is an interesting process. I
most cars, a liquid called brake fluid begi
the steps that stop the moving automobil
When the brakes are not being used, the flu
rests in the master cylinder and the brak

Main Idea Braking a car is an interesti

Supporting Details

a. In most cars, a liquid called brake flui
automobile.

b. When the brakes are not being used, t
tubes.

c. When the driver steps on the brake pe

d. The brake shoe presses against the bra

e. Each wheel has its own braking syster

On the next page, write the main idea and th

16

1. In the United States, almost everyone
life is linked to the auto industry. Most peopl
depend on a car, bus, or truck fo
transportation. More than 12 million peopl
earn their living in some part of the ca
industry by building, shipping, servicing, o
selling cars, buses, or trucks. These peopl
account for about one tenth of the labor forc
In fact, there are 500,000 automobile-relate
businesses in the United States.

2. Several steps go into designing a nev
car model. Automobile designers creat
hundreds of sketches on computers. Final idea
for the new model come from these sketche
Then a full-sized clay model is made. Furthe
improvements are made in the design.
fiberglass model is made. Finally, when ever
part has been approved, blueprints of the ca
are drawn so that the car can be cut out of ste
and built.

3. Most of the early automobile builde
were mechanics or knew about machin

112 **Lesson 40** *Identifying the main idea and supporti*

Lesson 42

Comparing Car Ads

17

If you are interested in buying a new car, reading ads in newspapers and magazines should start you in the right direction. The details in ads can help you decide what kind of car will suit your needs and your budget. After you decide on the best car for your needs, you shop around for the best price.

Carefully read the following ads to compare the two cars.

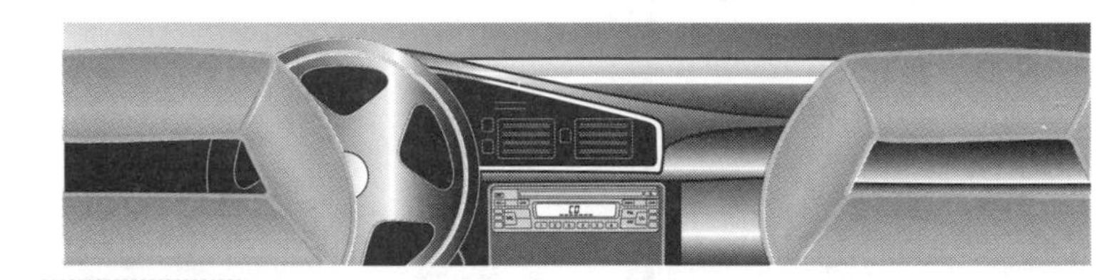

PASHUBI: WE DESIGNED OUR CAR FOR ~~YOU~~ *THE* DRIVER

At Pashubi, we think you are very important. So we created the 630-X, a fully equipped luxury sports car. The 630-X surrounds the driver with more window than other sports cars. The 630-X has a steering wheel and instrument panel that can be moved up or down.

The roomy bucket seats can be easily moved and can tilt back as far as you like. And the large storage area in back lifts up to become two additional seats.

There are 30 standard equipment features, including power disc brakes, power windows, electrically heated outside rearview mirror, two-tone paint, and CD player.

At $20,025, the 630-X offers more than other imported cars. And you'll save on gas—an exceptional 43 EST HWY MPG, [28] EST MPG. Use MPG for comparison. Mileage may differ depending on conditions. Highway mileage may be less.

The 630-X. By Pashubi. It's *not* for everyone—but it is for *you*.

TILTON:
The American way to get more for your money.

You get more for your money with our cars. Take the Star, for example. This compact car uses 3,000 computer-assisted robot welds, more than any other car. This helps to create an easy-to-maintain car which will give you more for your money for years to come.

The Star gives you more for your money because it's sensibly priced. It starts as low as $16,999*. The Star gives you more for your money with front-wheel drive. With the engine pulling in front and rack-and-pinion steering, you get the real feel of the road.

The six-passenger Star gives you more for your money with comfort.

And the Star gives you more for your money when you study the mileage figures:

41 EST HWY, [26] EST MPG.⁺

The Star's standard equipment includes power disc brakes, CD player, and 5-speed transmission (3-speed automatic is extra). Among the other extras are two-tone paint, luggage rack, leather steering wheel, power windows, and more.

Last year's Star was the best-selling compact car. See the Star today—and learn how to get more for your money the American way.

* $19,698 as shown in photograph

⁺ Use EST MPG for comparison. Mileage may vary depending on speed, trip length, and weather. Actual highway mileage lower.

116 **Lesson 42** *Comparing car ads*

15

Each brief Lesson focuses on one important skill and begins with instruction.

16

Students benefit from skills practice and reinforcement without full-length reading selections. (In Levels A, B, and C, phonic skills are reviewed in the Lessons.)

17

The last Lesson in each unit is on a practical skill—such as reading a bus schedule, filling out a job application, or following directions.

(See Level A, Lessons 40 and 42)

Whether students are reading a story for pleasure, skimming newspapers or magazines for information, or studying a chapter in a textbook, they need the following basic reading skills.

Word Recognition: the ability to recognize words.

Comprehension: the ability to derive stated and implied meanings from printed symbols.

Reading Rate: the ability to adjust reading rate to content and purpose.

Study Skills: the ability to apply what is already understood in a new context.

Word Recognition

In *Be A Better Reader*, specific skills instruction in word recognition is designed to provide students with a variety of word attack strategies needed to read an unfamiliar word.

Phonetic Analysis: recognizing and identifying the sounds of consonants, consonant blends, and digraphs; recognizing and identifying vowel sounds and their variant spellings.

Structural Analysis: recognition of root words, prefixes and suffixes, compound words, multisyllabic words, accent marks, and syllabication.

Context Clues: determining word meaning from a particular context clue.

Respellings, Footnotes, and Other Word Helps: using vocabulary aids typical of content-area textbooks.

Comprehension

Reading comprehension is a process that begins with word recognition, but does not end until students have derived meaning from the ideas both stated and implied in the text and have been able to evaluate these ideas. In *Be A Better Reader*, each lesson focuses on a specific reading skill that helps students recognize and understand a text pattern that is typical of a content area, as well as a variety of other reading materials that students encounter in their daily lives.

Literal Comprehension

Literal questions are included to help students process information that is stated explicitly in the text. These questions require students to recall from memory or to select from the text specific answers; in other words, to reproduce what has been stated in the text.

The literal comprehension activities and questions in the Understanding Facts and Skill Focus activities sections require students to do the following.

1. Identify stated main idea
2. Identify stated main idea and details
3. Recall details
4. Identify stated cause and effect
5. Recognize sequence of events
6. Recognize fact and opinion
7. Recognize elements of a short story (plot, character, setting, theme, etc.)
8. Recognize variety of literary types or genres (fiction, play, nonfiction, biography, primary sources, etc.)

Inferential and Critical Comprehension

Numerous activities and questions are included to encourage students to probe for deeper meanings that are implied but not explicitly stated in the text. These questions require students to think about the meanings that can be derived from their reading, not just reproduce what the text has stated. Inferential and critical comprehension begins with literal meanings, but advances to higher-level thinking and reasoning skills that require students to go beyond the printed symbol.

The inferential and critical comprehension questions in the Interpreting Facts and Skill Focus activities sections require students to do the following.

1. Infer unstated main idea
2. Infer cause and effect
3. Infer details
4. Infer conclusions
5. Infer comparisons and contrasts
6. Distinguish fact from opinion
7. Infer information about elements of a short story (plot, character, setting, theme, etc.)
8. Draw conclusions and make generalizations
9. Evaluate validity of ideas
10. Predict outcomes

Reading Rate

Studies indicate that students are ready for a variety of reading rates by the latter part of fifth grade or by sixth grade. Students who have acquired reading skills through reading fiction only need to learn that there are different rates at which they should read different content. Practice in adjusting reading rate is introduced in Level C of ***Be A Better Reader***. Emphasis is placed on adjusting the rate of reading to the content and the purpose of the material.

Study Skills

An analysis of questions, exercises, explanations, visuals, and directions in the various content area textbooks reveals that certain basic study skills are called for again and again in all subject areas. Most of these skills involve using comprehension skills to study and understand information in the content area. As students work with materials in literature, social studies, science, and mathematics, ***Be A Better Reader*** provides instruction and practice in the following study skills.

Selecting and Evaluating Information: the ability to select items from context and evaluate them in terms of conditions or specifications.

Organizing Information: the ability to put together or organize similar ideas.

Locating Information: the ability to find information in reference books and periodicals.

Reading Visuals: the ability to understand information presented in visuals, such as diagrams, maps, and graphs.

Following Directions: the ability to follow a specific sequence of steps.

Previewing: the ability to use previewing skills to understand the meaning and organization of a selection before reading it.

Reading Special Materials: the ability to read materials other than classroom textbooks.

Selecting and Evaluating Information

Just as word recognition skills are basic to reading, selection and evaluation are basic to study skills. Textbooks in the content areas contain many questions and directions that call for selection and evaluation skills. The skill of selecting and evaluating information requires students to select a piece of information and judge its worth in meeting the specifications of an activity or question. The answers to most literal comprehension questions need only to be selected from the text. However, inferential questions require students to go beyond the selection process to evaluation, the highest level of critical comprehension. In ***Be A Better Reader***, lessons on fact and opinion, primary sources, and propaganda teach students selection and evaluation skills.

Organizing Information

The skill of organizing information is important because of the frequency with which students must apply it in studying textbooks, listening in class, and writing papers and tests. This skill provides opportunity for applying comprehension of content to a different format. Organizing information calls for systematically putting together items or ideas that belong to a whole. ***Be A Better Reader*** includes lessons on the procedures most often used in organizing information: (1) classifying items that belong to one group or that occur in a certain order; (2) outlining to show the relationship among ideas; (3) summarizing important ideas.

Locating Information

The skill of locating information includes activities that range from using a table of contents and an index to using a dictionary, an encyclopedia, and the library database system. Skill in locating information begins with recognizing alphabetical order and advances to finding information in complex reference books. In ***Be A Better Reader***, lessons on locational skills are self-contained and include representative examples of typical dictionary and encyclopedia entries, indexes, and tables of contents.

Reading Visuals

Most content-area textbooks require students to read a variety of visuals, such as maps, timelines, diagrams, and graphs. Throughout ***Be A Better Reader***, in all content areas, students are taught how to extract specific information from visuals and how to compress textual information into a brief visual presentation.

Following Directions

Reading to follow directions is a fundamental skill needed in studying all content areas. In ***Be A Better Reader***, students are given directions for carrying out the activities that follow the reading selections. Thus, in addition to specific lessons in following directions, students acquire abundant experience in reading and following directions throughout each level of the program.

Previewing

Previewing a selection is another organizational skill. Previewing results in an organized "picture" or understanding of the structure of the selection. In ***Be A Better Reader***, students learn to preview a selection by noting headings of sections, main ideas, and visuals.

Reading Special Materials

Students must be able to read special materials that they encounter outside the classroom. The last lesson in each unit of ***Be A Better Reader*** provides specific directions on how to read the yellow pages, a recipe, a floor plan, a travel brochure, and so on. Practice with these materials helps students make the transition from relatively controlled classroom reading situations to everyday reading situations.

Reading research has shown that different types of content require specialized reading skills. In preparing ***Be A Better Reader***, textbooks in four different content areas were analyzed.

Literature

Social Studies

Science

Mathematics

Books were analyzed for text patterns, visual programs, and study aids typical of each content area. The specific skills situations that occurred most often in each content area were selected for inclusion in ***Be A Better Reader***. The situations in which the skills were used were more abstract and higher levels of thinking were required in the books intended for the higher grades, but the skills situations are basically the same at all grade levels at which each subject is taught.

Literature

The literature selections in ***Be A Better Reader*** were carefully selected to appeal to student interest and are written at appropriate reading levels. The basic goal of the lessons with literature selections is threefold: (1) to acquaint students with various literary genres; (2) to increase students' awareness of the literary elements; and (3) to provide practice in applying comprehension skills to reading literature. A variety of genres is included in each level of ***Be A Better Reader***. In the instructional section of each lesson, an important literary concept is stressed in terms appropriate to the particular level.

Each level of ***Be A Better Reader*** provides a lesson that develops one of the following special skills required in understanding and appreciating literature.

Recognizing plot

Recognizing character

Recognizing conflict

Recognizing setting

Recognizing theme

Plot

Most short stories have a plot, or sequence of events. They have a beginning, a middle, and an end, and events are arranged to build to a climax. As students read stories, it is important for them to keep the events in order, to notice how one event leads to the next, and to be able to identify the climax, or turning point of the story.

Character

The characters in a story are as important as the plot. Students need to be able to identify the main character, or protagonist, in a story. They should think about what motivates characters to act as they do. They should also notice how characters develop and change by contrasting how the characters behave at the beginning of a story with how they behave at the end.

Conflict

Students should be able to recognize a story's central conflict, or problem. Most stories are built around one of three common conflicts.

1. The main character is in conflict with himself or herself.
2. The main character is in a conflict with other characters.
3. The main character is in conflict with nature, society, or some outside force over which he or she may not have any control.

Setting

Setting is the time and place of the events in a story. Awareness of setting is essential to understanding the characters and their conflicts. Students must be shown how to interpret setting and its impact on the story's characters and events.

Theme

The theme, or idea, of a story is usually the most difficult concept for students to formulate by themselves. Students need to use higher-level comprehension skills to infer the author's underlying message.

Social Studies

Social studies texts have their own characteristic text patterns that require special reading skills. For example, social studies texts include frequent references to visuals, such as maps, graphs, and pictures. These references may require students to find information in a specific visual and then combine that information with information in the text.

Students need to become familiar with the text patterns typical of social studies textbooks. ***Be A Better Reader*** teaches some of the skills that are necessary to aid in comprehension of the patterns.

Reading visuals, such as pictures, maps, and graphs

Recognizing cause-and-effect relationships

Understanding sequence of events

Making comparisons and contrasts
Understanding detailed statements of fact
Thinking and reading critically

Visuals

Pictures in social studies textbooks are selected to depict historical concepts and events. The ability to read pictures and captions that accompany them results in students gaining information and implied meanings that go beyond the text. Reading pictures requires close attention to detail.

Reading maps and graphs is a highly specialized kind of reading skill. Map reading requires recognition and interpretation of symbols for rivers, mountains, lakes, towns and cities, boundary lines, and such features as scales of miles, color keys, and meridians. When reading graphs, students need to know how to extrapolate data and use it to make generalizations, thereby supplementing information in the text.

Cause and Effect

While the cause-and-effect text pattern occurs to some extent in most content areas, it occurs with the highest frequency in social studies, especially history. Every major event in history comes about as the result of some cause or set of causes, and when the event happens its effect or effects are felt. Sometimes the effect of one event becomes the cause of another event. Thus, the student often encounters a chain of causes and effects. Students who are adept at recognizing cause-and-effect patterns will find this to be a valuable asset in studying social studies textbooks.

Sequence of Events

Another text pattern encountered in social studies presents events in specific time sequences accompanied by dates. Students should read this pattern for two purposes: (1) to grasp the chronological order of large periods or whole blocks of events and (2) to grasp times of important happenings within each period or block—stopping long enough to associate events with dates and to think about how each event led to others.

Social studies textbooks include several kinds of visual aids designed to help students understand time relationships. These aids include charts of events and dates, chronological summaries, timelines, outline maps with dates and events, and so on. Each of these visual aids requires special reading skills.

Comparison and Contrast

A text pattern calling for the comparison of likenesses and/or contrast of differences is common in social studies textbooks. This pattern occurs most frequently in discussions of such topics as the theories of government or policies of different leaders; physical features, products, or industries of different countries; and so on. Students who recognize a comparison and contrast chapter or section of a text can approach it with the foremost purpose of noting likenesses and differences.

Detailed Statements of Fact

Much social studies text contains many details and facts. Facts, however, are usually included within one of the characteristic text patterns already discussed. The facts in social studies textbooks are not as dense as they usually are in science textbooks, nor are they as technical. Because they are often associated with sequential events or with causes and effects, they are more easily grasped.

Critical Thinking

Many social studies texts require students to interpret material critically. Students are expected to make inferences from facts, to distinguish fact from opinion, to analyze propaganda, to interpret primary sources, to draw conclusions and make generalizations, and to answer open-ended questions. Students need specific instruction and practice in these skills if they are to probe for deeper meanings and respond to higher-level questions.

Combination of Patterns

A single chapter in social studies may contain several text patterns. For example, a chapter may contain biographical material similar to the narrative pattern, a chronology of events during a certain time period, maps and charts depicting those events, and cause-and-effect relationships. If students who start to study such a chapter have not acquired the skills necessary to recognize and process each of these text patterns and instead use the same approach in reading all of them, the resulting understandings of the concepts presented will be extremely limited.

Science

Science text, like all other types of text, calls for the use of such comprehension skills as identifying main ideas and making inferences. However, an analysis of science textbooks reveals text patterns unique to science text that call for other approaches and special reading skills.

As in social studies textbooks, science texts include frequent references to such visuals as diagrams and pictures. Students need continued practice in combining text reading with visual reading in order to process all the information that is available on a science text page.

Be A Better Reader provides lessons on the following special reading skills that are needed for science textbooks.

- Understanding classification
- Reading an explanation of a technical process
- Recognizing cause and effect relationships
- Following directions for an experiment
- Understanding detailed statements of fact
- Recognizing descriptive problem-solving situations
- Understanding abbreviations, symbols, and equations
- Reading text with diagrams

Classification

The classification pattern is characteristic of science text. In this pattern, living things, objects, liquids, gases, forces, and so on are first classified in a general grouping that has one or more elements in common. This group is further classified into smaller groups, each of which varies in certain respects from every other group in the general grouping. Students who recognize the classification text pattern will concentrate on understanding the basis of the groupings and the chief characteristics of each one.

Explanation of a Technical Process

Another text pattern particularly characteristic of science is the explanation of a technical process. Explanation is usually accompanied by diagrams, necessitating very careful reading of text with continuous references to diagrams. The diagrams themselves require students to use special reading skills in addition to those needed to grasp the text explanations.

Cause and Effect

A text pattern sometimes encountered in science textbooks, but not unique to science, is the cause-and-effect pattern. In this pattern the text gives information that explains why certain things happen. In reading this type of pattern, students first read to find the causes and effects. A careful rereading is usually necessary to determine how and why the causes had the effects that they did.

Following Directions for an Experiment

This text pattern consists of explicit directions or instructions that must be carried out exactly. The common study skill of following directions is essential in reading this science pattern, but experiments also call for the mental activities of making discriminating observations, understanding complex explanations, and drawing considered conclusions.

Detailed Statements of Fact

Another pattern frequently encountered in science textbooks is detailed statements of fact. This pattern in science differs from factual text in the other content areas in two respects: (1) the facts are more dense and (2) they frequently lead to or embody a definition or a statement of a principle.

In reading this text pattern, students can make use of the reading skill of finding the main ideas and supporting details. Students first locate the most important thought or main idea in each paragraph, then proceed to find details that reinforce the main idea— noting particularly any definitions or statements of principles.

Descriptive Problem Solving

This text pattern describes problem-solving situations by taking the reader through a series of scientific experiments conducted by one or by many people. Students should approach this pattern with the idea of finding out what each successive problem was and how it was solved.

Abbreviations, Symbols, and Equations

Another science text pattern that requires a special kind of reading makes liberal use of abbreviations, formulas, and equations. For example, grasping the meaning of the symbol ° (degree) and the formula $CaCO_3$ (calcium carbonate) when they are integrated with words in the text calls for special recognition skills in addition to the usual recognition of word symbols. This pattern is still further complicated when symbols and abbreviations are involved in equations or number sentences.

Diagrams

Science textbooks usually contain many diagrams. Students need to learn how to go from the text to the diagrams and back to the text if they are to understand the meaning of scientific concepts. Reading diagrams requires an understanding of the purpose of diagrams, ability to interpret color and other visual devices used to highlight parts of a diagram, and comprehension of labels.

Combination of Patterns

As in social studies textbooks, a single chapter of a science text at the higher levels may contain several text patterns. If students who start to study such a chapter have not acquired the skills necessary to recognize and process each of these patterns and instead use the same approach in reading all of them, then the resulting understandings of the concepts presented will be extremely limited.

Mathematics

The reading skills needed for reading mathematics are sharply different from the skills needed in other content areas. Many students who read narrative with relative ease have great difficulty in reading mathematics, especially word problems and abstract mathematical symbols. The mathematics selections in ***Be A Better Reader*** are not included for the purpose of teaching mathematics. Their function is threefold: (1) to develop in students an awareness of the difference between reading mathematics texts and reading other texts; (2) to give students practice in reading the different types of text and symbols used in mathematics textbooks; and (3) to apply basic reading skills to mathematics text.

One of the special characteristics of mathematics text is compactness. Every word and every symbol is important. Unlike reading in other content areas, skipping an unfamiliar word or guessing its meaning from context will impair students' progress in mathematics. Students should be aware of this difference.

Another adjustment students have to make in reading mathematics is a change in basic left-to-right eye movement habits. Mathematics text often requires vertical or left-directed eye movements for rereading portions of the text for better understanding or for selecting certain numbers or symbols. While some students read mathematics more rapidly than others, text patterns in mathematics are not appropriate for speed reading.

Reading in mathematics makes heavy demands on the comprehension skills that call for interpretation, critical reading, and creative reading. Many mathematical situations call for a careful weighing of relationships. Of great importance is the ability to discover principles as a result of studying pictures and diagrams.

The inferential reading skills and the study skills of reading pictures and diagrams emphasized throughout *Be A Better Reader* should transfer to the following skills and attitudes specifically needed in working with mathematics.

Reading word problems

Reading mathematical terms, symbols, and equations

Reading graphs and other mathematical visuals

Reading explanation for processes or principles, such as fractions, decimals, and percents

Word Problems

Because problem solving is a priority in mathematics and closely related to basic reading skills, the Seventh Edition of *Be A Better Reader* includes in each level two lessons on problem solving. A five-step strategy is introduced in the first problem-solving lesson and used throughout the series. The steps in the strategy closely parallel the steps used in most mathematics textbooks. However, *Be A Better Reader* emphasizes the reading and reasoning skills necessary to solve word problems.

While the problem-solving strategy remains the same throughout the series, each succeeding lesson focuses on slightly more sophisticated problems. For example, the first problem-solving lesson focuses on problems that involve one mathematical operation. At a later level, problems are introduced in which two operations are necessary.

Terms, Symbols, and Equations

In mathematics, students must read sentences composed of word symbols and number symbols, such as equations. Recognizing and understanding symbols of various types is reading and should be taught as such in mathematics.

In reading equations, students have to recognize the meaning of the entire mathematical sentence, as well as the symbols +, −, x, ÷, and =. They also have to recognize and understand the symbols x and n, just as they have to learn to recognize and grasp the meaning of a new word in reading.

Students have to learn to recognize and understand the properties of geometric figures, such as the octagon, pentagon, prism, cube, cylinder, and pyramid. Parentheses, >, <, and other symbols are used frequently.

Graphs and Charts

Other distinctive text patterns in mathematics are graphs, such as bar graphs and circle graphs. While these visual aids are used in social studies, science, and other subjects, they almost always represent mathematical concepts.

To get the most information from a graph, students should: (1) read the title to determine exactly what is being compared; (2) read the numbers or labels to determine what the figures or labels stand for; (3) study the graph to compare the different items illustrated; and (4) interpret the significance of the graph as a whole. Due to the prevalence of graphs and similar mathematical visuals in most content area textbooks, most students profit from instruction in reading these types of text patterns.

Explanation

The explanation text pattern in mathematics texts is similar to the explanation text pattern in science textbooks, except that in mathematics text explanations describe a mathematical principle or process rather than a scientific process. Mathematical explanations are comparatively short and often contain symbols other than words. They are usually accompanied by or are preceded by a series of exercises or questions designed to guide students in discovering the principle or process. This text pattern calls for very careful reading and rereading until the process is understood.

Administering Level Assessment Tests

Assessment tests for Level B are designed to measure students' level of achievement in each of the important comprehension and study skills that receive emphasis in *all* levels of ***Be A Better Reader***. The tests may be used as pre-tests and/or post-tests, depending on students' needs and your particular classroom management style. Combined with an overview of student performance on each lesson, the tests should enable you to refine your assessment of students' performance and determine students' readiness to advance to the next level.

The four tests in Level B can be administered separately or at one time, depending on time available. Because directions are provided for each test, students should be able to take the tests independently. However, enough time should be allowed for each student to complete the tests.

The skill for each test item is identified in the answer key below. Following the skill is the number of the lesson or the lessons in Level B where that skill is treated as a Skill Focus. To simplify the scoring process, you can use the answer key to make a scoring mask, which when placed over the answer sheet reveals only those items that are correct. The total score is equal to the number of correct items. Criterion scores are not specified, as the individual class or group situation should determine the appropriate criterion.

Answer Key and Skills Correlation

Test 1

1. b Understanding character (20)
2. c Understanding character (20)
3. a Understanding character (20)
4. a Understanding character (20)
5. a Identifying conflict and resolution (11)
6. b Identifying conflict and resolution (11)
7. c Identifying conflict and resolution (11)
8. b Identifying conflict and resolution (11)
9. b Identifying plot (50)
10. c Identifying plot (50)
11. b Identifying plot (50)
12. a Identifying plot (50)
13. b Identifying setting (1)
14. b Identifying setting (1)
15. b Identifying setting (1)
16. c Identifying setting (1)
17. a Inferring theme (41)
18. c Inferring theme (41)
19. c Inferring theme (41)
20. c Inferring theme (41)
21. b Identifying/Inferring the unstated main idea (18, 55)
22. b Identifying/Inferring the unstated main idea (18, 55)
23. c Identifying/Inferring the unstated main idea (18, 55)
24. a Identifying point of view (30)
25. a Identifying point of view (30)
26. c Identifying point of view (30)
27. b Identifying point of view (30)
28. c Using comparison context clues (3, 11)
29. b Recognizing multiple meanings of words (59)
30. c Recognizing multiple meanings of words (59)

Test 2

31. a Identifying the main idea (6)
32. b Identifying the main idea (6)
33. a Identifying the main idea (6)
34. c Identifying/Inferring the unstated main idea (18, 55)
35. b Identifying/Inferring the unstated main idea (18, 55)
36. a Identifying/Inferring the unstated main idea (18, 55)
37. c Identifying the main idea and supporting details (45)
38. b Identifying the main idea and supporting details (45)
39. c Identifying cause and effect (12, 22)
40. b Identifying cause and effect (12, 22)
41. a Identifying cause and effect (12, 22)
42. a Comparing and contrasting (51)
43. b Comparing and contrasting (51)
44. b Comparing and contrasting (51)

45. a Using appositive context clues (1,13, 20, 22, 42)
46. b Using detail context clues (21, 30, 32, 41, 52)
47. c Using detail context clues (21, 30, 32, 41, 52)
48. a Using synonym context clues (43)
49. a Distinguishing fact from opinion (17, 21, 35)
50. c Distinguishing fact from opinion (17, 21, 35)
51. b Distinguishing fact from opinion (17, 21, 35)
52. b Distinguishing fact from opinion (17, 21, 35)
53. c Making inferences (56)
54. b Making inferences (56)
55. a Making inferences (56)
56. b Recognizing multiple meanings of words (59)
57. b Reading a map (42)
58. a Reading a map (42)
59. c Reading a map (42)
60. b Reading a map (42)

Test 3

61. a Classifying (3, 32)
62. c Classifying (3, 32)
63. b Classifying (3, 32)
64. b Classifying (3, 32)
65. a Identifying cause and effect (12, 22)
66. c Identifying cause and effect (12, 22)
67. a Comparing and contrasting (51)
68. b Making inferences (56)
69. a Identifying the main idea (6)
70. c Identifying the main idea and supporting details (45)
71. b Identifying the main idea and supporting details (45)
72. c Recognizing multiple meanings of words (59)
73. a Reading text with diagrams (43)
74. b Reading text with diagrams (43)
75. b Reading text with diagrams (43)
76. c Reading text with diagrams (43)
77. b Solving word problems (23, 33)
78. a Solving word problems (23, 33)
79. b Solving word problems (23, 33)
80. a Solving word problems (23, 33)

Test 4

81. b Using a dictionary entry (48)
82. c Using a dictionary entry (48)
83. a Using a dictionary entry (48)
84. a Using a dictionary entry (48)
85. c Using a dictionary entry (48)
86. c Adding prefixes and suffixes to words (9, 15, 16)
87. b Adding prefixes and suffixes to words (9, 15, 16)
88. c Adding prefixes and suffixes to words (9, 15, 16)
89. c Adding prefixes and suffixes to words (9, 15, 16)
90. b Adding prefixes and suffixes to words (9, 15, 16)
91. c Adding prefixes and suffixes to words (9, 15, 16)
92. c Adding prefixes and suffixes to words (9, 15, 16)
93. a Dividing words into syllables (24, 25, 26, 27, 34)
94. b Dividing words into syllables (24, 25, 26, 27, 34)
95. b Dividing words into syllables (24, 25, 26, 27, 34)
96. b Dividing words into syllables (24, 25, 26, 27, 34)
97. b Recognizing root words (9, 15, 16, 25)
98. c Recognizing root words (9, 15, 16, 25)
99. b Recognizing root words (9, 15, 16, 25)
100. a Recognizing roots (28)

Annotated Student's Edition

Be A Better Reader

Level B

Seventh Edition

Nila Banton Smith

Upper Saddle River,
New Jersey

Pronunciation Key

Symbol	Key Word	Respelling
a	act	(akt)
ah	star	(stahr)
ai	dare	(dair)
aw	also	(awl soh)
ay	flavor	(flay vər)
e	end	(end)
ee	eat	(eet)
er	learn	(lern)
	sir	(ser)
	fur	(fer)
i	hit	(hit)
eye	idea	(eye dee ə)
y	like	(lyk)
ir	deer	(dir)
	fear	(fir)
oh	open	(oh pen)
oi	foil	(foil)
	boy	(boi)
or	horn	(horn)
ou	out	(out)
	flower	(flou ər)
oo	hoot	(hoot)
	rule	(rool)
yoo	few	(fyoo)
	use	(yooz)

Symbol	Key Word	Respelling
u	book	(buk)
	put	(put)
uh	cup	(kuhp)
ə	a as in	
	along	(ə lawng)
	e as in	
	moment	(moh mənt)
	i as in	
	modify	(mahd ə fy)
	o as in	
	protect	(prə tekt)
	u as in	
	circus	(ser kəs)
ch	chill	(chil)
g	go	(goh)
j	joke	(johk)
	bridge	(brij)
k	kite	(kyt)
	cart	(kahrt)
ng	bring	(bring)
s	sum	(suhm)
	cent	(sent)
sh	sharp	(shahrp)
th	thin	(thin)
z	zebra	(zee brə)
	pose	(pohz)
zh	treasure	(treszh ər)

***Be A Better Reader*, Level B, Seventh Edition**
Nila Banton Smith

Printed in the United States of America
9 10 11 12 13 14 04 03 02 01 00

C12
ISBN 0-8359-1919-6

Acknowledgments

We wish to express our appreciation for permission to use and adapt copyrighted materials.

The dictionary definitions in this book are reprinted with permission of Macmillan Reference USA, a Division of Simon & Schuster, from WEBSTER'S NEW WORLD DICTIONARY, Basic School Edition. Copyright © 1983 by Simon & Schuster Inc.

"The Giant Snake That Swallowed a Girl." Adapted from SOUTH AMERICAN WONDER TALES by Frances Carpenter, © 1969 by Follett Publishing Company, an imprint of Modern Curriculum Press, Simon & Schuster Elementary. Used by permission of MCP and the author's heirs.

Prentice-Hall, Inc., for "Humid Subtropics." From Oliver H. Heintzelman, Richard M. Highsmith, Jr., WORLD REGIONAL GEOGRAPHY, 4th Ed., © 1973. Adapted by permission of Prentice-Hall, Inc., Englewood Cliffs, N.J.

Photo Credits

p. 13: The Bettmann Archive; **p. 15:** UPI/Bettmann; **p. 42:** The Bettmann Archive; **p. 43:** Wendy Stone/Gamma Liaison; **p. 73:** Lisa Law/The Image Works; **p. 74:** (*left*) J. Spratt/The Image Works, (*right*) J. Spratt/The Image Works; **p. 75:** George Gardiner/The Image Works; **p. 75:** The Bettmann Archive; **p. 101:** Federal Information Department, Southern Rhodesia; **p. 102:** Kennecott Copper Corp.; **p. 130:** (*left*) De Wys Inc./Western Ways/Tad Nichols, (*top right*) Coleman/De Vore, (*bottom right*) Italian National Tourist Office; **p. 155:** courtesy of North Carolina Parks and Recreation Service; **p. 159:** (*left*) Culver Pictures, (*others*) National Library of Medicine; **p. 160:** (*top right*) Culver Pictures, (*bottom right*) National Library of Medicine, (*top right*) Culver Pictures, (*bottom right*) National Library of Medicine.

Contents

Unit Four **Seeing Both Sides** *90*

Unit Five **Mexico** *118*

Unit Six **Neighbors to the South** *146*

How to Use *Be A Better Reader*

For more than thirty years, ***Be A Better Reader*** has helped students improve their reading skills. ***Be A Better Reader*** teaches the comprehension and study skills that you need to read and enjoy all types of materials—from library books to the different textbooks that you will encounter in school.

To get the most from ***Be A Better Reader***, you should know how the lessons are organized. As you read the following explanations, it will be helpful to look at some of the lessons.

In each of the first four lessons of a unit, you will apply an important skill to a reading selection in literature, social studies, science, or mathematics. Each of these lessons includes the following seven sections.

Skill Focus

This section teaches you a specific skill. You should read the Skill Focus carefully, paying special attention to words that are printed in boldface type. The Skill Focus tells you about a skill that you will use when you read the selection.

Word Clues

This section teaches you how to recognize and use different types of context clues. These clues will help you with the meanings of the underlined words in the selection.

Reading a Literature, Social Studies, Science, or Mathematics Selection

This section introduces the selection that you will read and gives you suggestions about what to look for as you read. The suggestions will help you understand the selection.

Selection

The selections in the literature lessons are similar to those in a literature anthology, library book, newspaper, or magazine. The social studies selections are like chapters in a social studies textbook or encyclopedia. They often include maps and tables. The science selections, like a science textbook, include special words in boldface type and sometimes diagrams. The mathematics selections will help you acquire skill in reading mathematics textbooks.

Recalling Facts

Answers to the questions in this section—the first of three activity sections—can be found in the selection. You will sometimes have to reread parts of the selection to do this activity.

Interpreting Facts

The second activity includes questions whose answers are not directly stated in the selection. For these questions, you must combine the information in the selection with what you already know in order to *infer* the answers.

Skill Focus Activity

In the last activity, you will use the skill that you learned in the Skill Focus section at the beginning of the lesson to answer questions about the selection. If you have difficulty completing this activity, reread the Skill Focus section.

The remaining lessons in each unit give you practice with such skills as using a dictionary, an encyclopedia, and other reference materials; using phonics and syllabication aids in recognizing new words; locating and organizing information; and adjusting reading rate. Other reading skills that are necessary in everyday experience are also covered, such as reading a bus schedule and a menu.

Each time that you learn a new skill in ***Be A Better Reader***, look for opportunities to use the skill in your other reading at school and at home. Your reading ability will improve the more you practice reading!

UNIT 1

The Sea

Lesson 1

Setting

Reading a Literature Selection

▶ Background Information

This play is based on actual events that occurred after the Vietnam War. After the last Americans left Vietnam in April 1975, thousands of Vietnamese who had helped the United States still remained. After North and South Vietnam were reunited in 1976 under Communist rule, years of poverty and ongoing conflict drove a million and a half Vietnamese from their country. Some refugees relocated to the United States. These Vietnamese often sailed from their homeland in tiny boats that were not designed for the open sea. As a result, these people became known as the "Vietnamese boat people."

In this selection, you will read about a Vietnamese family that came to the United States after the war.

▶ Skill Focus

Setting is the time and place of the events in a story. Setting tells where and when the events occur. Events can happen in any place and at any time. A story can take place on city streets, on a country farm, or on a boat afloat in a faraway sea. The time can be the present, the past, or the future.

Sometimes a story set in the present includes events that happened earlier. A writer will interrupt the present-day events to describe a scene that took place before the story or play begins. This interruption is called a **flashback**. A flashback treats an event from the past as if it were taking place in the present. The writer usually signals to the reader that a flashback is about to begin by using such phrases as "I remember" or "I recall."

The following questions will help you keep track of the setting as you read a story containing flashbacks. Ask yourself these questions as you read the story.

1. Where does the story take place?
2. When does it take place?
3. Does the time or the place change? Why does this change take place?

▶ Word Clues

Read the sentence below. Look for context clues that explain the underlined word.

> The setting changes from a present-day suburban home in the United States to a small boat fleeing, or moving quickly from, the coast of Vietnam in 1979.

If you do not know the meaning of the word *fleeing,* the appositive phrase, *or moving quickly from,* can help you. *Fleeing* means "moving quickly from a place."

Use **appositive phrases** set off by dashes or commas to find the meaning of the three underlined words in the play.

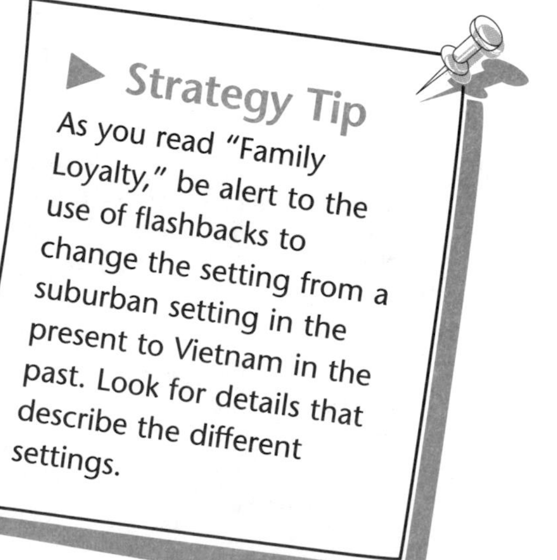

Family Loyalty

Cast

Pham Kim, known as Kim, a seventh-grade student whose family is from Vietnam
Kim's grandfather
Kim's mother
Jake, Kim's friend and classmate
Kim's father
Kim's older brother at age five
Tran Bay, a man in charge of a boat leaving Vietnam
Stranger, a Vietnamese refugee— a man hurrying from danger

The setting changes from a present-day suburban home in the United States to a small boat fleeing, or moving quickly from, the coast of Vietnam in 1979. When the setting is in the present, the actors are on the left side of the stage; the right side of the stage is dark. When the setting is in the past, the actors are on the right side of the stage; the left side of the stage is dark. As the setting changes, the lights on one side of the stage dim and go out while the lights on the other side get brighter. The play begins in the present.

Scene 1

The lights slowly come up on a suburban kitchen. An elderly Vietnamese man sits at the table. A middle-aged Vietnamese woman is preparing breakfast. A teenaged boy runs into the kitchen, dressed in a football uniform.

Kim: *Tieng chao buoi sang!* Good morning, Grandfather. Good morning, Mother! *(stops to look at the breakfast that his mother is cooking)* Hmmm, looks great, Mom. You know, Jake is stopping by this morning before practice. Do you have enough for him?

Mother *(chuckles softly)*: The way you've been eating lately, I'm not sure I have enough for YOU!

Kim *(turns to his grandfather and speaks respectfully)*: Grandfather, you remember Jake, don't you?

Grandfather *(smiles)*: Nice boy, that Jake.

There is a knock at the kitchen door, and a red-headed teenaged boy sticks his head into the room. He is also dressed in a football uniform.

Jake: Anyone home? I could smell breakfast a block away! *(greets Kim's mother and grandfather)* Good morning, Mrs. Pham. Good morning, sir.

Kim: Jake! Great game last night, huh? Boy, you really made some nice plays!

Jake: Yeah, we're really coming together as a team. *(smiles at Kim's grandfather as he sits down at the table)* You know, Mr. Pham, I've done gymnastics and cross-country running, but being on a team is special. You know, working together, everyone helping each other, putting the team first . . .

Grandfather: Whether it is a family or a team, Jake, loyalty is very important. I remember when our family first began our journey to America. You were not yet born then, Kim, and your brother was only five years old . . .

Lights on the left side of the stage fade out.

Scene 2

The lights come up on the right side of the stage. A small boat somewhere on the South China Sea in Vietnam is tied to the side of a makeshift*, or temporary, dock. It is dark and lanterns light the scene. The boat is filled with people—men, women, and children. Kim's father, mother, brother, and grandfather are moving toward the boat. Grandfather looks noticeably tired and weakened. A man speaks to them.*

Tran Bay: *Nug lai!* Stop! The boat is almost full, can't you see? *(He points to Kim's mother and brother.)* We may have room for the woman and child, but there is no room for the two men.

Father *(politely but with force, voice edged with fear)*: Please, sir, my father can no longer stay in this country! I can survive here, but he is weak and tired. He must leave today.

Grandfather: *Thoi dii!* Enough, my son. I will stay behind with you.

Father: No, Father! You must leave now!

Tran Bay: All right. We will take the woman and child—and the grandfather. The stories of the old will help preserve our past, to

remind us in our new home of where we've been. *(motions to the other people in the boat)* Move over! Make room!

Kim's mother, brother, and grandfather climb into the boat. Lights on the right side of the stage fade out.

Scene 3

The lights come up on the left side of the stage. In the kitchen of Kim's home, Kim, his grandfather, and Jake are sitting around the kitchen table. Kim's mother is resting against a kitchen counter. She is engrossed in what they are saying—giving her full attention to their words.

Jake *(turns to Kim)*: I don't understand! Your father is here with you. What happened?

Kim: Well, it was so strange! Of course I wasn't there, but . . . *(turns respectfully to his grandfather)* Grandfather, you tell it.

Grandfather: In Vietnam, the family is very important. It was good for us that the people of Vietnam feel this way. I recall the words of the man who helped our family. They are words I will never forget. . . .

Lights on the left side of the stage fade out.

Scene 4

The lights come up on the right side of the stage. Kim's mother, brother, and grandfather are sitting in the crowded boat. Kim's father is on the dock. Kim's brother is crying loudly, his arms stretched out to his father. Then a stranger in the boat speaks out.

Stranger *(stands and calls loudly)*: Tran Bay! Listen to me. We cannot separate this family. No good will come of it.

Tran Bay: I want as many people as possible to leave the country on this boat, but it isn't safe to put another full-grown man on board. We're already over the limit!

Stranger: I, too, had a family. My wife and children were killed in the war. I do not know what happened to my mother and my father. All my brothers have disappeared. I know how difficult it is to live alone and isolated. *(He begins to climb out of the boat.)* Give him my space on the boat.

Father: But I cannot . . . *(Kim's brother again begins to cry and reach out for his father.)*

Grandfather *(looks carefully at the stranger, pauses, and then speaks)*: Listen to the cries of your child, Son. Join your family in the boat.

Father *(climbs into the boat as the man steps out)*: Thank you! Thank you! I cannot thank you enough!

Stranger: I will see you soon, my friend. Do not worry.

Lights on the right side of the stage fade out.

Scene 5

Lights come up on the left side of the stage. Grandfather is finishing his story. Kim's mother is placing breakfast on the table.

Jake *(sighs)*: That's amazing! The man gave up his own safety so that your family could be together! I don't know many people who would do that!

Grandfather: In Vietnam, the family is everything. Here in America, we still consider family to be most important.

Mother: Yes, Jake. That is why we asked a lonely man from our country to join us when we settled here. We met him through some Vietnamese friends here in America. *(The kitchen door opens and she smiles. Kim's father walks in with another man. They are talking and laughing.)*

Kim *(gestures politely as he makes introductions)*: Jake, you know my father. This is Father's business partner and my uncle, Bac Gan.

Jake *(stands to shake hands with Bac Gan)*: Nice to meet you, sir. *(stares at him for a moment and then shakes his head in confusion)* Are you . . . ?

Grandfather *(smiles)*: Yes, Jake. Kim's uncle is the stranger who gave up his seat for my son. Now I am pleased to say that he is also a son of mine.

Curtain.

RECALLING FACTS

Write the answers to the following questions on the lines provided. You may go back to the selection to find an answer.

Recalling details

1. How does Jake know Kim and his family?

Jake is Kim's friend and classmate. Kim and Jake also play football together.

Recalling details

2. Where did Kim's family live before coming to America?

They lived in Vietnam.

Identifying setting

3. Where do the events in this play take place?

The events take place in a small boat leaving Vietnam in 1979 and in a present-day suburban home.

Identifying cause and effect

4. What did the man in the boat do to help Kim's family?

The man gave up his space in the boat so that Kim's father could leave Vietnam with his family.

Recalling details

5. How did Kim's family meet the man in the boat again?

When they were living in America, friends from Vietnam introduced them to the man.

Using context clues

6. Circle the correct meaning of the underlined word in each sentence.

a. The refugee left his homeland by boat.

person who is very poor

person who travels by boat

(person hurrying from danger)

b. A makeshift dock had been built overnight.

(temporary) permanent unsafe

c. The story told by the elderly man engrossed the people around him.

surprised and shocked

(captured the attention of)

bored and annoyed

INTERPRETING FACTS

Not all questions about a selection are answered directly in the selection. For the following questions, you will have to figure out answers not directly stated in the selection. Write the answers to the questions on the lines provided.

Inferring cause and effect

1. How might Kim's life be different if the man in the boat had not given up his seat to Kim's father?

Answers may vary. Kim's father may never have escaped from Vietnam. The rest of the family might not have gone to the United States. The family would not be enjoying the life that they have now.

Understanding character

2. In Scene 4, the stage directions state that Kim's grandfather looked carefully at the stranger in the boat and paused before he told his son to join the rest of the family in the boat. Why do you think he did this?

Answers may vary. The grandfather was deciding if it would be wise to accept his offer.

Drawing conclusions

3. How do you think Kim's father felt about the man who gave up his seat in the boat?

Answers may vary. Kim's father was very grateful and perhaps surprised that a stranger would do this for him.

Making inferences

4. Why did Kim's family ask the stranger to join their family in the United States?

Answers may vary. The man had no family of his own. He had saved Kim's family by helping them to stay together while escaping from Vietnam.

Making inferences

5. Why do you think this play is called *Family Loyalty*?

Answers may vary. The play shows the importance of being loyal and respectful to family members. It also shows that this loyalty can extend to others who respect the unity of family life.

SKILL FOCUS

The writer of this play gives you many clues about the setting of the action. Use these clues to answer the questions that follow.

1. At what time of day does the opening scene take place? How do you know?

It takes place in the morning. Kim's mother is fixing breakfast. Kim says good morning to his grandfather and his mother.

2. What other two scenes take place in the same setting as the opening scene?

Scene 3 and Scene 5

3. The setting of Scene 2 and Scene 4 is the same. Briefly describe the time and place.

The time is 1979. It is night. The place is Vietnam. A boat filled with refugees is tied to a dock on the South China Sea.

4. Does the action in Scenes 1, 3, and 5 take place on the left side or the right side of the stage? Explain your answer.

The action takes place on the left side of the stage because these scenes are set in the present.

5. a. In which two scenes does the author use flashbacks?

Flashbacks are used in Scene 1 and Scene 3.

b. Reread the dialogue in these scenes. Which sentences signal the beginning of each flashback? Circle those sentences.

▶ **Real Life Connections** Put yourself in the stranger's shoes. What would you have done when Tran Bay tried to separate Kim's family?

Lesson 2
Reading a Timeline

Reading a Social Studies Selection

▶ Background Information

The *Titanic* was a great ocean liner that was considered the most luxurious ship of its time. It was also said to be unsinkable because of its 16 watertight bulkheads. However, on its very first sea voyage, from England to the United States, the *Titanic* struck an iceberg in the North Atlantic Ocean on April 14, 1912, and sank the next day. Of the 2,224 people on board, 1,513 were drowned. The "unsinkable" *Titanic* only carried enough lifeboats for a little over half of its passengers. In fact, some of the lifeboats that left the sinking ship weren't even filled to capacity.

Several books have been written about this horrible sea disaster, including *A Night to Remember* by Walter Lord, a minute by minute account of the tragedy. In 1889, Morgan Roberts wrote a book called *The Wreck of the Titan*. It is the story of a huge luxury liner that hit an iceberg and sank. The name of the ship is the *Titan*. The book was written 14 years before the *Titanic* sank!

You might want to read a more recent telling of the *Titanic* in Robert Ballard's *Finding the Titanic.*

In this selection, you will read another account about the sinking of the *Titanic.*

▶ Skill Focus

A **timeline** is a type of chart that shows the sequence or order of events that took place. By showing major events in chronological order, a timeline helps you keep track of when important events happened. A timeline can also show the time span of important historical developments.

A timeline usually identifies the events and the date when each took place. Each section on a timeline stands for a specific period of time. This period can cover different lengths of time, such as a day, a year, ten years, or a century. Pay attention to how much time each section on a timeline stands for. Reading a timeline completely and carefully will help you understand the order in which important historical events took place.

▶ Word Clues

Read the sentence below. Look for context clues that explain the underlined word.

> People had thought for years that the *Titanic* sank because of a <u>gash</u>—a long, deep cut—in her hull.

If you do not know the meaning of the word *gash,* read the rest of the sentence. It tells you what the word *gash* means. A word meaning that is stated directly can often be found in the same sentence before or after a new word. A gash is a long, deep cut.

Use **definition** context clues to find the meaning of the three underlined words in the selection.

▶ Strategy Tip

Look at the timeline as you read the story of the *Titanic.* This will help you better understand the sequence of events that took place before and after the *Titanic* sank.

The *Titanic*

The *Titanic* measured two blocks long and 11 stories high. In 1912, she was the largest ship in the world. She was also considered the safest ship afloat. The *Titanic*, people said, was something new and amazing: she could not sink.

The hull, or frame of the ship, was divided into 16 watertight sections. This meant that no water could get in or out. The ship could stay afloat even if two of these sections filled with water. The *Titanic* was considered so safe that she carried only enough lifeboats for half the people aboard.

When the *Titanic* began her first voyage on April 10, there were about 2,200 men, women, and children aboard. Many of the passengers were rich and famous, like John Jacob Astor. At the age of 56, he was one of the richest men in the world. With him was his young wife Madeleine. Also aboard were Mr. and Mrs. Isidor Straus, who owned Macy's Department Store in New York. These and other first-class passengers had rooms decorated like expensively decorated hotels. The rooms for second-class passengers were not as grand but were still very comfortable. All of these passengers could eat in fine dining rooms, exercise in the gym, and swim in the heated pool.

The *Titanic* also carried over 700 immigrants traveling to a new land. Their rooms, located down below, had four bunks and a washbasin. These passengers, too, had much to enjoy: games, singing, even a Scotsman playing bagpipes.

Warnings at Sea

On April 14, the *Titanic* was traveling full steam ahead in the North Atlantic. The weather was clear and cool, as it usually was in April. However, the wireless telegraph operator began to receive messages warning of icebergs ahead. Over the next few hours, a total of six messages came from other ships.

The captain of the *Titanic*, E. J. Smith, received some of these messages. But he did not receive all of them. The *Titanic* had no set system for passing messages from the operator to the crew to the captain. Because of this, no one person saw all of the messages. If the six warnings had been mapped out, they would have shown a wall of ice in the path of the *Titanic*. Captain Smith simply asked the men on lookout to watch for icebergs. The lookouts could use only their eyes, because they had no binoculars with them on the lookout platform.

Disaster at Sea

Shortly before midnight, one of the men on lookout stared into the darkness. He saw a large white shape straight ahead. The lookout rang bells and telephoned a message to the bridge: an iceberg was dead ahead. And the *Titanic* was headed straight for it.

Ship officers rushed to order the ship turned so that she would miss the iceberg. But they were too late. The *Titanic* struck the iceberg. Chunks of ice fell on the deck, and the ship slowly came to a stop. In one of the

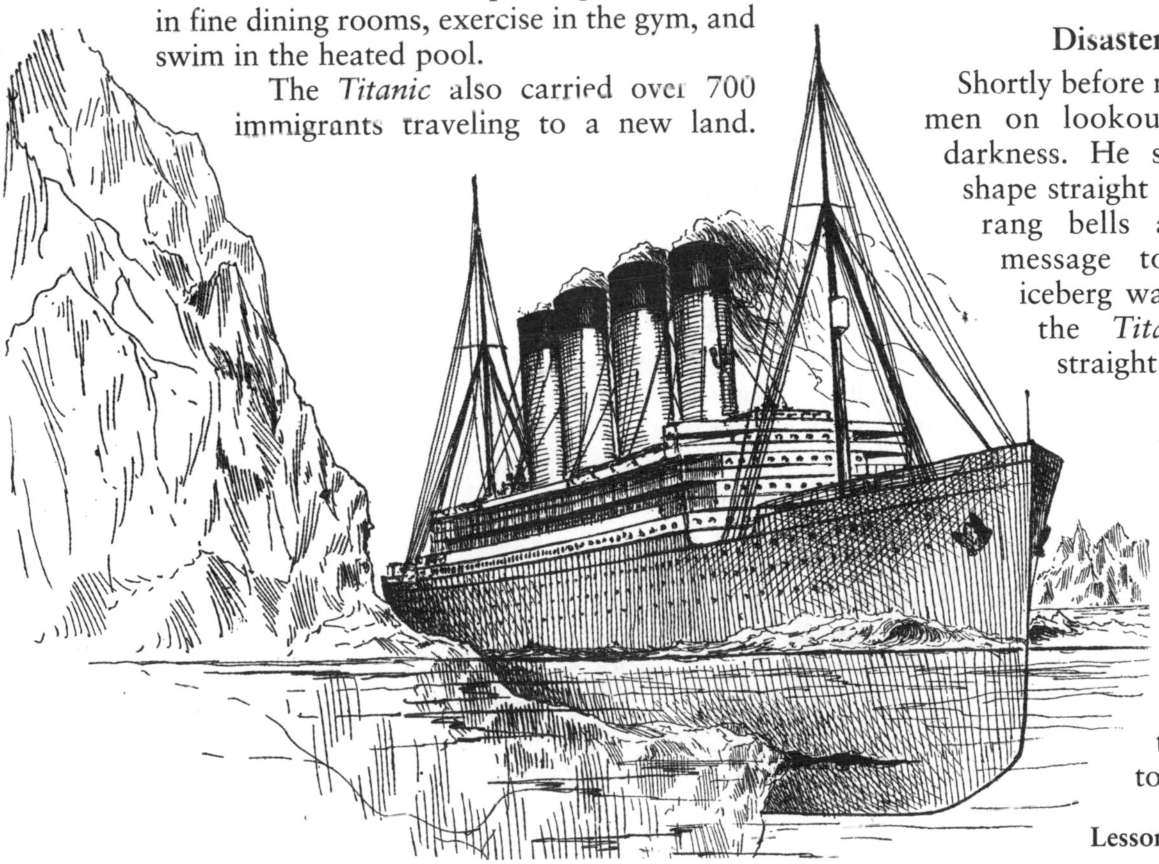

1912 April 10	April 11	April 12	April 13	April 14
Titanic leaves Southampton, England.	*Titanic* at sea.	*Titanic* at sea.	*Titanic* at sea.	**Morning** *Titanic* receives message warning of icebergs. **Lunchtime** Two more warnings received. **Afternoon and evening** Three more warnings received. **11:40 P.M.** Lookout sees iceberg, sends alarm. **A few minutes later** *Titanic* hits iceberg.

boiler rooms, alarms went off. A wall gave way, and water began to rush in. Captain Smith soon learned what had happened to the ship. The *Titanic* was filling up fast with water.

The crew rushed to call other ships for help. Ships hearing the call began to change course to come to the aid of the *Titanic*. One ship, the *Californian,* was nearby. But the radio operator did not get the message. He had gone off duty at 11:30 P.M., the time that he usually left for the night. Then he had gone to bed.

As water gushed into the *Titanic,* lifeboats were lowered. Women and children were asked to get into them, but they did not know how great the danger was. Some saw no reason to take a ride in the icy sea. Some men laughed as they helped their wives into boats. All would be well by breakfast, they thought.

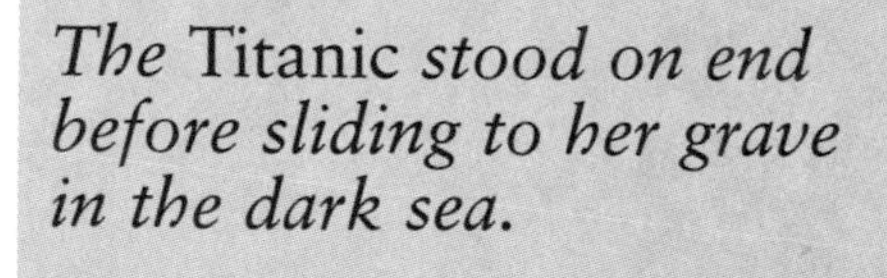

The crew sent rockets into the sky, trying to attract the attention of other ships. Then the passengers began to realize that the *Titanic* was sinking. Through the sound of shouting and crying, the ship's band could be heard playing ragtime songs. The band kept playing as the front deck of the ship was covered with water. Soon, the sound of hymns was heard in the darkness.

The *Titanic* stood on end before sliding to her grave in the dark sea. At 2:20 A.M., the great, "unsinkable" ship sank in the cold waters of the North Atlantic. Over 1,500 people, including the captain, died in the disaster.

The Survivors

Some people were in the freezing water, struggling to reach the lifeboats. Most boats still had room in them, but very little effort was made to pick up the swimmers.

By 2:40 A.M., a ship had spotted the boats. By 4:10 A.M., the *Carpathia* had begun to take people aboard. There were about 700 survivors, including women, children, and some men. At sunrise, they saw the huge iceberg that the *Titanic* had hit.

Other ships racing to the rescue learned that they were too late. The *Californian,* the one ship that had been nearby, saw the rockets that the *Titanic* sent up. But the crew was uncertain about what they meant. At about 5:40 A.M., one crew member woke up the radio operator. The operator turned on his radio and contacted another ship. He learned that the *Titanic* had hit an iceberg and had sunk.

News of survivors was slow in reaching relatives. Newspaper stories were based on only a few facts, and many reports were false. Over 30,000 eager people waited in New York as the *Carpathia* arrived. As the survivors left the ship, they began to tell the story of the *Titanic.*

April 15	April 16	April 17	April 18
Shortly after midnight Water gushes into ship. **12:25 A.M.** SOS sent to other ships. Nearby *Californian* fails to respond. **12:30 A.M.** People loaded into lifeboats. **2:30 A.M.** *Titanic* sinks. **2:40 A.M.** *Carpathia* spots lifeboats. **4:10 A.M.** *Carpathia* picks up survivors.	*Carpathia* at sea.	*Carpathia* at sea.	*Carpathia* arrives in New York with survivors.

The Investigations

In the weeks following the tragedy, the United States Senate and the Board of Trade in England held investigations. The reports stated that the *Titanic* had not been carrying enough lifeboats. The boats that had been available were not fully loaded. Because no lifeboat drills had been held, officers were slow in loading people into the boats. If the boats had been full, at least 400 more lives could have been saved.

Investigators also found that the *Titanic* had been traveling too fast. As warnings about ice had reached the ship, the *Titanic* should have been moving at a slower speed. There also should have been more people on lookout to spot the icebergs.

Much of the blame for the lost lives went to the *Californian*. The crew of the *Californian* had seen the rockets that the *Titanic* sent up. If the *Californian* had helped the *Titanic* right away, many, if not all of the passengers, might have been saved. The *Californian* did not receive the calls for help

because the ship's radio operator was not on duty. In 1912, the law did not require ships to have a radio operator on duty at all times.

Exploring the Wreckage

The story of the *Titanic* has continued to unfold. In 1985, a group of scientists found the wreckage of the ship. This team was led by Robert E. Ballard of the United States and Jean-Louis Michel of France. The scientists removed samples of the ship and then studied them. People had thought for years that the *Titanic* sank because of a gash—a long, deep cut—in her hull. But the steel used in the hull was the real problem. It was too brittle for the cold waters and broke easily when the ship hit the iceberg.

Stories, articles, and films have described the greatest sea tragedy in history. The film *Titanica* shows the wreckage of the ship, over two miles down on the ocean floor. Two submarines were used in the filming. One submarine filmed the other as it entered the site of the wreck. People viewing the film can see the remains of the ship's railing, where people stood as they waited for the *Titanic* to sink.

Recalling Facts

Write the answers to the following questions on the lines provided. You may go back to the selection to find an answer.

Recalling details

1. In what year did the *Titanic* begin her voyage? 1912

Recalling details

2. What did people say about the new and amazing *Titanic*?

People said that she could not sink.

Identifying cause and effect

3. What was the reason that Captain Smith did not receive all of the messages that warned about icebergs ahead?

The *Titanic* had no system for passing messages from the operator to the crew to the captain.

Identifying cause and effect

4. Why did the lookout ring bells and telephone a message to the bridge?

He had seen an iceberg straight ahead.

Recognizing sequence of events

5. What happened in the boiler room after the ship hit the iceberg?

Alarms went off. A wall gave way, and water began to rush in.

Identifying cause and effect

6. Why didn't the radio operator on the nearby *Californian* receive the *Titanic*'s call for help?

He had gone off duty at 11:30 P.M. and had gone to bed.

Recognizing sequence of events

7. What was the order of events that enabled some of the passengers to arrive safely in New York?

They got into lifeboats. The *Carpathia* spotted the boats and took the passengers on board. This ship then carried the passengers to New York.

Identifying cause and effect

8. Why did investigators blame the *Californian* for loss of life?

The *Californian* did not go to the aid of the *Titanic* when the rockets were first seen.

Recalling details

9. What did scientists learn about the sinking of the *Titanic*?

They found that the steel in the hull had been the problem. It was too brittle for the cold waters and had broken easily when the ship hit the iceberg.

Using context clues

10. Decide if each statement is true or false. Write *true* or *false* on the line provided.

a. A hull of a ship is the framework that supports the sails. false

b. If a container is watertight, no water can get inside. true

c. If a seashell is brittle, it may easily break. true

Interpreting Facts

Not all questions about a selection are answered directly in the selection. For the following questions, you will have to figure out answers not directly stated in the selection. Write the answers to the questions on the lines provided.

Making inferences

1. Was Captain Smith concerned about the safety of his ship when he received the messages about icebergs? Explain.

No. He simply asked the men on lookout to watch for icebergs. He did not add more lookouts.

Making inferences

2. What do you think the captain expected to happen if the men on lookout spotted any icebergs?

He expected the ship to change course and avoid any icebergs.

Making inferences

3. Why did the people in lifeboats make little effort to pick up swimmers?

They feared for their own lives. Rowing toward swimmers in the darkness could be dangerous. Pulling swimmers on board might cause the boat to overturn. The boats might become overloaded.

Making inferences

4. Why do you think the *Californian* did not respond to the rockets the *Titanic* sent up?

Answers may vary. Because the radio operator was off duty, the *Californian* was not aware of how great the danger was.

Making inferences

5. Why were there many false newspaper reports about the disaster?

Answers may vary. Communication was much slower in 1912 than it is today. Some newspapers made up details when they could not get the facts.

Drawing conclusions

6. Why do you think the story of the *Titanic* has been retold so many times?

Answers may vary. It has all the elements of great drama: disaster at sea, the forces of nature, and human error.

Skill Focus

The timeline on pages 14 and 15 shows when events took place during the *Titanic* disaster. Use the timeline to answer the questions below.

1. How long was the first, and last, voyage of the *Titanic*?

It was a little over five days.

2. For how many days were iceberg warnings received?

Warnings were received for one day.

3. When did the *Titanic* hit the iceberg?

It hit on April 14, 1912, shortly before midnight.

4. When were there signs that the ship had been badly damaged?

Signs were noted April 15, 1912, shortly after midnight.

5. About how long did it take the *Titanic* to sink after hitting the iceberg?

It sank in about two and three-quarters hours.

6. About how long did the survivors spend in lifeboats?

Survivors spent over three and a half hours in the lifeboats.

7. What ship rescued the survivors?

The *Carpathia* rescued them.

8. Where did the ship take the survivors?

They went to New York.

Real Life Connections Name an event at school or in your community for which a timeline would be useful. Tell why.

Lesson 3

Classifying

Reading a Science Selection

Background Information

The following selection describes three classifications, or groups, of water animals—spiny-skinned animals, hollow animals, and sponges. Most of the animals that you will read about live in the ocean; however, the hydra is a freshwater animal. Preview the selection before you read it. Look at the headings that identify the names of the three groups. Under each heading you will see, in boldfaced type, the names of some water animals. These are the names of animals that belong to that group. After each boldfaced name, you will find information about the water animal.

Skill Focus

Sometimes information is organized by **classifying** similar objects, living things, or ideas into groups. Similarities and differences among these groups are easier to see. Classifying is especially helpful for people such as scientists who study different animals or ideas.

When scientists classify plants and animals, they divide the members of large groups into smaller groups. The members of each smaller group are similar in certain ways. For example, different kinds of animals live in water. To study these water animals, scientists have classified them according to their body structures and body functions. Water animals with similar body structures and body functions are grouped together.

When reading information about animals that have been classified into groups, notice the headings. They will help you to understand important details about each group. Ask yourself questions such as the following.

1. What is similar about the animals that scientists classify in the same group?
2. How are the animals in one group different from animals in another group?

Word Clues

Read the sentence below. Look for context clues in the same sentence that explain the underlined word.

> The starfish's body has a central disk from which five arms extend like those of an octopus.

If you don't know the meaning of the word *extend*, the phrase, *like those of an octopus,* can help you. The arms that stretch out from the body are compared to the arms of an octopus.

Use **comparison** context clues to find the meaning of the three underlined words in the selection.

Strategy Tip

As you read "Spiny-Skinned Animals, Hollow Animals, and Sponges," look for the similarities and differences among the animals in each group. Also think about the similarities and differences among the groups.

Spiny-Skinned Animals, Hollow Animals, and Sponges

Group 1: Echinodermata

Starfish, brittle stars, sea urchins, and sea cucumbers all are members of a group called **Echinodermata** (i ky nə der MAH tə). The word *Echinodermata* means "spiny-skinned." All of these animals have a hard, spiny skin. They also have a central body from which arms or spines branch out.

Starfish The starfish is not a fish. A better name for it would be *sea star.* Its body has a central disk from which five arms extend like those of an octopus. Most starfish have five arms, but some kinds have a greater number. The starfish has no head. The mouth of a starfish is in the center of the underside of the disk.

✔ The starfish has many tiny tubes on the underside of its arms. These tubes are connected to canals inside the arms. The starfish draws water into the canals through the tubes. By forcing water in and out of the canals, it opens and closes the tubes. This creates a suction like that caused by a vacuum cleaner. As a result, the tubes stick to a surface and are used as tiny feet. That is how the starfish moves across the ocean floor.

The starfish feeds on clams, which are slow-moving, and oysters, which do not move at all. After climbing on top of a clam, the starfish attaches its tube feet to the clam's shell using suction. It pulls on the shells of the clam, using its many tube feet in relays. When the muscles that hold the clam's shell together are tired out, the shell opens. The starfish then turns the lower part of its stomach inside out and extends it through its mouth. The stomach surrounds the soft part of the clam and digests it.

Certain animals are able to **regenerate** (ri JEN ə rayt). The starfish is one of these animals. This means that it can replace lost parts of its body. In fact, if a starfish is cut into several pieces, each piece can grow into another starfish.

Brittle Stars The brittle star is so called because its arms break off easily. However, like the starfish, it can regenerate. The brittle star crawls over the ocean floor with quick movements of its arms. Most brittle stars have five arms, but some have as many as eight. The brittle star has a mouth in the center of its underside, similar to that of the starfish. It feeds on worms and mollusks.

Sea Urchins The sea urchin does not look like a starfish, yet it has a similar body structure. The sea urchin looks like a large ball with long, sharp spines. It moves by using its spines and its tube feet. The spines also protect the sea urchin from its enemies. The mouth of the sea urchin is on its underside. Around its mouth is a set of five teeth arranged in a circle. The sea urchin lives near rocky shores, feeding on plants and decaying materials in the sea.

Sea Cucumbers The sea cucumber is a fleshy animal shaped something like a cucumber. The sea cucumber has spines that are very tiny. It can crawl along the ocean floor by muscular movements of its body. The sea cucumber has five rows of tube feet. It uses the tube feet to attach itself to rocks. At one end of its body is the mouth, which is surrounded by **tentacles** (TEN tə kəlz). The tentacles are like tiny arms and can trap small animals.

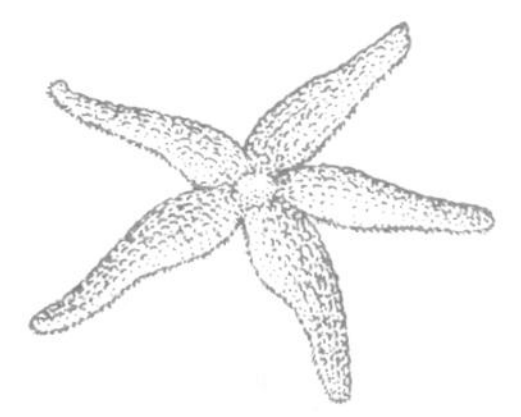

Starfish

Brittle Star

Sea Urchin

Sea Cucumber

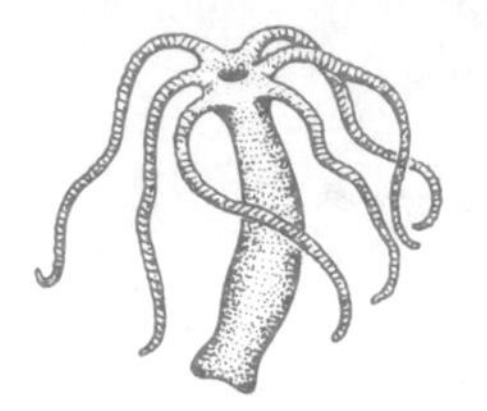

Hydra

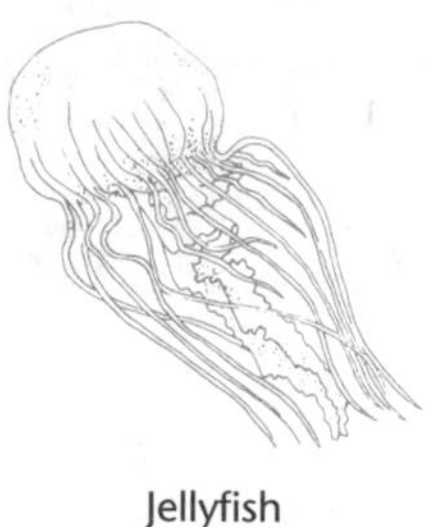

Jellyfish

Sea Anemone

Corals

Group 2: Coelenterata

Hydras, jellyfish, sea anemones, and corals all belong to a group called **Coelenterata** (si len tə RAH tə). The word *Coelenterata* means "hollow insides." All of these animals are hollow in the middle.

Hydra The hydra is a simple animal. Its body is a hollow tube only a quarter of an inch long. The hydra's mouth is at one end of the tube. The other end of the tube is closed, and the animal uses this end as a foot. From six to ten long tentacles grow out from around the mouth. The hydra is not a sea animal. It lives in fresh water. It clings to weeds, sticks, and stones.

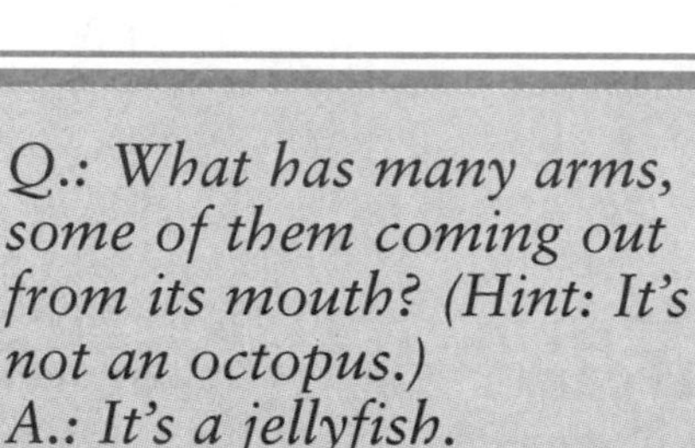

Q.: What has many arms, some of them coming out from its mouth? (Hint: It's not an octopus.)
A.: It's a jellyfish.

Jellyfish The jellyfish is not a fish. This coelenterate has a jellylike body in the shape of a bell. Its mouth is in the center of the underside of the bell. From the corners of its mouth extend arms that can grasp small animals. The bell of the jellyfish has many other arms around its edge. The jellyfish can swim slowly by contracting and expanding its bell. The swimming jellyfish looks like a balloon being filled with air and then being emptied of air over and over again. Jellyfish bells range in size from about 3 to 12 inches in diameter.

Sea Anemone The sea anemone (ə NEM ə nee) is so named because it looks like a many-colored, beautiful flower called an anemone. The sea anemone attaches itself to a rock or shell and stays there. Its mouth is surrounded by many tentacles. The sea anemone feeds on crabs and fish. It has a slimy disk or foot on which it can slide along. The sea anemone has the ability to regenerate a lost or injured part of its body.

Corals The stony coral is like the sea anemone. It remains attached to one spot and produces a cup of limestone material into which it can retreat. Millions of tiny corals live together. In warm seas, they build reefs of limestone. Coral jewelry is made from the colorful coral houses built by some of these tiny animals.

Group 3: Porifera

Many types of sponges belong to the group called **Porifera** (po RIF ə rə). The word *Porifera* means "pore bearer." Sponges have many pores, or holes. Sponges grow in different shapes. They may be dome shaped or fan shaped. The basket sponge, deadman's fingers, and vase sponge are named because of the way they look.

Sponges attach themselves to the ocean floor and do not move about. Like the starfish, brittle star, and sea anemone, sponges can regenerate. All sponges have one thing in common. They are made up of colonies of many tiny animals. Each cell of the sponge is able to feed itself and get rid of its waste.

The sponge has many whiplike parts, each called a **flagellum** (fle JEL əm). As the flagellum whips about, it causes a flow of

Deadman's Fingers

Bath Sponge

Vase Sponge

Basket Sponge

water. The movement of many flagella causes water to enter the sponge through the pores or openings in its outer surface. Tiny plants and animals are thus brought in as food for the sponge.

A sponge has a framework that supports the soft mass of its living cells. This framework is the part that is sold in stores as a natural sponge. Most sponges provide living quarters for many other animals. Worms, shrimps, small crabs, and some small fish find homes in the canals and chambers of sponges. They also get food from the water that passes through the sponge's body.

RECALLING FACTS

Write the answers to the following questions on the lines provided. You may go back to the selection to find the answer.

Recalling details

1. What happens if a starfish loses one of its arms?
   It can regenerate its lost arm.

Recalling details

2. What do all Coelenterata have in common?
   They are hollow in the middle.

Recalling details

3. What is a flagellum?
   It is a tiny whiplike part.

Recalling details

4. What does *Porifera* mean?
   Porifera means "pore-bearer."

Recalling details

5. Where does the hydra live?
   It lives in fresh water.

Identifying the main idea

6. Go back to the selection and reread the paragraph with a check mark next to it. Underline the sentence that contains the main idea.

Using context clues

7. Underline the word that correctly completes each sentence.
   a. Milk can be drunk through a straw using ________.
      suction **tentacles** **flagellum**
   b. You are ________ your stomach when you hold it in.
      expanding **extending** **contracting**
   c. A tire is ________ when air is being pumped into it.
      regenerating **expanding** **contracting**

INTERPRETING FACTS

Not all questions about a selection are answered directly in the selection. For the following questions, you will have to figure out answers not directly stated in the selection. Write the answers to the questions on the lines provided.

Making inferences

1. What purpose might be served by the skin of Echinodermata?
   The skin might protect the animal.

Making inferences

2. Why might it be an advantage for brittle stars to have arms that break off easily?
   Answers may vary. Possible answer: If another animal catches a brittle star by one of its arms, the brittle star could escape when its arm breaks off.

Making inferences

3. The sand dollar has skin that is covered with short spines. It has tube feet and a mouth in the center of its underside. To what group does it probably belong?
   Echinodermata

Drawing conclusions

4. Why do you think the sand dollar belongs to that group?
   It has spiny skin.

SKILL FOCUS

A. Write the name of each of the three groups mentioned in the selection. Under each group name, write the names of the animals that belong to it.

Group 1 Echinodermata	Group 2 Coelenterata	Group 3 Porifera
starfish	hydra	basket sponge
brittle star	jellyfish	deadman's fingers
sea urchin	sea anemone	vase sponge
sea cucumber	coral	

B. Go back to the selection and reread the description of each type of Echinodermata. Complete the chart below by adding the characteristics of each animal. The first one is started for you.

ECHINODERMATA

Responses will include some of the following.

	Starfish	Brittle Star	Sea Urchin	Sea Cucumber
Body Structure	Central disk with five arms Mouth in center of underside of disk	Body, arms, and mouth similar to those of starfish Arms break off easily	Round body with long, sharp spines Five teeth around its mouth	Body like cucumber with tiny spines Mouth surrounded by tentacles
Motion	Possible answers: Uses tubes to draw water into canals in its arms Forces water in and out and creates suction	Crawls by quick movements of its arms	Moves using its spines and tube feet	Crawls by muscular movements of its body

▶ **Real Life Connections** Name at least two categories for the items in your desk or book bag. What items would you classify in each category? How are the items in each category the same? How are the two categories different?

Lesson 4

Decimals

Reading a Mathematics Selection

▶ Background Information

The following selection explains decimals, which is a way of writing about numbers. You will learn the names for place values to the right of the decimal point. The suffix *th* is an important clue in reading decimals.

The word *decimal* comes from the Latin word for ten, *decem.* The decimal system was named because it is a base-ten system. That means that the value of each place is ten times greater than the value of the place to its right.

Mathematicians developed the decimal system in India more than 2,000 years ago. However, no one knows exactly when or where in India this number system was invented. In 876 C.E., the use of a new symbol in the number system was recorded. This symbol is what we now call zero. People who lived in Central America also invented a similar system and used a zero by 300 C.E.

In the 700s C.E., Arabs conquered parts of India. As a result of this conquest, they learned the decimal system that was in use there. Over the next 300 years, the Arabs spread the use of this system throughout their empire—through the Middle East to northern Africa and into Spain.

An Italian pope introduced the decimal system into Europe about 1000 C.E. However, at this time books were copied by hand and weren't available to many people. As a result, many people still didn't know about the decimal system. After the invention of the printing press in the mid-1400s, however, arithmetic books were published. These books explained the use of the decimal system, which was then taught in schools and universities throughout Europe.

▶ Skill Focus

A period in a number is called a **decimal point**. It is there to separate the digits to the left of the decimal point from the digits to the right of the decimal point. The digits to the left of the decimal point are whole numbers. The digits to the right of the decimal point are less than one.

6.2

In the number above, the decimal point tells you that 6 stands for a whole number. The decimal point also tells you that the number to its right stands for part of a whole number. When reading this number, you use the word *and* in place of the decimal point. The number is read as: six *and* two tenths.

▶ Word Clues

When the suffix *th* is added to a number word, such as ten, hundred, or thousand, the meaning of the word is changed. With the suffix *th,* the word describes a value of less than one whole. The difference in value between *ten* apples and a *tenth* of an apple is great. Ten tenths would make *one* whole apple. When you buy *ten* apples, you have a hundred times more apples than a *tenth* of an apple.

▶ Strategy Tip

When reading this selection about decimals, remember the names of the place values to the right of the decimal point. These numbers are always less than one.

Reading Decimals

These four place values all show whole numbers.

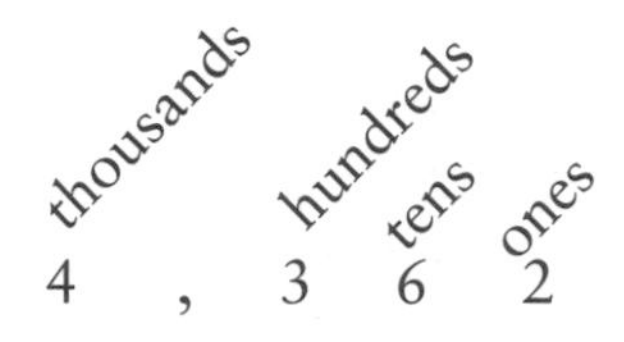

There are also place values to the right of the ones place. These are called **decimal places.** A decimal point separates the ones place from the first decimal place. The places to the right of the decimal point show values of less than one.

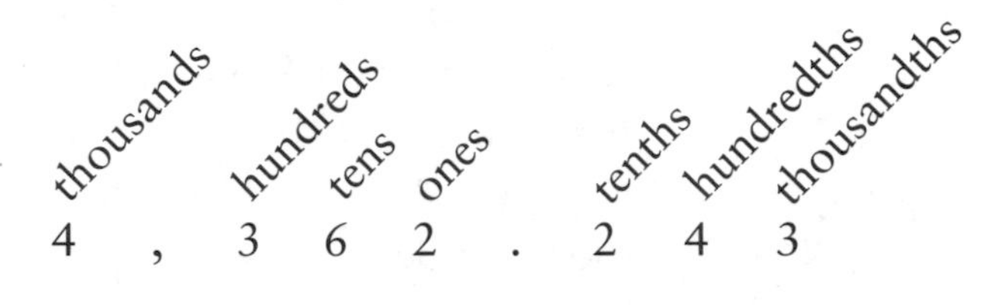

The first three places to the right of the decimal point are tenths, hundredths, and thousandths. A number in the tenths place is $\frac{1}{10}$ as large as the same number in the ones place.

Think about a dollar bill. It takes ten dimes to make a dollar. A dime is one-tenth of a dollar. One-tenth can be written as a decimal, 0.1, or as a fraction, $\frac{1}{10}$.

A number in the hundredths place is one-hundredth of the same number in the ones place. It takes 100 pennies to make a dollar. A penny is one-hundredth of a dollar. One-hundredth can be written as a decimal, 0.01, or as a fraction, $\frac{1}{100}$. It takes one hundred dimes to make ten dollars. A dime is 0.01 or $\frac{1}{100}$ of ten dollars.

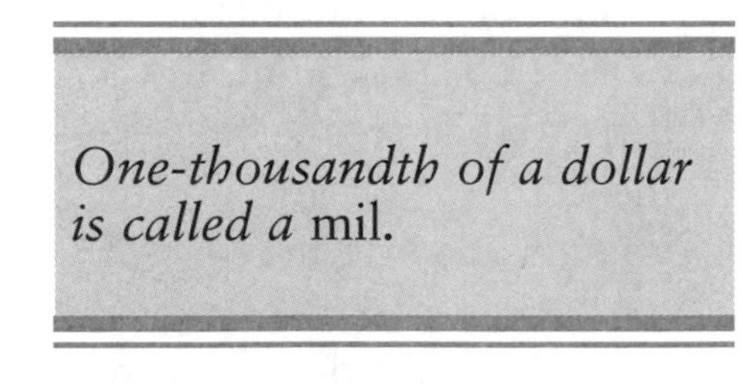
One-thousandth of a dollar is called a mil.

A number in the thousandths place is one-thousandth of the same number in the ones place. This is a very small part of a dollar. It is so small that there is no coin made for that value. One-thousandth of a dollar is called a *mil.* Mils are used in the financial world. It takes 1,000 mils to make a dollar. One-thousandth can be written as a decimal, 0.001, or as a fraction, $\frac{1}{1,000}$.

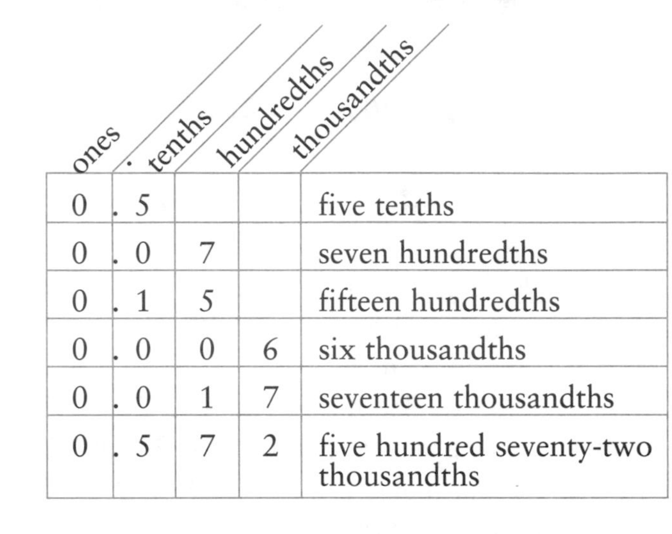

ones	.	tenths	hundredths	thousandths	
0	.	5			five tenths
0	.	0	7		seven hundredths
0	.	1	5		fifteen hundredths
0	.	0	0	6	six thousandths
0	.	0	1	7	seventeen thousandths
0	.	5	7	2	five hundred seventy-two thousandths

If a number less than one is written as a decimal, a zero may be used to the left of the decimal. When reading a decimal number that has no whole numbers, ignore the zero. Read the number to the right of the decimal as though it were a whole number. Then add the name of the place value.

Numbers that include digits on both sides of the decimal point are always read in two groups. Look at the following number.

376.4

First, read the number to the left of the decimal. Say the word *and* when you reach the decimal point. Then read the number to the right of the decimal point as though it were a whole number, and add the name of the place value. The number should be read as: three hundred seventy-six and four-tenths.

The same number could also be written as a whole number and a fraction. The number to the left of the decimal point is a whole number. The number to the right of the decimal point is a fraction. The 4 is in the tenths place, so the denominator of the fraction is 10. The number is written as follows:

$$376\frac{4}{10}$$

Look at the following number.

496.15

Read the number to the left of the decimal point first. Say the word *and* when you reach the decimal point. Read the number to the right of the decimal point. Since the last digit is in the hundredths place, add the word *hundredths*. The number is read as: four hundred ninety-six and fifteen-hundredths. The number is written as a whole number and a fraction as follows:

$496\frac{15}{100}$

Look at the following number.

537.207

It is read as: five hundred thirty-seven and two hundred seven thousandths.

Remember, the decimal point separates the whole numbers from the numbers that are less than one. The numbers that appear to the right of the decimal point are always less than one.

RECALLING FACTS

Write the answers to the following questions on the lines provided. You may go back to the selection to find an answer.

Recalling details

1. What are the names, in order, of the three places to the right of the decimal point?

tenths, hundredths, thousandths

Recalling details

2. What word is said when you reach the decimal point in a number?

and

Recalling details

3. If a dollar bill is one whole, what part of a dollar is a dime? A penny? Write each as a fraction and as a decimal.

$1.00 = 1

$0.10 = $\frac{1}{10}$ 0.1

$0.01 = $\frac{1}{100}$ 0.01

INTERPRETING FACTS

Not all questions about a selection are answered directly in the selection. For the following questions, you will have to figure out answers not directly stated in the selection.

Making inferences

1. How are a decimal and a fraction the same?

They both show part of the whole number one.

Making inferences

2. What is the function of zero in a decimal?

It holds a place value.

Making inferences

3. For each group of three decimals, circle the number with the largest value.

a.	b.	c.
(0.5)	0.4	(0.6)
0.07	0.02	0.02
0.01	(0.7)	0.3

Skill Focus

A. Write each number in the correct column.

	thousands	hundreds	tens	ones	tenths	hundredths	thousandths
4 tenths				.	4		
9 tenths				.	9		
23 and 8 tenths			2	3 .	8		
4,496 and 5 tenths	4,	4	9	6 .	5		
3 hundredths				.	0	3	
12 hundredths				.	1	2	
5 and 17 hundredths				5 .	1	7	
6 thousandths				.	0	0	6
47 thousandths				.	0	4	7
526 thousandths				.	5	2	6
7 and 93 thousandths				7 .	0	9	3
92 and 5 thousandths			9	2 .	0	0	5
143 and 12 thousandths		1	4	3 .	0	1	2
800 and 8 hundredths		8	0	0 .	0	8	
2,002 and 2 thousandths	2,	0	0	2 .	0	0	2

B. Rewrite each decimal number as a fraction or as a whole number and a fraction.

0.6 $\frac{6}{10}$ 4.2 $4\frac{2}{10}$ 423.001 $423\frac{1}{1,000}$ 591.93 $591\frac{93}{100}$

0.42 $\frac{42}{100}$ 8.96 $8\frac{96}{100}$ 1,492.013 $1,492\frac{13}{1,000}$ 783.486 $783\frac{486}{1,000}$

0.157 $\frac{157}{1,000}$ 12.07 $12\frac{7}{100}$

C. Draw lines to match each decimal in the first column with the fraction in the second column that has the same value. Then match each fraction with a written-out number in the third column.

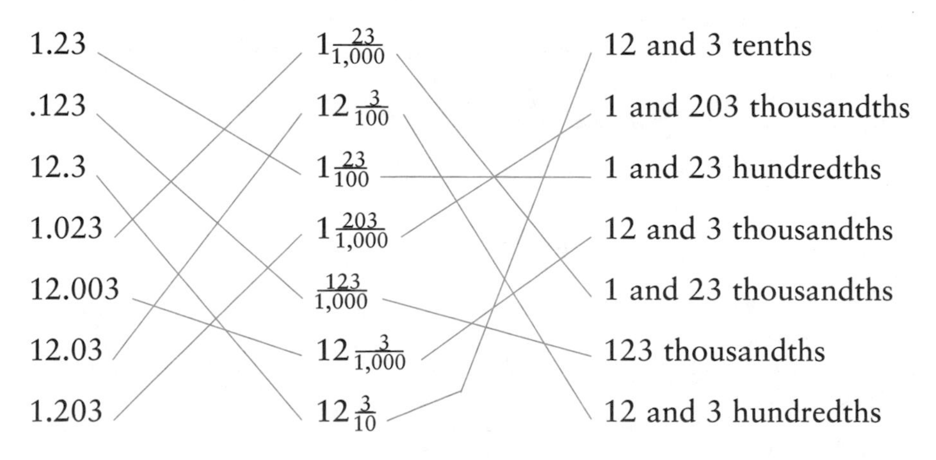

▶ **Real Life Connections** Describe three occasions when you had to read or use decimals.

Silent Letters

In studying vowels, you learned that when a one-syllable word contains two vowels, one of which is a final *e*, the final *e* is usually silent. You also learned that when two vowels come together in a one-syllable word, the second vowel is usually silent.

Cross out the silent vowel in each word below.

hole	boat	tribe
sea	shore	fire
line	coast	gleam
reach	home	coat

Consonants, as well as vowels, can be silent. Below are some cases when a consonant is silent.

k before *n,* as in *knee*

w before *r,* as in *write*

c before *k,* as in *kick*

b after *m,* as in *lamb*

gh after *au, ou,* or *i,* as in *caught, thought,* and *light*

t in the middle of a one-syllable word, as in *hatch*

d in the middle of a one-syllable word, as in *hedge*

Say each word below to yourself. Cross out the silent vowels and consonants.

1. wrap	11. dough	21. knot
2. file	12. night	22. high
3. badge	13. patch	23. truck
4. meat	14. toad	24. beak
5. bought	15. wreck	25. fudge
6. limb	16. nine	26. dime
7. cute	17. watch	27. latch
8. crack	18. train	28. steam
9. hose	19. struck	29. stone
10. fight	20. tape	30. taught

Lesson 6

Main Idea

The main idea is the most important idea in a paragraph. Often the sentence giving the main idea is the first or last sentence. You can find the sentence that gives the main idea if you ask yourself which sentence states what the paragraph is about.

Read the following paragraphs. Below each one are three sentences that appear in the paragraph. Underline the sentence that is the main idea of the paragraph.

Woodpeckers

1. Several kinds of woodpeckers live in North America. The flicker, a brown-backed woodpecker with red markings, is fairly common. The little downy woodpecker, another common woodpecker, usually lives in orchards. The ivory-billed woodpecker is one of the rarest birds in North America. It is a large, wild, shy bird with a high, scarlet crest.

a. The little downy woodpecker, another common woodpecker, usually lives in orchards.

b. Several kinds of woodpeckers live in North America.

c. The flicker, a brown-backed woodpecker with red markings, is fairly common.

2. The red-headed woodpecker is one of the most common kinds of woodpeckers. It lives in the central and eastern parts of the United States. It looks for grubs by boring holes in the bark of trees. But it doesn't live on grubs alone. It also eats fruit, especially berries. This woodpecker is about ten inches in length. It is a very colorful bird. Its head, neck, and throat are red. Its back, tail, and upper wings are black. Its lower wings and under sections are white.

a. It is a very colorful bird.

b. Its back, tail, and upper wings are black.

c. The red-headed woodpecker is one of the most common kinds of woodpeckers.

3. The woodpecker's bill is sharp and strong. With it, the woodpecker chisels holes in trees where food will be. Its tongue is long and sharp. The woodpecker uses its tongue to spear insects, insect eggs, and grubs. One kind of woodpecker sucks sap from the tree. This woodpecker has a brush on the end of its tongue to collect the sap. The woodpecker's bill and tongue help it get food.

a. The woodpecker's bill is sharp and strong.

b. One kind of woodpecker sucks sap from the tree.

c. The woodpecker's bill and tongue help it get food.

4. Woodpeckers build their nests in holes in trees. Sometimes they dig a new hole in a live tree. Sometimes they find a hole in a dead tree. The female looks the hole over carefully while the male is digging into it. After the female decides that the hole is suitable, she helps the male with the digging. They line the hole in the nest with sawdust and wood chips.

a. Sometimes they dig a new hole in a live tree.

b. They line the hole in the nest with sawdust and wood chips.

c. Woodpeckers build their nests in holes in trees.

5. You may think that the deep holes woodpeckers bore in trees are harmful. However, these holes have little effect on the health of the trees. In fact, woodpeckers possibly save many trees by destroying the harmful insects that bore into trees. The drilling helps trees more than it hurts them.

a. However, these holes have little effect on the health of the trees.

b. The drilling helps trees more than it hurts them.

c. In fact, woodpeckers possibly save many trees by destroying the harmful insects that bore into trees.

Lesson 7

Reference Books

How can you find information about a subject you are studying or want to know more about? You can use **reference books** in the library or at home. You need to know what kind of information each reference book contains in order to select the one you need. It is easy to locate information if you use the right reference books.

Suppose a friend is going to give you a sitar, but you are not certain what a sitar is. You can find the word *sitar* in the **dictionary.** You know that a dictionary defines words. It also shows how words are spelled, pronounced, and divided into syllables, and what parts of speech they are. Some dictionaries include a picture with the entry.

si·tar (si tär′) ***n.*** a musical instrument of India with a long neck, and strings that vibrate along with those being played. *See the picture.*

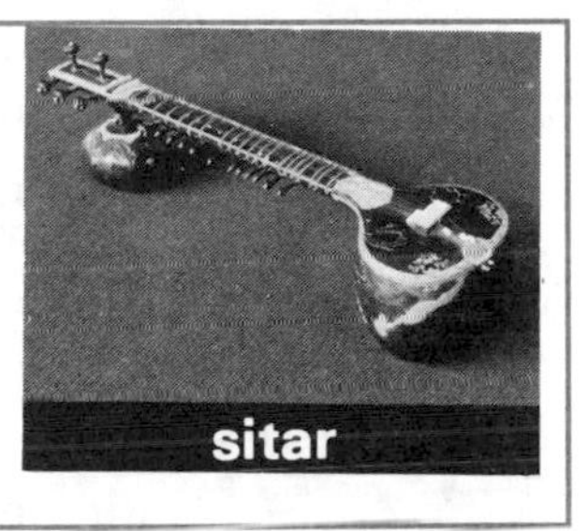

sitar

Once you find out what the word *sitar* means, suppose you want to learn more about the instrument. You might want to know what kinds of sounds it makes, where it was developed, or how it is played. What reference book could you use? You may already know that an **encyclopedia** is a book or set of books containing articles on many subjects. An encyclopedia would provide the kind of information you want.

Sitar, *sih* TAHR, is a stringed instrument that originated in India or Persia. It is used in the classical music of northern India, Pakistan, and Bangladesh. The sitar has a long, broad neck made of wood and a pear-shaped body made from a large gourd. It has 7 main strings, which the musician plucks with a wire pick worn on the right index finger. It also has 12 or more *sympathetic strings.* These strings vibrate when the main strings are played. Adjustable metal strips called *frets* are attached to the neck of the instrument. They serve as fingering guides for the left hand.

The sitar probably was developed in the A.D. 1200's. It reached its present form during the 1800's and 1900's. It serves chiefly as a solo instrument, usually accompanied by a drum called a *tabla* and a lute called a *tambura* that produces a *drone* (continuous pitch). A sitarist improvises within a certain melodic framework known as a *raga* and a metrical framework called a *tala.* The instrument has become more familiar in the West since the 1960's. The Beatles and other rock groups have used it in their music.

Valerie Woodring Goertzen

While reading the encyclopedia, you may become curious about India, the country where the sitar was first developed. You may wonder how many people live there today. To find out, you would use an **almanac.** Although an encyclopedia may give the population of India, the figure may not be current. An almanac is a book with the most up-to-date information on many different subjects. Because it is printed every year, the information is more current than information found in other references. An almanac contains weather reports, statistics, or facts, about the United States and other countries, current events, sports facts, world records, and interesting information about people.

Area and Population by Country
Mid-1993 Estimates

Country	Area	Population	Country	Area	Population
Afghanistan	250,000	17,400,000	Hungary	35,920	10,300,000
Albania	11,100	3,300,000	Iceland	39,770	300,000
Algeria	919,590	27,300,000	India	1,269,340	897,400,000
Angola	481,350	9,500,000	Indonesia	741,100	187,600,000
Antigua and Barbuda	170	100,000	Iran	636,290	62,800,000
Argentina	1,068,300	33,500,000	Iraq	167,920	19,200,000

A. Write the name of the correct reference material next to the kind of information it contains.

1. book with important facts printed yearly ___almanac___
2. meanings, spellings, and pronunciations of words ___dictionary___
3. articles on many different subjects ___encyclopedia___

B. Complete each situation by underlining the name of the correct reference material.

1. Sergio wants to go mountain climbing with his older sister and brother. They tell him that he may go along if he has enough stamina. Sergio doesn't know what the word *stamina* means. Before he goes on the trip, he should use the ________.

   almanac **dictionary** **encyclopedia**

2. Angela heard someone say that there was a "baby boom" last year—that more babies were born last year than in quite a few years before. To check if this information is correct, Angela should use the ________.

   almanac **dictionary** **encyclopedia**

3. Jamal and his mother are moving from Phoenix to Baltimore. Jamal wants to learn about Baltimore's population, weather, history, and recreation. To find such facts about his new city, Jamal should use the ________.

   almanac **dictionary** **encyclopedia**

4. José is writing a letter to his grandfather. José wants to write about his new pet parakeet, but he is not sure how to spell the word *parakeet.* He needs to check the ________.

   almanac **dictionary** **encyclopedia**

5. May Ling's class is going to visit Mount Vernon, the home of George Washington. Before the visit, May Ling wants to find out more about the first president and his life at Mount Vernon. To find this information, she should use the ________.

   almanac **dictionary** **encyclopedia**

6. Yousef is studying a floor plan of his new school. He doesn't recognize the word *gymnasium* on one of the rooms. He looks up the word and sees that it is pronounced jim nā ′zē əm. He realizes he will play basketball in that room. To find this information, Yousef uses the ________.

   almanac **dictionary** **encyclopedia**

7. Mr. Gordon's class is studying weather. The students are interested in learning about the places and dates of the highest and lowest temperatures, as well as the greatest rainfalls and snowfalls. They should look in the ________.

   almanac **dictionary** **encyclopedia**

8. Viktor is making a graph comparing the number of votes the candidates for governor of his state received in each of the last four elections. To find the information he needs, he should use the ________.

   almanac **dictionary** **encyclopedia**

9. Abby is copying a report she has written. She is almost at the end of a line on her paper and finds that she can fit only part of the word *manufacturing* on the line. To find out where to divide the word into syllables, she should use the ________.

   almanac **dictionary** **encyclopedia**

Lesson 8

Hard and Soft *c* and *g*

The consonant *c* has two sounds, soft *c* as in *cent* or hard *c* as in *can*. The consonant *g* has two sounds, soft *g* as in *gem* or hard *g* as in *goose*.

When you come to a new word that contains either *c* or *g*, you may wonder if the letter has the hard sound or the soft sound. There is a guide that can tell you which sound to use in pronouncing the word.

Write an answer to each of the questions in the headings.

	What vowel comes after c?	*Does* c *have the hard or soft sound?*
1. cape	a	hard
2. common	o	hard
3. curve	u	hard

Fill in the words necessary to complete the following guide.

> Usually *c* has the ___hard___ sound when followed by the vowel ___a___, ___o___, or ___u___.

	What vowel comes after c?	*Does* c *have the hard or soft sound?*
1. center	e	soft
2. cider	i	soft
3. cycle	y	soft

Fill in the words necessary to complete the following guide.

> Usually *c* has the ___soft___ sound when followed by the vowel ___e___, ___i___, or ___y___.

	What vowel comes after g?	*Does* g *have the hard or soft sound?*
1. gate	a	hard
2. goblet	o	hard
3. gulf	u	hard

Fill in the words necessary to complete the following guide.

> Usually *g* has the ___hard___ sound when followed by the vowel ___a___, ___o___, or ___u___.

	What vowel comes after g?	Does g have the hard or soft sound?
1. gentle	e	soft
2. giant	i	soft
3. gym	y	soft

Fill in the words necessary to complete the following guide.

> Usually *g* has the ___soft___ sound when followed by the vowel ___e___, ___i___, or ___y___.

Now make a guide that can be used with both *c* and *g*.

> **Guide:** Usually *c* and *g* have the hard sound when followed by the vowel ___a___, ___o___, or ___u___ and the soft sound when followed by the vowel ___e___, ___i___, or ___y___.

This guide has a few exceptions, as in *get, girl,* and *give.* In most cases, however, the vowel letter following *c* or *g* will show what sound to use in pronouncing a new word.

Below are some words that contain either *c* or *g*. Say each word to yourself. Decide which sound the *c* or *g* has in each word. Write *hard* or *soft* on the line next to the word.

1. general	soft	9. gypsy	soft	17. gunpowder	hard
2. gush	hard	10. oxygen	soft	18. giraffe	soft
3. civilian	soft	11. citizen	soft	19. cinder	soft
4. curtain	hard	12. certain	soft	20. captain	hard
5. cymbals	soft	13. gull	hard	21. germ	soft
6. cabin	hard	14. cite	soft	22. care	hard
7. compare	hard	15. rage	soft	23. current	hard
8. garden	hard	16. cash	hard	24. gyrate	soft

Read the story below. Underline every word that has a hard or soft *c* or a hard or soft *g*. If the letter has the hard sound, write *h* above it. If the letter has the soft sound, write *s* above it.

The Magic Boat of Lake Geneva

Once there was a strange boat on Lake Geneva. It had no engine. White swans with silken cables in their beaks gently pulled it.

This was a magic boat. A fairy princess stood in it. Her hair was golden yellow. Her head covering was set with gems. She wore a gown of many colors.

Whenever the boat came to the shore, corn and wheat began to sprout, and cypress trees came up in all the gardens.

Very few of the country people ever saw the boat. When one of them happened to catch a view of it, his purse was filled with gold. He never had to go to work again. He always had plenty of cash.

Lesson 9

Prefixes and Suffixes

A **prefix** is a word part that is added to the beginning of a word to change its meaning. Circle the prefix in each of the words below.

discover	enlarge	superhighway	renew
unhappy	preview	depart	subway
misspell	dislike	redo	indoors

A **suffix** is a word part that is added to the end of a word to change its meaning. Circle the suffix in each of the words below.

statement	swiftly	national	quickest
straighten	helpful	sweetness	clearly
loudness	darken	hopeless	teacher

Write one of the prefixes below in the blank to the left of each word to make a new word with a meaning that agrees with the given definition.

Prefix	*Meaning*
un	not
re	back, again
in	in, toward
pre	before

1. un wanted not wanted
2. in coming coming in
3. re sew to sew again
4. un usual not usual
5. pre heat to heat before
6. re patch to patch again
7. pre pay to pay before
8. in land toward land
9. re plant to plant again
10. un tied not tied

Write one of the suffixes below in the blank to the right of each word to make a new word with a meaning that agrees with the given definition.

Suffix	*Meaning*
er	one who does
ful	full of
en	made of, to become
ness	quality or state of

1. farm er one who farms
2. near ness quality of being near
3. wood en made of wood
4. wonder ful full of wonder
5. kind ness quality of being kind
6. sweet en to make sweet
7. joy ful full of joy
8. sing er one who sings

Lesson 10

Following Directions

A recipe is a set of instructions for making something to eat or drink. The ingredients, which tell what and how much to use, are listed first. The steps to follow in preparing the food are next. It is important to follow the steps in the right order. If you read the directions carefully, you can follow any recipe.

Study the following recipe. Notice the abbreviations in the list of ingredients and the metric conversions in parentheses.

SEAFOOD AND SPAGHETTI

1 doz uncooked shrimp, peeled and deveined
$\frac{1}{2}$ lb (.225 kg) sea scallops
40 small to medium mussels, rinsed well
1 onion, sliced thin
1 garlic clove, chopped fine
3 T (45 mL) olive oil
1 lemon, sliced thin
1 large can of Italian plum tomatoes, mashed and drained
$\frac{1}{2}$ can tomato paste
$\frac{1}{2}$ c (.12 L) clam juice
1 t (5 mL) dried basil
1 T (15 mL) oregano
$\frac{1}{2}$ t (2.5 mL) pepper
1 t (5 mL) salt
1 lb (.45 kg) spaghetti

1. Cook onion and garlic in oil in large pot.
2. When onion is soft, add lemon, tomatoes, tomato paste, basil, oregano, salt, and pepper. Simmer for 25 minutes, stirring occasionally.
3. Add clam juice and simmer until sauce thickens, about 15–20 minutes.
4. Cook spaghetti according to directions on package.
5. Add shrimp, scallops, and mussels to sauce. Cover and cook on high heat until mussels open, about 5 minutes. Lower heat and simmer uncovered until spaghetti is done.
6. Drain the spaghetti. Empty into large bowl. Pour sauce and seafood over spaghetti. Serve immediately.

SERVES 4–6 PEOPLE

A. Below, in correct order, are the steps to follow for the seafood and spaghetti recipe. Write 1 in front of the step to follow first, 2 in front of the step to follow next, and so on.

__2__ Add the lemon, tomatoes, tomato paste, basil, oregano, salt, and pepper, simmering for 25 minutes.

__5__ Add the shrimp, scallops, and mussels, cooking on high heat until mussels open.

__4__ Cook the spaghetti according to directions on package.

__1__ Cook onion and garlic in oil in large pot.

__6__ Empty the drained spaghetti into large bowl and pour sauce and seafood over.

__3__ Add clam juice and simmer until sauce thickens.

B. Fill in the circle next to the answer to each question.

1. What kinds of seafood are used in this recipe?
   - ● shrimps, scallops, mussels
   - ○ onion, garlic, oil
   - ○ scallops, mussels, lemon

2. What do you need to do to the onion before you cook it?
   - ○ Wash it well.
   - ● Slice it thin.
   - ○ Chop it fine.

3. Once the onion is soft, about how long does the sauce simmer before the seafood is added?
   - ○ 25 minutes
   - ○ 15–20 minutes
   - ● 40–45 minutes

4. Why do you think you have to stir the sauce occasionally while it is cooking?
   - ● so it doesn't stick to the bottom of the pot
   - ○ so all of the ingredients will cook for the same amount of time
   - ○ so you won't forget that you have something cooking on the stove

5. Why doesn't the recipe explain how to cook the spaghetti?
   - ○ There probably wasn't enough room in the recipe.
   - ○ Everybody already knows how to cook spaghetti.
   - ● The directions for cooking the spaghetti are on the spaghetti package.

6. How do you know that you are to cook the shrimps without their shells?
   - ○ The recipe calls for uncooked shrimp.
   - ● The recipe calls for peeled shrimp, so you must remove the shells.
   - ○ The recipe calls for covering and cooking the shrimp on high heat.

7. Why do you think the recipe calls for covering the pot once the mussels are in?
   - ● The cover keeps the heat in the pot, which makes the mussel shells open.
   - ○ The cover allows the heat to escape from the pot, which keeps the mussel shells closed.
   - ○ The cover keeps the mussels in the pot so that they do not jump out.

8. The recipe serves four to six people. What does that mean?
   - ○ Depending on the size of the shrimp and scallops, it will serve about 46 people.
   - ○ It serves four adults or six children.
   - ● Depending on how large the portions are, it will be enough for four, five, or six people.

9. How could you prepare this recipe for two or three people?
   - ● Use half the amount of each ingredient.
   - ○ Double the ingredients.
   - ○ Triple the ingredients.

C. Read the words below. Then read the abbreviations from the recipe. On the line next to each abbreviation, write the word it stands for.

pound	kilogram	tablespoon	cup
milliliter	liter	dozen	teaspoon

1. T tablespoon
2. L liter
3. lb pound
4. t teaspoon
5. kg kilogram
6. mL milliliter
7. doz dozen
8. c cup

UNIT 2

Challenges

Lesson 11

Conflict and Resolution

Reading a Literature Selection

Background Information

The Sioux, or Lakota—a Plains Indian nation—lived in the mid-1800s in what is now Minnesota, the Dakotas, and Nebraska. These Native Americans were famous for their bravery and fighting ability.

The following selection is about one Lakota boy who was always looking for opportunities to prove his courage as a hunter and a warrior.

Skill Focus

Often the characters in a story have a goal to achieve or a problem to solve. The struggle to achieve this goal or to solve this problem is called the **conflict**. This conflict drives the plot of the story.

A character can face three main types of conflict.

Conflict with Self

A character may struggle with inner emotions or feelings. An example is a person who has to climb a mountain despite a fear of heights.

Conflict with Another Character

A character may struggle against another person or an animal. An example is two runners competing against each other in a marathon race.

Conflict with an Outside Force

A character may struggle against nature, society, or some danger over which he or she has no control. An example is a sailor fighting to keep a ship afloat during a terrible storm at sea.

By the end of the story, the character facing the conflict succeeds or fails in achieving a goal or solving a problem. The way a conflict is settled is called the **resolution.** Every conflict has a resolution. Conflict and resolution are part of a story's plot or main action.

Look for the conflicts in the stories that you read. Be sure to find the resolution for each conflict.

Word Clues

Read the following sentences. Look for context clues that explain the underlined word.

> A long line of Lakota hunters slithered silently through the waving prairie grass in what now is South Dakota. As they moved like rattlesnakes, their feet whispered over the ground.

If you don't know the meaning of the word *slithered,* the phrase, *moved like rattlesnakes,* can help you. The way the hunters moved is compared to the way that snakes move, using the word *like.*

Use **comparison** context clues to find the meaning of the three underlined words in the selection.

Slow-to-Let-Go

A long line of Lakota hunters slithered silently through the waving prairie grass in what is now South Dakota. As they moved like rattlesnakes, their feet whispered over the ground. In the front were the best hunters. In the rear was a ten-year-old boy.

A herd of grazing buffaloes moved slowly down the plain toward the hunters. The hunters spread out and quietly crept toward the buffaloes. When they had almost reached the herd, they froze, arrows ready. They waited, hidden by the tall grass.

A lick of wind brought the animals' scent to the hunters. The boy watched closely through the crooked branches of a bush. Big and shaggy-haired, the buffaloes passed some of the lead hunters. Some of them were taller than his father, Jumping Bull. They would soon be nearing the boy.

Suddenly, the quiet of the prairie was broken by the roar of pounding hoofs. The animals had smelled the hunters and started to run. Hunters jumped from cover, sighted along arrows, and let them fly. The buffaloes were running hard now. The ground shook beneath their hoofs as the animals rumbled toward the boy.

The boy fitted an arrow to his bow. He picked out a red-eyed bull running toward him. He aimed just above and behind the animal's front shoulder. The arrow shot from his bow and pierced the galloping animal. Although the arrow stabbed the buffalo like a bolt of lightning, the animal kept running, pushed on by the others, thundering close behind.

The boy grabbed another arrow and ran after the bull. The herd swung away, but his buffalo slowed. The herd had left the wounded buffalo behind. The boy ran hard, seeking a second shot. Suddenly, the great animal stopped. Its legs folded. The heavy beast fell to the ground, rolled twice, then lay still.

It was dead. Slow-to-Let-Go had killed his first buffalo with only one shot.

Slow-to-Let-Go was given his name when he was a baby. Given food, he studied it, turning it this way and that before eating it, even when he was hungry. Given a rattle, he never wanted to let it go. He was careful about everything he did. And he learned from everything he did. He was careful and not afraid to try new things.

A Lakota man must be a good hunter. Slow-to-Let-Go killed his first buffalo at ten. Above all, a Lakota boy must grow to be a brave warrior. When he was only 14, Slow-to-Let-Go became a warrior. On that day in 1851 when he became a warrior, he earned a new name. Under this name he became one of the most famous Indian leaders in American history.

It was one of the long golden days of summer. The young boy watched his father and the other warriors ride out of the village. The village was camping for the summer on the heights above the Grand River in South Dakota. A few miles away was a creek. There the warriors would join Sioux from other villages for a war party against the Crows.

Whenever Slow-to-Let-Go talked of going on these war parties, his family told him that he was not old enough. They said he was not yet a man. And his father always agreed.

Above all, a Lakota boy must grow to be a brave warrior.

This time, Slow-to-Let-Go would try something instead of talk. When the men were out of sight, Slow-to-Let-Go jumped onto his horse and followed them. No one noticed him. He caught up with the men at the creek and rode to where his father stood.

"What are you doing here?" asked Jumping Bull.

"I am going, too," said Slow-to-Let-Go.

"Warriors are not made in 14 winters, my son."

Slow-to-Let-Go said nothing but looked calmly at his father.

"Warriors must be brave," Jumping Bull told him.

Slow-to-Let-Go nodded. "That is why I am here," he said. "To show I am brave."

Jumping Bull looked at his only son. Then he raised his hand. "My son will ride with us," he said.

He stepped closer to the boy. "You are not old enough to carry a warrior's arrows," he said. "But you can prove your courage with this." He handed his son a stick with a feather on it.

To the Lakota and other Plains Indians, war was a testing ground to prove a warrior's courage. One way to show courage was to "count coup." A warrior counted coup by touching an enemy with a coup stick. When a fight began, the bravest warriors raced ahead to touch the enemy with their coup sticks. Getting away without being killed was more honorable than killing the enemy. These fast and brave warriors were considered as noble as a king. "Your horse is fast," said Jumping Bull. "You must show that your heart is brave."

The Lakota rode for several days, but the scouts found no sign of the Crows. One day, the party made camp behind a low hill. A scout called down from the hilltop. There was something far off—perhaps only a dust cloud or some buffaloes.

Others joined the scout. They watched until they were sure. An enemy party about the size of the Sioux party was coming at a gallop. The men grabbed their weapons and ran for their horses.

Slow-to-Let-Go was quickly painted bright yellow from head to foot. His gray horse was painted red. He grabbed his coup stick and leaped onto his horse. The wind whistled past him as he thundered down the hill and across the plain.

The Crows pulled up short. They began to turn their horses back. They were going to run! The Sioux bellowed with anger as they chased the Crows across the plain.

Slow-to-Let-Go thumped his heels against his horse's flanks, causing it to sprint like a jackrabbit. The Lakota were catching up with the fleeing Crows. Slow-to-Let-Go had the honor of being the first into battle.

Suddenly Slow-to-Let-Go could see the Crows' faces as they looked back. The enemy drew their bows and arrows. They turned, aiming for the leaders of the Sioux charge.

Very quickly, Slow-to-Let-Go was among the Crows. He caught up with a Crow warrior who drew his bow and turned to shoot at the Lakota. The boy cut his horse closer to the enemy. He lashed out with his coup stick. The stick struck the Crow's arm just as he shot his arrow. The arrow flew into the ground.

The running battle ended in a few minutes. The Lakota gathered the horses and weapons they had won and turned for home. When they got to the village, Jumping Bull painted his own horse black. This was the sign of victory and honor. Then he put his son on the horse and led him around the village.

"Hear me!" he cried. "My son has counted coup in his first battle! He was first to strike the enemy! My son is brave!

"From this day my son is a warrior. Today I give him a new name. From this day his name is Sitting Bull!"

Directions for Recalling Facts and Interpreting Facts are given in Unit One only.

RECALLING FACTS

Identifying sequence of events

1. What happened to the buffalo after Slow-to-Let-Go shot it with his arrow?
The buffalo ran on, slowed, fell to the ground, rolled over twice, and then lay still.

Identifying cause and effect

2. What did Slow-to-Let-Go prove when he killed his first buffalo?
Slow-to-Let-Go proved that he was a good hunter.

Understanding character

3. After Slow-to-Let-Go proved his skill as a hunter, what else did he want to prove?
Slow-to-Let-Go wanted to prove that he was a brave warrior.

Recalling details

4. How did Slow-to-Let-Go prove his courage as a warrior?
Slow-to-Let-Go was the first to touch the enemy with a coup stick.

Recalling details

5. What new name did Jumping Bull give his son upon his becoming a man?
He gave him the name Sitting Bull.

Identifying setting

6. Where do the events in this story take place?
They take place in what is now South Dakota.

Using context clues

7. Write the word below that could be used in place of the underlined word(s) in each sentence.

pierced   sprinted   honorable

a. The lion <u>ran fast for a short distance</u>.
sprinted

b. The <u>noble</u> factory owner helped to find new jobs for the laid-off workers.
honorable

c. The cook <u>stabbed</u> the steak with a knife to check if it was done.
pierced

INTERPRETING FACTS

Making inferences

1. How did Slow-to-Let-Go live up to his name when he hunted his first buffalo?
Answers may vary. Slow-to-Let-Go carefully selected his target and continued to hunt the same animal until he was successful.

Making judgments

2. Do you think Slow-to-Let-Go's new name, Sitting Bull, fits him? Explain.
Answers may vary. Yes, because while sitting on a horse he struck his prey as fiercely as a bull.

Making inferences about character

3. Why was Jumping Bull proud of his son?
Answers may vary. Jumping Bull was proud of his son because Slow-to-Let-Go showed that he was a good hunter and a brave warrior.

Drawing conclusions

4. Do you think Slow-to-Let-Go was brave when he counted coup? Explain.
Answers may vary. Yes, because according to Lakota custom, counting coup required more courage than killing because weapons were not used.

SKILL FOCUS

Think about the conflicts Slow-to-Let-Go faced and how he resolved them. Write your answers on the lines provided.

1. What is Slow-to-Let-Go's goal?

Answers may vary. Slow-to-Let-Go wants to prove that he has courage. He also wants to show that he is a good hunter and a brave warrior.

2. a. To prove that he is a good hunter, what conflict does Slow-to-Let-Go face at age ten?

He faces a herd of running buffaloes.

b. How is this conflict resolved?

Answers may vary. Slow-to-Let-Go selects his target and pursues it until he successfully kills his first buffalo.

c. What has Slow-to-Let-Go learned as a result of this experience?

Answers may vary. He has probably learned that he has courage and that he is a good hunter.

d. Think about the three kinds of conflict. What kind of conflict is this?

The conflict in this story is conflict with another character.

3. a. To prove that he is a brave warrior, with whom does Slow-to-Let-Go come into conflict?

He comes into conflict with a Crow war party.

b. How is this conflict resolved?

Slow-to-Let-Go counts coup in his first battle.

c. What has Slow-to-Let-Go learned as a result of this experience?

Answers may vary. Slow-to-Let-Go has learned that he has courage and is recognized as a brave warrior.

d. What kind of conflict is described in c above?

This incident describes conflict with another character.

4. How has Slow-to-Let-Go changed as a result of these conflicts?

Answers may vary. Slow-to-Let-Go is no longer a child. He has become a man and a Lakota hunter and warrior.

▶ **Real Life Connections** Think about Slow-to-Let-Go's character. Do you think that he would be a good leader today? Explain.

Lesson 12

Cause and Effect

Reading a Social Studies Selection

Background Information

Little was known of the history of the hundreds and thousands of African Americans kidnapped from Africa and sold into slavery in the Americas until historian and writer Alex Haley searched for his roots. His search took him to Africa and Europe. He spent nine years researching the background of one of his ancestors. He then spent another three years writing a book called *Roots: The Saga of an American Family*.

Roots was a great success. Millions of people bought the book. It was awarded the Pulitzer Prize in 1977 and was made into a popular television miniseries in the same year. In 1988, a second television miniseries, *Roots: The Gift,* appeared.

Skill Focus

The events above are connected by **cause and effect**. A cause is a reason, condition, or situation that makes an event happen. An effect is the result of a cause.

Sometimes one cause can have more than one effect. The following chart shows how one cause results in two effects.

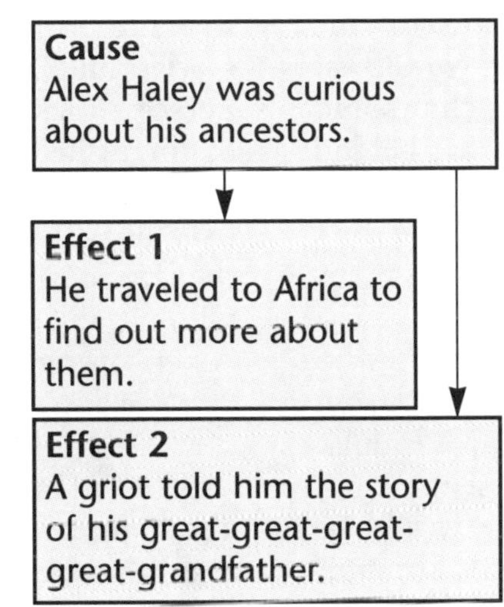

Sometimes the effect can be the result of more than one cause. The following chart shows this kind of relationship.

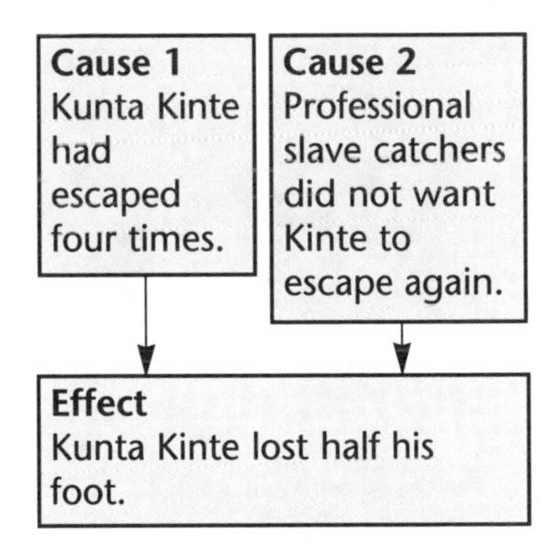

When you read, try to identify the events that are connected by cause and effect. For each event, think about the event or events that caused it to happen.

Word Clues

Read the following sentences. Look for context clues that explain the underlined word.

> During this time, Haley distinguished himself by writing revealing interviews with African Americans who usually avoided publicity, such as Miles Davis, the jazz musician, and Malcolm X, the activist who organized groups that fought for African American rights.

If you do not know the meaning of the word *activist,* read on. The rest of the sentence states what the word means. A word meaning that is stated directly can often be found near the new word.

Use **definition** context clues to find the meaning of the three underlined words in the selection.

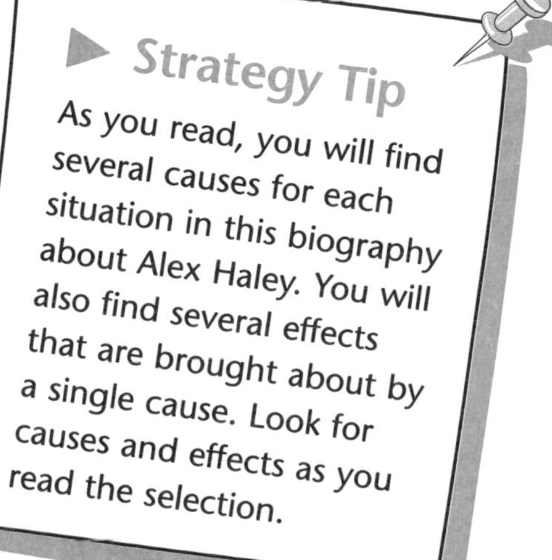

Alex Haley

When Alex Haley was a young boy growing up in Henning, Tennessee, his family lived in the home of his grandparents. On many summer evenings, he remembers great-aunts and other older women in his family who visited for weeks on end. In the afternoon and early evening, they would sit out on the front porch in rocking chairs and tell stories about the family. Haley sat behind his mother's rocking chair and listened.

One story that he remembered hearing over and over again was about his great-great-great-great-grandfather, who was described as "the African." This man, who called himself Kintay, was brought from Africa on a ship to Spotsylvania, Virginia. Time after time, Kintay tried to escape from his owner. Each time, however, he would be captured and beaten. On the fourth attempt, professional slave catchers caught him and, to discourage any more escapes, cut off half his foot. This slave called Kintay survived and had a family. Alex Haley is one of his descendants.

As a boy, Haley did not realize it, but this story would eventually take him to Africa and shape many events in his life.

Becoming a Writer

As an adult, Haley went to college briefly. He then joined the U.S. Coast Guard and was assigned to a ship in the Pacific Ocean during World War II. Bored by being at sea for two or three months at a time, Haley began writing. For eight years, he wrote. He wrote dramas about the sea. He also wrote letter after letter back home to everyone he knew. Lonely sailors asked him to write love letters to their girlfriends. Then Haley began to write stories and articles for magazines. He sent the stories to publishers and received hundreds of rejection slips, but he kept on writing. Finally, a magazine accepted a story, and Haley's writing career began.

At 37, Haley retired from the Coast Guard and moved to New York City. Then he began to write professionally. Magazines bought his stories and asked him to interview famous personalities. During this time, Haley distinguished himself by writing revealing interviews with African Americans who usually avoided publicity, such as Miles Davis, the jazz musician, and Malcolm X, the activist who organized groups that fought for African American rights.

Curiosity About Roots

Alex Haley had always been curious about his ancestors, but he knew very little about his family's history. Walking through a library one day, he saw people studying their genealogy, or account of their ancestors. By studying their genealogy, they were really trying to find out who they were. Haley suddenly wanted to find out about his own family history, a task that would be difficult at best.

Haley knew that it was difficult for African Americans to find out about their ancestors' history. Many slaves brought over from remote parts of Africa often did not know the white man's name for the region where they came from originally. Moreover, once the slaves were brought over to the Americas, wives, husbands, and children were often separated from one another and sold to different owners.

On a trip to London, Haley found himself standing in front of the Rosetta Stone in the British Museum. He was fascinated by the sets of puzzling hieroglyphics, or picture-like characters that

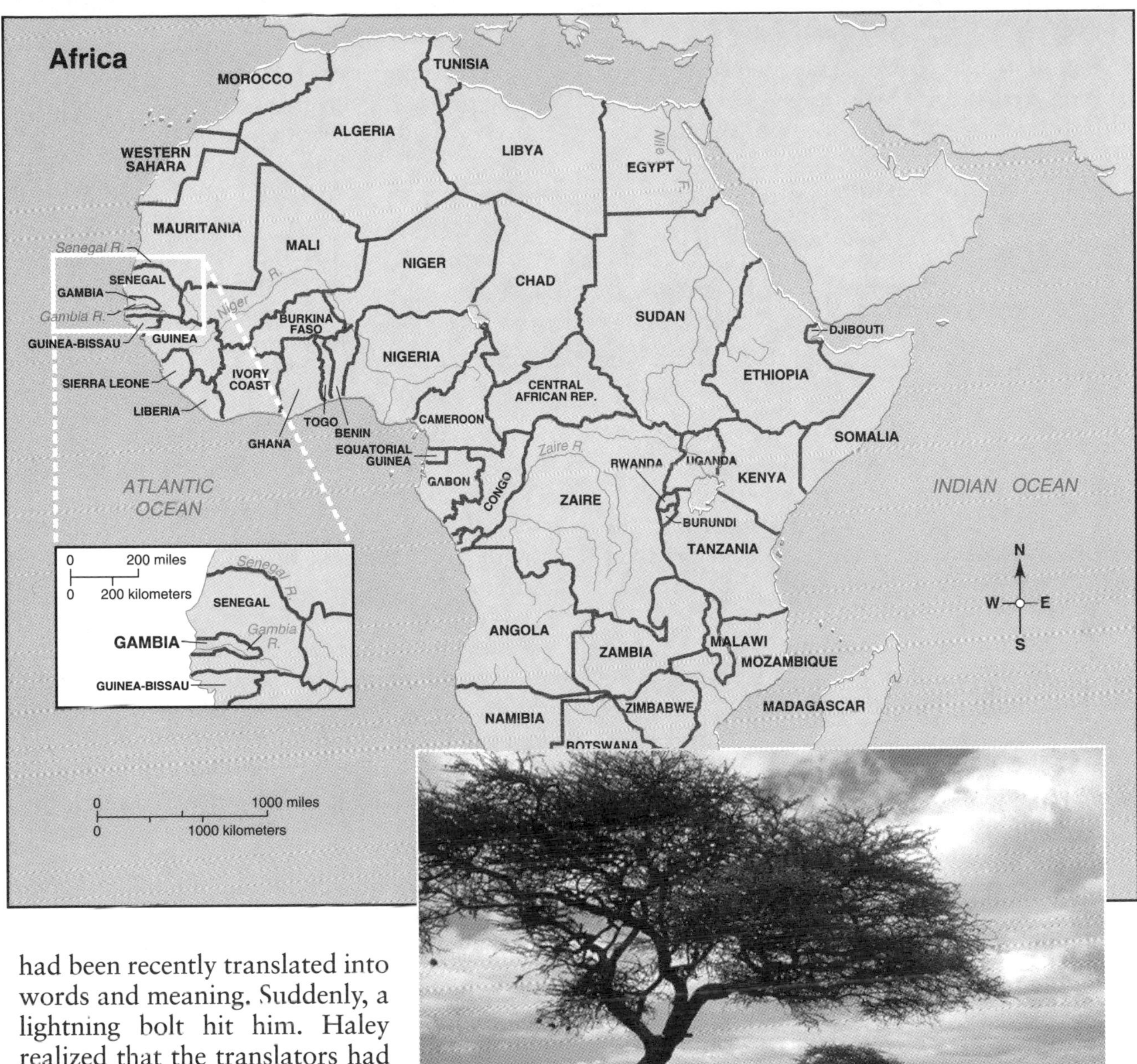

A Maasi griot, or storyteller, addresses a captive audience with his tales.

had been recently translated into words and meaning. Suddenly, a lightning bolt hit him. Haley realized that the translators had merely used what they knew to figure out the unknown.

Haley returned to the United States determined to find out about his roots. He took what he remembered and began to fit together the missing puzzle pieces. From the stories about "the African" that he had heard as a child, Haley remembered that his ancestor's name was Kintay. He knew that Kintay went out to find wood for a drum one day and was kidnapped by slave traders. He also knew that Kintay played a ko, an African musical instrument that looks like a harp. Haley was told that Kintay was a slave in Virginia near a river called Kamby Bolongo. With only these clues, Haley began his search.

When he spoke with a professor of African languages in Madison, Wisconsin, the professor identified the words ko and Kintay, or Kinte. He said that the words were spoken in the country of Gambia. He also said that Kamby Bolongo was Kambelongo, the Gambia River.

Thrilled by this discovery, Haley went to Africa four days later. There he found out that griots, or historical storytellers, could help him. But how could he ever locate the right griot?

Haley returned to the United States. A few days after his return, he received a letter stating that a griot who knew the history of the Kinte clan had been located. Because this griot knew the history of the area where the Kinte people had lived, he could help Haley.

So Haley returned to Africa and organized a safari of 14 people. They traveled with him far up the Gambia River to a settlement called Juffure. When he arrived, he was surrounded by 70 people in the village who were seeing an African American for the first time in their lives. Haley stared at the African villagers, and they stared back at their American visitor. Suddenly, the griot emerged from the crowd.

Kunta Kinte has become a universal ancestor, a symbol of heritage of all African Americans.

The griot began speaking. Haley waited patiently, fearing it might take a few days to hear the story that he was waiting for. Two hours later, he sat spellbound, listening to a story about a man named Omoro Kinte, who had four sons. Then he heard the words, ". . . the oldest of these sons, Kunta, went away from his village to chop wood, . . . and he was never seen again."

Haley knew that he had started to find the background information that he needed to write his story. He returned to the United States and began his research. He searched the shipping logs in Annapolis and found the landing where his great-great-great-great-grandfather had been sold into slavery. Haley wanted to experience how it might have felt to be aboard a slave ship for 90 days, as his ancestor had. He slept ten nights in the cargo hold of a ship coming from Africa to the United States. Each night, he tried to imagine what it felt like to be Kinte—chained, alone, and traveling to a place that he didn't know.

Haley also read all he could find about slavery, Africa, and plantation life in the South. Then he wrote the story about his family's history. He started at the beginning of that fateful day when Kunta Kinte was kidnapped in Africa, the day that he went out to chop wood for a drum.

Success at Last

Twelve years after he first began writing the book, in 1976, Haley delivered the final manuscript of *Roots* to his publishers. *Roots* was an immediate success. Millions of copies were sold. About 130 million Americans watched the made-for-TV miniseries of the book.

Perhaps the book's greatest achievement was its description of Kunta Kinte's life, both in Africa and in the United States. For many African Americans who knew little about their family history, Kunta Kinte became a universal ancestor, a symbol of the heritage of all African Americans.

RECALLING FACTS

Recalling details

1. What happened to Alex Haley when he was a sailor and went to sea for months at a time?

He became bored and began writing letters. He wrote love letters for other sailors. Then he began writing stories and articles for magazines.

Recalling details

2. What did Alex Haley know about his great-great-great-great-grandfather?

He knew that his name was Kintay and that he was born in Africa and played a ko. He also knew that one day Kintay went out to chop wood and was kidnapped by slave traders.

Comparing and contrasting

3. a. How was Alex Haley like the relatives he found in Africa?

He was descended from Omoro Kinte and his son Kunta Kinte.

b. How was he different from the people he found in Gambia?

He had lived in America; the people in Gambia still lived in a small village in Africa.

Recalling details

4. What happened to Kunta Kinte once he arrived in Virginia?

He tried to escape four times. On the fourth attempt, slave catchers cut off part of his foot.

Recalling details

5. How did seeing the Rosetta Stone help Alex Haley discover his roots?

When he saw how others had used the known to discover the unknown, he decided to do the same thing to learn about his family's history.

Recalling details

6. How did Alex Haley research the book *Roots*?

He traveled to Africa, he read books, and he studied shipping logs. He also spent ten nights on a sea freighter from Africa.

Recalling details

7. How did the African griot help Haley?

He told him about his ancestors who lived in Gambia.

Using context clues

8. Write the letter of the correct meaning on the line next to each word.

c genealogy

a hieroglyphics

b griot

a. picture-like characters

b. a storyteller who tells about historical events

c. an account of the history of one's ancestors

INTERPRETING FACTS

Making inferences

1. How do you think Alex Haley felt as he listened to stories about his family when he was a child?

Answers may vary. He probably felt excited and proud to have Kintay, or Kinte, as his ancestor. He might have felt angry, though, that Kintay was taken away from his family in Africa and sold into slavery.

Drawing conclusions about character

2. Based on what you have read, how would you describe Alex Haley's character?

Answers may vary. He is resourceful and very persistent. His family history is obviously very important to him.

Drawing conclusions

3. Why do you think Alex Haley called his book *Roots*?

Answers may vary. He described his search for his own roots, or his own beginnings and identity.

Making inferences

4. Why do you think Alex Haley wrote a book about his family?

Answers may vary. He wanted to tell a story that all African Americans could relate to and even claim as their own.

SKILL FOCUS

A. Write the cause of each of the following effects.

1. **Cause** Alex Haley was bored at sea.

   Effect Alex Haley started writing.

2. **Cause** Haley received a letter that said a griot who knew the history of the Kinte clan had been located.

   Effect Alex Haley returned to Africa and organized a safari.

3. **Cause** Alex Haley wrote a book called *Roots.*

   Effects
   a. The book sold millions of copies.
   b. Kunta Kinte became a universal ancestor for many African Americans.

B. Write the effect of each of the following causes.

1. **Causes**
   a. Slaves kidnapped from remote parts of Africa did not know the white man's name for the region they came from.
   b. Families of slaves were often separated from one another.

   Effect African Americans had difficulty finding the history of their ancestors.

2. **Causes**
   a. Kunta Kinte went out alone to chop wood for a drum.
   b. Kunta Kinte was kidnapped by slave traders and taken by ship to America.

   Effect Kunta Kinte was sold into slavery.

3. **Causes**
   a. Alex Haley saw people studying their genealogy to find out who they were.
   b. Alex Haley visited the Rosetta Stone and became inspired.

   Effect Alex Haley searched for his roots and wrote a book about it.

▶ **Real Life Connections** Discuss why it would be important for people to find out about their family history.

Lesson 13

Following Directions

Reading a Science Selection

Background Information

The following selection discusses the raw materials that plants need to produce food. It also describes how these raw materials are changed into food in a plant.

Skill Focus

Following directions is an important skill. For example, to carry out an experiment described in a science textbook, you must follow the directions that are provided.

Directions for an experiment are set up in a certain way. Most sets of directions have five parts: Problem, Aim, Materials, Procedure, and Observations or Conclusions. The following paragraphs describe each part.

Problem
The question that you should be able to answer at the end of the experiment.

Aim
What will be done in the experiment.

Materials
Objects or equipment needed for the experiment.

Procedure
The steps that must be carried out to complete the experiment.

Observations or Conclusions
Questions to answer or conclusions to draw about the outcome of the experiment.

Like recipes, science experiments are set up this way so that they can be performed repeatedly exactly as they were performed the first time. When you read directions for an experiment, notice the headings for the five parts. Read the paragraphs that come before the directions to help you understand the experiment.

Use the following steps to help you read a selection with directions for an experiment.

1. Read the paragraphs that explain the ideas. Be sure that you understand the ideas.
2. Read the five parts of the directions carefully. Be sure that you understand all the scientific words.
3. Study the pictures or diagrams. Be sure to read the captions and labels.
4. Reread the Problem, Aim, Materials, Procedure, and Observations or Conclusions. Be sure that you understand what to do before you carry out the experiment.

Word Clues

Read the sentence below. Look for context clues that explain the underlined word.

> The energy for the food-making process, a method for producing something, is supplied by sunlight.

If you do not know the meaning of the word *process,* the appositive phrase, *a method for producing something,* can help you. The word *process* is explained by this appositive phrase. Appositive phrases come before or after the word that they explain.

Use **appositive phrases** to find the meaning of the three underlined words in the selection.

Strategy Tip

After you read the paragraphs in this selection explaining how plants make their own food, study the directions for the experiment on page 49. Use the four steps described in the Skill Focus to help you understand the experiments.

How Plants Make Their Own Food

Plants need certain raw materials to manufacture food. These raw materials are water and carbon dioxide. Plants use these raw materials to make a simple form of sugar.

Plants get water from the soil and carbon dioxide from the air. Water passes through the roots into the stem and leaves of the plant. Carbon dioxide from the air enters a plant through tiny openings in the leaves called **stomates** (STOH mayts). See Figure 1 below.

Chlorophyll helps photosynthesis take place by trapping energy from sunlight.

To change the raw materials to food, plants need sunlight. The energy for the food-making process, a method for producing something, is supplied by sunlight. The food-making process is called **photosynthesis** (foh to SIN thə sis). See Figure 2. Most photosynthesis takes place in the plant's leaves.

This food-making process is made possible by **chlorophyll** (KLOR ə fil). Chlorophyll gives leaves and stems their green color. Chlorophyll helps photosynthesis take place by trapping energy from sunlight. This energy is held until it can be used to produce sugars and oxygen from the raw materials. Plants need oxygen to make use of their food. Extra oxygen is given off through the stomates. Some of the sugar is used for the plant's growth. Some of it is changed to starch and stored in the roots, stem, or seeds. Many of the foods eaten by people come from plants.

The roots of plants grow into the soil, holding the plant in the soil. Plant roots have another important function. The experiment on page 49 will demonstrate, or show, what that function is.

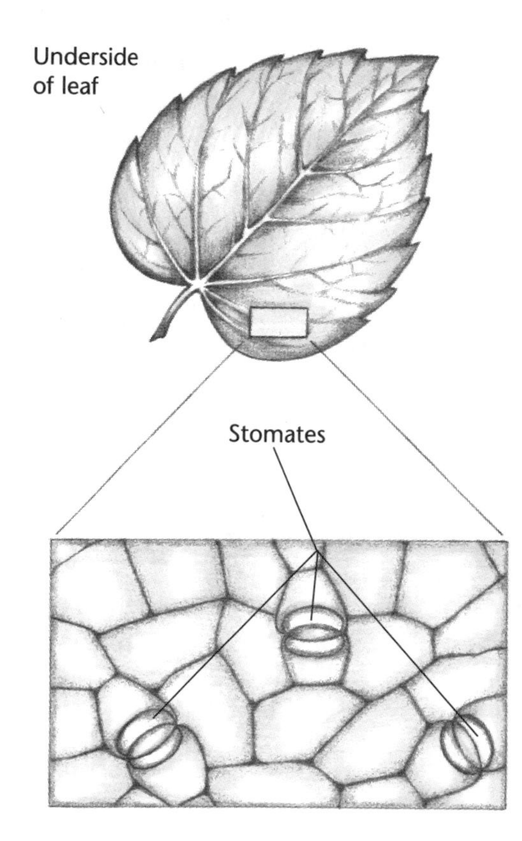

Figure 1. The stomates are on the underside of the plant leaves. Carbon dioxide enters the plant through the stomates, and oxygen is given off through the stomates.

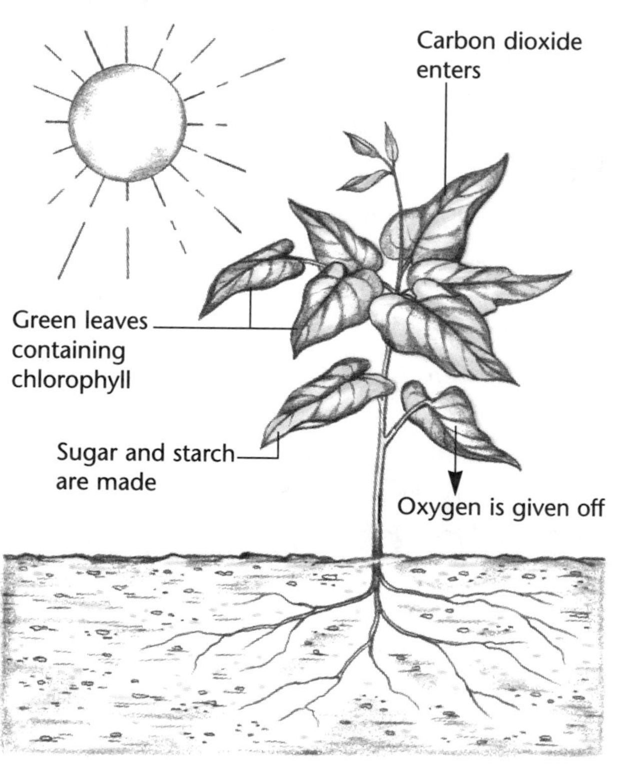

Figure 2. What raw material necessary for photosynthesis is not shown in this diagram?

Experiment

Problem

What is an important function of plant roots?

Aim

In this experiment, you will learn about the role that plant roots play in the food-making process.

Materials

You will need some young pea or radish plants. Choose plants whose roots are about one-half inch long. You will also need a small jar, a piece of wire <u>gauze</u>—a thin, loosely woven material—some red ink, and scissors. Have on hand a <u>magnifying</u> glass, a glass that makes something look larger.

Procedure

1. Fill the jar with water. Add a few drops of red ink and stir.

2. Place the piece of wire gauze on the open mouth of the jar. Place the plants on the wire gauze. Gently push the plant roots through the wire and into the water. See Figure 3.

3. After two to three days, carefully remove one of the young plants. Cut the roots and examine the inside with a magnifying glass. What do you notice?

4. Remove another young plant. Study the root carefully. Notice the tiny hairs on each of the larger root parts.

Observations or Conclusions

The insides of the roots and the root hairs are red. Think about what this shows. Also think about why the roots are important to the food-making process of a plant.

Figure 4 shows the roots of a plant that is growing in soil. The root hairs of plants that grow in soil function the same way as do those in the experiment.

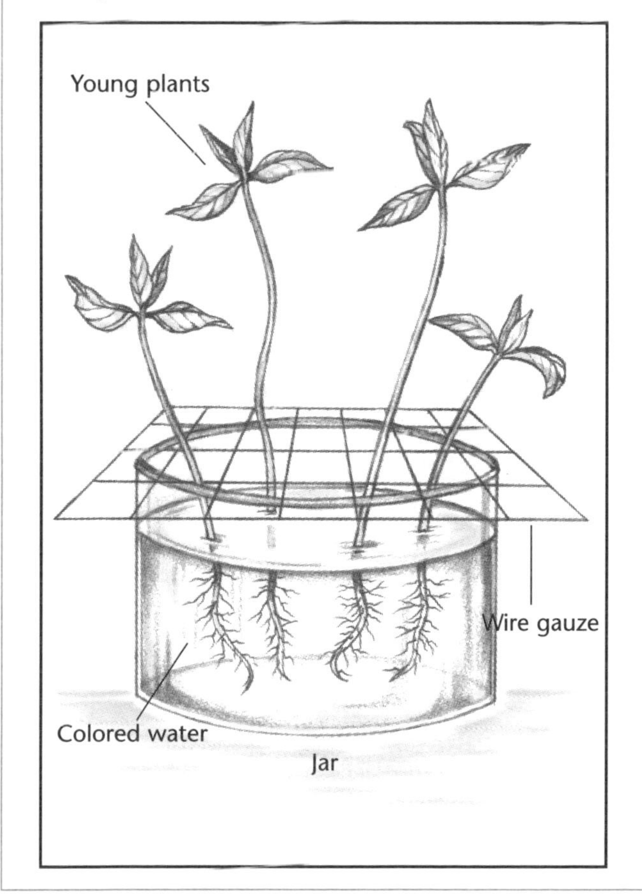

Figure 3. Be sure that the water level in the jar is high enough so that some of the roots are in the water.

Figure 4. Root hairs are tiny hair-like structures.

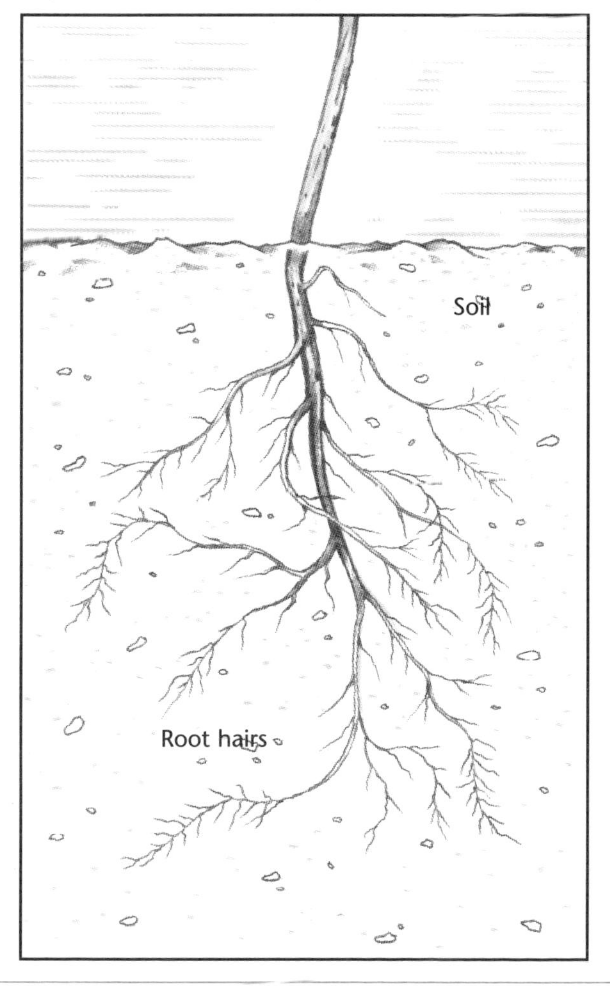

Recalling facts

Recalling details

1. What is photosynthesis?

It is the food-making process in plants.

Reading text with diagrams

2. Look at Figure 1. How does carbon dioxide enter the plant?

Carbon dioxide enters through the stomates on the underside of the leaves.

Reading text with diagrams

3. Look at Figure 2. The raw material not shown is water. How does water enter the plant?

Water enters through the roots.

Recalling details

4. How does chlorophyll help the plant make food?

It traps energy from sunlight and holds it until it can be used to produce sugars and oxygen.

Recalling details

5. In what parts of the plant is chlorophyll found?

It is found in the leaves and the stem of the plant.

Summarizing

6. In your own words, describe the food-making process (photosynthesis) shown in Figure 4.

Water is taken in through the roots. Carbon dioxide is taken in through the stomates. Chlorophyll traps energy from the sun. Sugars and oxygen are produced, and the excess oxygen is given off.

Recalling details

7. What does chlorophyll give to plant leaves and stems?

Chlorophyll gives leaves and stems their green color.

Using context clues

8. Write the letter of the correct meaning on the line next to each word.

b demonstrate	a.	making something look larger
c gauze	b.	show
a magnifying	c.	thin, loosely woven material

Interpreting facts

Making inferences

1. In an experiment, what is the purpose of listing the materials?

Answers may vary. The person carrying out the experiment can gather the materials in advance.

Making inferences

2. In the procedure section for an experiment, why is it important to follow the steps exactly as written and in the exact order?

Answers may vary. If this is not done, the experiment might not work.

Inferring cause and efffect

3. In the experiment described on page 49, what caused the insides of the roots to turn red?

Answers may vary. Water that was colored with red ink was taken in by the roots.

Making inferences

4. Look at Figure 3. Would a piece of wood have worked as well as the wire gauze? Why or why not?

Answers may vary. No. The roots couldn't have reached the water through the wood.

Drawing conclusions

5. Minerals are substances that are found in soil. How do they enter plants?

Answers may vary. They are in the water that is taken in through the plant roots.

Inferring cause and effect

6. If you don't give a plant enough water, what will probably happen to it? Why?

The plant will probably die because it needs water from the soil to produce food.

SKILL FOCUS

Write a summary of the experiment on page 49 in your own words. Do not look back. Then check your summary by rereading the experiment. Make any necessary corrections.

Answers may vary. A jar is filled with water to which red ink was added for color. Young plants are placed over the jar on a piece of wire gauze. The plant roots are pushed through the gauze into the water. After two to three days, one of the plants is removed. The roots are cut and examined through a magnifying glass. The inside of the roots are red. The root hairs are also examined.

Do the following experiment to show whether a plant needs light to make food for itself. Complete the directions for your experiment using the experiment on page 49 as a model. Use two plants in the experiment. One plant should get plenty of light. The other plant should get no light at all. Be sure to number the steps in the Procedure part. Draw a diagram in the box to show what is to be done. Write labels and a caption for your diagram. The Problem and Aim have been completed for you.

Experiment

Problem

How does light affect food production in plants?

Aim

In this experiment, you will find out how plants are affected by light and by darkness.

Materials

Answers may vary. You will need two healthy plants of the same type and size. You will also need a place near a window for one plant and a place in a closet for the other.

Procedure

1. Give each plant the same amount of water.
2. Put one plant near the window.
3. Put the other in a dark closet with the door closed.
4. After four or five days, observe both plants.

Observations or Conclusions

The plant that was in the closet is yellow and limp. The plant that was near the window is green and healthy. This is because plants need light to make food.

Real Life Connections Describe a simple science experiment that you could do at home.

Lesson 14

Roman Numerals

Reading a Mathematics Selection

Background Information

Have you ever watched the Super Bowl? If you have, you might remember seeing Super Bowl XXIX or Super Bowl XXX. What this really means is Super Bowl 29 and Super Bowl 30. Roman numerals are used when referring to the Super Bowl.

Roman numerals are simply another system of numbers. It is a different language for numbers. If you went to Spain or Germany, the people would speak Spanish and German, respectively. If you could travel back in time and you lived during the Roman Empire, you would see people using Roman numerals.

Roman numerals were invented by the ancient Romans. However, the early Roman numeral system in use around 500 B.C.E. differed from the Roman numeral system that we use today. For example, people used different symbols for numbers that can be divided by 1,000.

Roman numerals were used in Europe until the 1500s C.E. In the late 1500s, people began to use Arabic numerals. It was easy to use Roman numerals to add and subtract. However, the Arabic numbers were easier to use when people wanted to do more difficult problems.

In the following selection, you will learn about Roman numerals, which is a system of symbols that stand for certain numbers. By learning what different symbols in this system stand for, you will learn how to read Roman numerals.

Skill Focus

Roman numerals were widely used before Arabic numerals became common. When people started to record numbers and use them to solve problems, they found that Roman numerals were difficult to use.

Today Arabic numerals have largely replaced Roman numerals. However, Roman numerals are still used in outlines and research papers. You may also notice them on the cornerstones of certain buildings. The Roman numerals on a cornerstone tell the date that the building was built.

Roman numerals are read differently from Arabic numerals. When reading Arabic numerals, the position of each digit, or place value, helps you to read the number. The Roman numeral system is not based on place value. Before reading Roman numerals, you often have to add some of the symbols. Some Roman numerals require you to subtract and then add before you can read the numeral.

Word Clues

When reading the selection, look for the following words: *Arabic, symbol.* Be sure that you understand the meaning of the word *symbol.*

Strategy Tip

As you complete the activities in this lesson, remember to read Roman numerals from left to right. If a smaller value appears to the left of a larger value, you must subtract the smaller value from the larger one.

Reading Roman Numerals

Roman numerals were first used thousands of years ago. People started to use numerals because they needed to count and record numbers. The first symbol used was a vertical line. It became the Roman symbol for the number one.

I = one

Other numbers were written using the symbol for one.

III = three

IIIIIIIII = nine

As you can imagine, it would take time and space to write the number thirty-eight using just the symbol for the number 1. It also would take time to read the number thirty-eight. New symbols were invented for numbers larger than three. These numerals made reading larger numbers easier. For example,

People started to use Roman numerals because they needed to count and record numbers.

V = five

X = ten

Roman symbols can be used over and over again. For example, in the Roman numeral XXXII, the symbol X appears three times and the symbol I appears twice. The value of a Roman symbol does not depend on place, as it does in Arabic numbers. For example, in the number XXXII, each X stands for the value of ten and each I for the value of one.

To read a Roman number, you must add the values of the symbols. In the following example, the largest value is at the far left. Then comes the symbol with the next largest value, and so on. The symbol that stands for the smallest value is at the far right.

XVI = 10 + 5 + 1 = 16

If a smaller value symbol appears to the left of a larger value, you need to use another step before you add. The smaller value to the left is subtracted from the larger value to the right. Then the symbols are added.

XIV = (1) IV = 5 − 1 = 4
(2) XIV = 10 + 4 = 14

XXIX = (1) IX = 10 − 1 = 9
(2) XXIX = 10 + 10 + 9 = 29

In the Roman numeral system, four or more of the same symbols are never used in a row. For example, instead of IIII, the numeral for four is written as five minus one. Instead of IIIIIIIII, the numeral for nine is written as ten minus one.

IV = 4
IX = 9

Following are the steps for reading Roman numerals.

1. Check whether the symbols are in that order from greatest value to least value.

2. If the symbols are in that order, add the values of the symbols.

3. If the symbols are not in that order, subtract the symbol for the smaller number from the symbol to its right. Then add the values.

As the Romans needed larger and larger numbers, they used other symbols. Here are some.

L = fifty
C = one hundred
D = five hundred
M = one thousand
$\overline{\text{V}}$ = five thousand
$\overline{\text{X}}$ = ten thousand

The following examples show how these numerals are used to make larger numbers.

LXVII = 67
XLIX = 49
XC = 90
DCCX = 710
MMCM = 2,900
$\overline{\text{V}}$MCCXVII = 6,217
M$\overline{\text{V}}$CX = 4,110
$\overline{\text{XXX}}$CC = 30,200

Roman numerals can be used only for very simple arithmetic. When using Roman numerals, difficult arithmetic must be done with an abacus.

Recalling Facts

Recalling details
1. When were Roman numerals first used?
They were first used thousands of years ago.

Recalling details
2. What was the first symbol the Romans used? What was its value?
I = one

Recalling details
3. Why were new symbols invented for numbers larger than three?
They made reading large numbers easier.

Identifying cause and effect
4. In a Roman numeral, when are the values of the symbols subtracted?
when a smaller value symbol appears before a larger value symbol

Recalling details
5. What is the symbol for 10,000?
$\bar{X}$

Recalling details
6. When using Roman numerals, how must difficult arithmetic be done?
It should be done with an abacus.

Identifying sequence of events
7. What are three steps for reading a Roman numeral?
1. Check whether the symbols are in order.
2. If the symbols are in order from greatest to least, add.
3. If the symbols are not in that order, subtract and then add.

Interpreting Facts

Drawing conclusions
1. What symbol is lacking in the Roman system?
zero

Inferring cause and effect
2. If the order of the symbols in a Roman numeral were changed, what would happen to the value of the numeral?
The value of the numeral would change.

Drawing conclusions
3. In the Roman system, why do you think four or more of the same symbol are never used in a row?
Answers may vary. It would take too much time and space.

Drawing conclusions
4. Why do you think Romans found this number system useful in daily life?
Answers may vary. They could use the system to figure out how much things cost.

Skill Focus

A. Give the value for each Roman numeral below. Because the symbols are in order from the largest value to the smallest, you will only have to add the values.

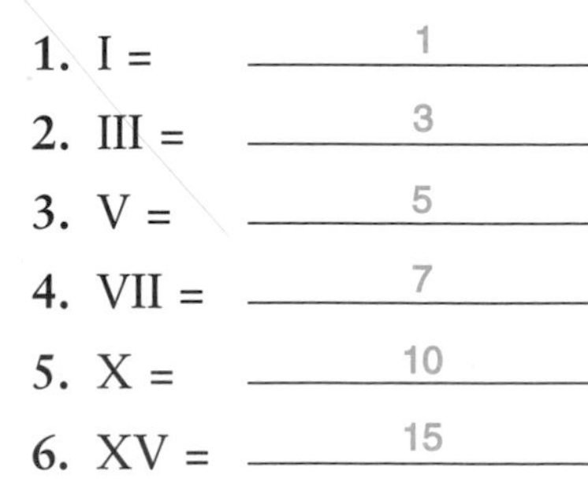

1. I = 1
2. III = 3
3. V = 5
4. VII = 7
5. X = 10
6. XV = 15
7. XVI = 16
8. XXX = 30
9. XXII = 22
10. XXVIII = 28
11. L = 50
12. LX = 60

13. LXV = 65
14. LXX = 70
15. C = 100
16. CL = 150
17. CX = 110
18. CLXV = 165
19. CC = 200
20. CCCLXXXVIII = 388
21. D = 500
22. DXXVI = 526
23. MMLXVIII = 2,068
24. MMM = 3,000
25. $\overline{V}$ = 5,000
26. $\overline{X}$ = 10,000
27. $\overline{XX}$ = 20,000
28. XXXII = 32

B. Give the value of each Roman numeral below. You will sometimes have to subtract before you add.

1. XIV = 14
2. XXXIX = 39
3. LXVI = 66
4. CDXIX = 419
5. XLVII = 47
6. DLXIV = 564
7. MCM = 1,900
8. MCML = 1,950
9. M$\overline{V}$CCIX = 4,209
10. M$\overline{X}$CMXCIX = 9,999

C. Give the Roman numeral for each Arabic number below.

1. 18 = XVIII
2. 188 = CLXXXVIII
3. 15,000 = $\overline{XV}$
4. 220 = CCXX
5. 550 = DL
6. 250 = CCL
7. 1,700 = MDCC
8. 4,000 = M$\overline{V}$
9. 75 = LXXV
10. 59 = LIX
11. 400 = CD
12. 48 = XLVIII
13. 4,500 = M$\overline{V}$D
14. 9,500 = M$\overline{X}$D
15. 1,800 = MDCCC
16. 1,425 = MCDXXV
17. 3,450 = MMMCDL
18. 26 = XXVI
19. 8 = VIII
20. 13 = XIII
21. 5,250 = $\overline{V}$CCL
22. 17,000 = $\overline{XV}$MM
23. 650 = DCL
24. 29 = XXIX
25. 68 = LXVIII
26. 12 = XII
27. 72 = LXXII
28. 4 = IV

▶ **Real Life Connections** Name two places where you can see Roman numerals in your community.

Lesson 15

Prefixes and Suffixes

A **prefix** is a word part that is added to the beginning of a word to change its meaning. Four common prefixes and their meanings are given below.

Prefix	*Meaning*
mis-	wrong or badly
out-	away from or better than
under-	below or not enough
over-	above or too much

Change the meaning of each word below by adding a prefix. Write the new word in the first column. Write the meaning of the new word in the second column.

1. over + head = overhead — over one's head
2. mis + treat = mistreat — to treat someone or something badly
3. under + fed = underfed — not fed enough
4. out + run = outrun — to run faster or better than someone else

Use a prefix from the list at the top of the page to make each phrase below into one word. Write the new word in the blank to the right of each phrase.

1. to eat too much overeat
2. not sold for enough undersold
3. to behave badly misbehave
4. to do better than outdo

A **suffix** is a word part that is added to the end of a word to change its meaning. Three frequently used suffixes are *-ion, -ition,* and *-ation.* All three suffixes have similar meanings: act of, result of, or state of.

Add one of the suffixes to each word below to make a new word. If the word ends with *e,* cross out the *e* before adding the suffix. If you are unsure of the spelling, you may use a dictionary.

1. direct ion
2. define ition
3. inform ation
4. locate ion
5. oppose ition
6. declare ation

Use one of the words above to complete each sentence below.

1. Squanto gave the Pilgrims valuable information about planting corn.
2. The Pilgrims wanted a location in Virginia for their settlement.
3. When the Pilgrims landed, they faced no opposition from the Native Americans.
4. The Declaration of Independence was adopted on July 4, 1776.
5. The definition of a pilgrim is "a person who travels about."
6. The direction the Pilgrims traveled from England to Massachusetts was west.

Lesson 16

Prefixes and Suffixes

Read the following prefixes and their meanings.

Prefix	*Meaning*
dis-	away or opposite of
super-	bigger, greater, or larger
trans-	over, across, or beyond

Write the correct prefix before each word below.

1. dis appear — opposite of appear
2. super market — big market
3. dis place — away from its place
4. trans atlantic — across the Atlantic
5. super highway — large highway
6. trans port — to carry across

Use one of the words above to complete each sentence below.

1. A supermarket contains many kinds of food.
2. Large jet planes make many transatlantic trips every day.
3. Cargo ships transport many of this country's products to other countries.
4. The magician made the rabbit disappear from view.

Read the following suffixes and their meanings.

Suffix	*Meaning*
-al	belonging to, or the act of
-ment	state of being, act
-y	full of, or covered with
-able	capable of doing something
-ist	one who does a certain thing
-less	without

Add one of the suffixes above to each word below to make a new word.

1. move ment — state of being in motion
2. art ist — one who does artwork
3. water less — without water
4. tropic al — belonging to the tropics
5. accept able — capable of being accepted
6. length y — having length

Use one of the words above to complete each sentence below.

1. The 800-page book seemed lengthy to Jane.
2. The movement of the earth around the sun takes one year.
3. John's homework was messy. His teacher said it was not acceptable.
4. The soil of most deserts is almost waterless.
5. Michelangelo was a famous Italian sculptor and artist.
6. The tropical rain forest had many beautiful plants.

Lesson 17

Fact and Opinion

Do you know the difference between a fact and an opinion? A fact is a piece of information that can be proved. An opinion is a statement that someone believes is true but may not be able to prove. An opinion often tells how someone feels or thinks about a subject.

Fact: Mexico is our neighbor to the south.
Opinion: Mexico has the greatest art treasures in the world.

Read this letter written by a student to the editor of a newspaper. Think about which statements are facts and which are opinions.

Dear Editor:

Last week our local art museum held an exhibit called "Art from Around the World." Hundreds of people saw the show. Your own paper praised the museum for its fine work. I saw the show and thought it was very good. However, I feel that the country of Mexico was neglected.

Mexico is our neighbor to the south. It is a large country with a long history. The ancient cultures of the Maya, Toltec, and Aztec people are important in Mexican history. I think the art of these people is some of the most interesting in the world. It seems to me that some of this art should have been included in the exhibit.

When Spanish settlers came to Mexico, they brought with them their own style of art and design. Their influence is still seen today in Mexico, as well as in the United States. Yet, the exhibit did not include any art from the Spanish colonial period.

Some of the greatest painters in Mexico worked after the Mexican revolution. Artists, such as José Orozco and Diego Rivera, painted colorful murals to show the story of the revolution. These murals were painted on the walls of public buildings. In my opinion, photos of these murals also should have been shown.

Today Mexico is home to many young artists. The exhibit at the art museum included only two of their paintings. I believe that the talented young artists of Mexico deserve more attention. Their work is some of the most interesting new art being produced today!

I hope that the next time the museum has an exhibit of world art, they will not forget Mexico. The artists of ancient Mexico, old Mexico, and modern-day Mexico have given me much pleasure. It's time that other people in our city had a chance to enjoy them!

Paul Ramon

Read each of the following statements. On the line next to each statement, write the letter **F** for fact or the letter **O** for opinion.

F 1. Your own paper praised the museum for its fine work.
O 2. However, I feel that the country of Mexico was neglected.
F 3. Mexico is a large country with a long history.
O 4. I think the art of these people is some of the most interesting in the world.
O 5. It seems to me that some of this art should have been included in the exhibit.
F 6. Yet, the exhibit did not include any art from the Spanish colonial period.
F 7. These murals were painted on the walls of public buildings.
O 8. In my opinion, photos of these murals also should have been shown.
F 9. Today Mexico is home to many young artists.
O 10. I believe that the talented young artists of Mexico deserve more attention.

Lesson 18

Unstated Main Idea

When you read a textbook or reference book for information, you often find the main idea of each paragraph stated in a sentence. The supporting details, which give more information about the main idea, are found in the rest of the paragraph.

Sometimes the main idea of the paragraph is not stated. You may need to figure out, or **infer**, the main idea yourself. To do this, think about the supporting details. Then think of a sentence that summarizes the supporting details.

Read the following selection. As you read each paragraph, think about whether the main idea is stated or unstated.

1. Monkeys are small lively mammals that rank high among the most intelligent animals. Scientists classify monkeys in the highest order of mammals. This order is the **primates.** Because monkeys are so intelligent, they can learn many tricks. Their liveliness makes them favorites of zoo visitors.

2. The New World monkeys, one of two major groups of monkeys, live in Central and South America. The Old World monkeys live in Asia and Africa. The nostrils of New World monkeys are spaced more widely apart than those of the Old World monkeys. Most kinds of New World monkeys have 36 teeth. All Old World monkeys have 32 teeth. Some New World monkeys can hold things with their tail, but no Old World monkeys can.

3. Many people believe that apes, which include chimpanzees, gibbons, gorillas, and orangutans, are like monkeys. But monkeys and apes differ in several ways. For instance, apes are more intelligent than monkeys. Apes do not have tails, while most monkeys do. Most species of apes are larger than monkeys.

4. Monkeys use their long arms and legs to help them climb and leap. They grasp the branches of trees with their hands and feet. Most types of monkeys have a long tail that helps them keep their balance. While moving through trees, some monkeys use their tail to grasp branches.

5. Almost from the moment of birth, a baby monkey hangs on to its mother by grasping her fur. The infant clings to its mother's chest at first. Later, it rides on her back. Until the baby can travel safely on its own, its mother carries it. A baby monkey feeds on its mother's milk. Depending on the species, a baby monkey receives its mother's milk for a few weeks up to two years.

For each paragraph in the selection, if the main idea is stated, write the word *stated* on the line. If the main idea is unstated, choose a main idea from the sentences given below and write its letter on the line.

a. Baby monkeys are easy to care for.
b. A monkey's body enables it to move easily through trees.
c. New World monkeys are smaller than Old World monkeys.
d. The two major groups of monkeys are the New World monkeys and the Old World monkeys.
e. Baby monkeys are very dependent on their mothers.

Paragraph 1 stated　*Paragraph 3* stated　*Paragraph 5* e

Paragraph 2 d　*Paragraph 4* b

Now go back to each paragraph that has a stated main idea and underline the sentence with the main idea.

Lesson 19

Reading the White Pages

What can you do if you want to call a friend on the phone but you can't remember his or her number? The best thing to do is to look up your friend's telephone number in the white pages of the phone book. Names in the white pages are listed alphabetically, last names first. After a person's last name, the first name or initial, the address, and the phone number are given.

You can quickly find the name you are looking for by using the guide words at the top of each page. The guide words give the last name of the first entry on the page and the last entry on the page. Guide words help you to know if the name you are looking for is on that page of the phone book.

Study the listings below from the white pages of a phone book. Notice that the names of businesses that are initials only are listed alphabetically before the other names.

B — BARNES

B & B Sporting Goods 11 Forest Av 555-3600
BJ's Bicycle Shop 232 Hampton Rd 555-0880
BWI AIRLINES –
Reservations & Information. 555-3000
Bach Richard J 16 Ridge Rd 555-7942
Baddleman Mrs P 2 Stoney Hill La 555-1024
Bader John R 406 Walter St. 555-7033
Ball Lee & Connie 208 Bark Rd 555-3794
Banks I 29 Piedmont Dr 555-1132
BARBARA'S BARGAIN STORE
20 Forest Av. 555-5299
BARBER – See Also BARBOUR
Barber C L 47 Spruce Hollow Rd 555-3583
Barber George 24 Shoreline Dr 555-4552
Barber Gina 28 Woodstock Rd 555-4921
Barber Stuart 113 Brookville St. 555-9844
Barbera Julio 239 Huntington Rd 555-0384
BARBI-LEE DANCE STUDIO
24 Annandale Rd 555-9456
Barbini Sonia 609 Meadowlark La. 555-1891
BARBIZON HOTEL 400 Main St. 555-6666
Barbour Alice 192 Huntington Rd 555-1276
Barbour J 4099 Afton Ct. 555-8268
Barbour J 841 Juniper Av 555-4811
Barbour William K 189 Kings Point Rd . . . 555-6831
Barclay Ken 5993 Oakwood St. 555-4218
Barclay Margaret 135 Roanoke St 555-7263
Barclay Scott D 127 Mountain Rd. 555-3181
Bark Edith 345 Ocean Blvd. 555-5217
Barkas Maurice 289 Hollycrest La. 555-6950
Barker Eugene J 100 Centershore Rd . . . 555-1937
Barker Harry C 2904 Cobb St. 555-2287
Barker Harry Q 824 Treehouse Ct 555-8604
Barker L 2938 Village St. 555-8352
Barker Zachary 99 W. Fordham St 555-5733
BARKER'S PHARMACY 406 Main St. . . . 555-0288
Barkley Kam C 835 Laurelwood Dr. 555-3501
Barksdale William L 77 Darnell Dr. 555-1493
BARNACLE BILL'S RESTAURANT
92 Dune Rd 555-3400
Barnes A 4273 Yardley Blvd 555-5441
Barnes Arthur 14 Rolling Woods La 555-6635
Barnes Brooke 4273 Yardley Blvd. 555-5441

A. Use the phone listings to write the answer to each question.

1. a. How many businesses are listed?

8

b. What are the names of two of them?

Responses may include any two: B & B Sporting Goods, BJ's Bicycle Shop, BWI Airlines, Barbara's Bargain Store, Barbi-Lee Dance Studio, Barbizon Hotel, Barker's Pharmacy, Barnacle Bill's Restaurant.

2. Which five last names have more than one listing?

Barber, Barbour, Barclay, Barker, Barnes

3. You have to speak to Edith Bark. What is her address and phone number?

345 Ocean Blvd. 555-5217

4. What is the phone number of the Harry Barker who lives on Cobb Street?

555-2287

5. What is the address of a Mr. Barnes whose phone number is 555-6635?

14 Rolling Woods La

6. a. How can you find the phone number of your friend Alissa Barclay if you don't know her mother's or father's first name but you do know that she lives on Roanoke Street?

Look under Barclay and find one listed on Roanoke St.

b. Whose name is the phone number listed under?

Margaret Barclay

7. You want to call your soccer coach, James Barber, but you're not sure of the spelling of his last name. He lives on Afton Court. What is his phone number?

555-8268

8. Which two people named Barnes do you think are related? Why?

A. Barnes and Brooke Barnes because they have the same address and phone number.

9. a. If Terry Barber was listed in the phone book, whose name would be right before hers?

Stuart Barber

b. Whose name would be right after hers?

Julio Barbera

10. Why isn't the Briarwood School listed on this page?

Briarwood isn't between *B* and *Barnes*.

B. Use the following information to make a sample phone book page on the lines below. Remember to list the names in alphabetical order, last name first. The first entry has been done for you.

Adriano Rodriguez 58 Cres Rd 555-3506
ROD TOOL CO 35 Second Av 555-7630
Freddie Rodriguez 470 West Rd 555-1034
A Rodriguez 85 Audubon Rd 555-7724
Barbara Rizner 7812 Ridge Ter 555-8614
James O Rodney 280 Bart Dr 555-0385
Fernando Rodriguez 7 Steve Rd 555-5539
Al Rodriguez 5401 Water St 555-4823

RIZNER - ROF

Rizner Barbara 7812 Ridge Ter 555-8614
ROD TOOL CO 35 Second Av 555-7630
Rodney James O 280 Bart Dr 555-0385
Rodriguez A 85 Audubon Rd 555-7724
Rodriguez Adriano 58 Cres Rd 555-3506
Rodriguez Al 5401 Water St 555-4823
Rodriguez Fernando 7 Steve Rd 555-5539
Rodriguez Freddie 470 West Rd 555-1034

UNIT 3

Different Ways of Living

Lesson 20

Character

Reading a Literature Selection

Background Information

"Ana's Crusade" is an example of realistic fiction—a kind of fiction that describes true-to-life characters, places, or events that could really exist. In fact, the characters in realistic stories, plays, or books could easily be people you know or go to school with. Realistic fiction is very different from fantasy, which takes place in an unreal, made-up world, where animals can talk and people can perform magical acts.

In this story Ana is not content to leave things as they are. She wants to help other people and children who are less fortunate than she.

Skill Focus

The people in a story are called the **characters.** A story can have a few or many characters. Most stories, however, have only one **main character**, who plays an important part in the story's action. The other characters are not as important as the main character.

The main character usually has a goal to achieve or a problem to solve. Most of this character's actions are directed toward achieving the goal or solving the problem. Often this character changes as he or she tries to achieve the goal or solve the problem.

When you read a story, keep in mind the following questions. They will help you to understand the main character.

1. Who is the main character?
2. What is the main character's goal or problem?
3. What does the main character do to achieve the goal or solve the problem?
4. How does the main character change as a result of these actions?

Word Clues

Read the sentence below. Look for context clues that explain the underlined word.

> The next week, Ana and Mrs. Eisen thought of a strategy, or plan, to solve the problem.

If you do not know the meaning of the word *strategy*, the phrase following the word *or* can help you. The word *strategy* is explained by the appositive phrase, "plan to solve the problem." An appositive phrase comes before or after the word that it explains. This phrase is set off by commas or dashes. A strategy is a plan used to solve a problem.

Use **appositive phrases** as context clues to find the meaning of the three underlined words in the selection.

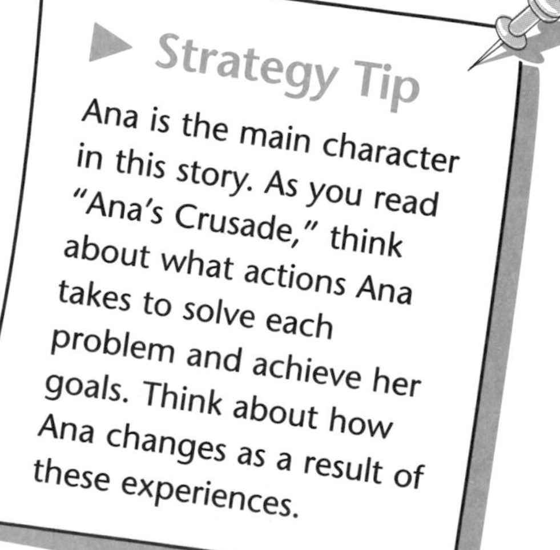

Strategy Tip

Ana is the main character in this story. As you read "Ana's Crusade," think about what actions Ana takes to solve each problem and achieve her goals. Think about how Ana changes as a result of these experiences.

Ana's Crusade

"Hurry up, Ana!" her brother Pablo yelled from the soccer field. "The game is starting!"

Ana grabbed her shoes and socks from the car and slammed the door. A boy she knew from school stood beside the car, watching.

"Are you playing soccer today?" Justin asked.

"Sure!" Ana said. "Aren't you?"

"No, I can't," was all that he said. Then he walked away, looking wistfully at the soccer field.

Later that night, Ana asked her parents about Justin. "Why doesn't he play soccer with us?" she asked.

"Not everybody can afford it," her mother replied. "We had to pay a fee for you to play."

"Why can't he afford it?" Ana asked.

"I don't know. Maybe his parents don't have the extra money."

"It doesn't seem fair that both Pablo and I can play and Justin can't. Could we pay the fee for him?" Ana asked.

"Your mother and I can't afford that," her father replied. "According to your coach, there are ten kids who want to play soccer, but their parents can't afford to pay the fee. I'm afraid that there's nothing we can do to help them."

But Ana couldn't stop thinking about Justin. Even though her parents couldn't do anything to help him, maybe she could find a way!

The next day, Ana contacted Mrs. Eisen, the president of the Parent-Teachers Association of her school, and told her about Justin's problem.

"We don't have extra money for that," Mrs. Eisen said. "But perhaps I can help you kids do something—that is, if you want to work."

The next week, Ana and Mrs. Eisen thought of a strategy, or plan, to solve the problem. Ana organized all the students in her class to sponsor a bake sale. They spent several days baking pies, cakes, cookies, and brownies. Saturday morning, they set up a table at the mall in their community. Many shoppers stopped to buy the baked goods. By the end of the afternoon, they had earned $450.00.

In the meantime, Ana and Mrs. Eisen spoke with the owner of Parton's Electronics. Mr. Parton donated, or contributed, a 31-inch television set. Ana's soccer team then sold raffle tickets for the television set. At the end of the second week, the team had earned another $600.

A few weeks later, Ana's soccer team was playing a game. Her mother had come to watch. Justin waved to them before he joined the other players on the field. "I'm so glad that Justin is playing today," Ana's mother said. "Are you feeling good about what you did for him and the other kids?"

"Well, sort of," Ana said. Then she paused. "No, not really. I think that I should do more to help people."

Ana had no idea what she wanted to do or how she should do it. Then late in the summer, she read a newspaper story about floods that had destroyed homes in nine states along the Mississippi River. She realized that children probably lived in many of those homes. They had probably lost all their clothes and toys. Ana imagined how sad they must be feeling. "There must be a way to help them," she thought.

On the Internet, Ana explained the problem and what she and Project Flood were trying to do.

Ana asked her soccer team to help her begin a clothing drive, or group effort, for the flood victims. Soon, everyone brought boxes filled with clothes to Ana's garage. People who didn't have clothes to bring donated money. Ana used this money to pay for shipping costs. In a few weeks, all the townspeople found out about Ana's project. Even the local news broadcast a story about the work that Ana and her soccer team were doing.

"You're doing a great thing," Ana's mother said to her after the last box was sent to the Salvation Army in Arkansas. But Ana just shook her head.

"What's wrong, Ana?" her father asked.

"It's not enough!" Ana cried. "There are thousands of people who are homeless. They need clothes and food. They'll need millions of dollars to rebuild their homes."

"Ana, you can't help everybody," her mother said. But Ana was not convinced.

Later that night, Ana's father was working at his computer. He told Ana that he was on-line, or connected, to other computer users by a modem on the Internet.

"Whom can you talk to on the Internet?" Ana asked.

"Just about anybody," her father said. "Anybody who has a modem and is connected to the Internet, that is."

Then Ana had an idea. It was a big idea. "About how many people would that be?" she asked her father. "Thousands?"

"More."

"A million?"

"Oh, yes, easily," her father said. "I'm sure it would be millions. The Internet connects people all over the world."

"And could I talk to big companies—companies that could make donations?" Ana asked.

"Sure," her father replied. "You could leave messages on their home pages."

"Then I've got a plan!" Ana shouted. "But I'll need your help."

The next week, Ana and her father were very busy. First, he helped her set up a nonprofit organization. They named their company Project Flood. Ana and the soccer team asked their coach, the school principal, Mrs. Eisen, and Ana's parents to be on the board of directors.

With Ana's father's help, Project Flood went on-line. On the Internet, Ana explained the problem. She then described what Project Flood was trying to do. She asked for clothing for the flood victims. She contacted children's clothing companies and asked for clothes of all sizes. She contacted shoe companies and asked for free shoes.

Every day after school, Ana and the soccer team opened letters containing checks and boxes of clothing. They sorted the clothing according to size and deposited the money in a special checking account. Clothes had been sent from all over the United States and Canada. A large box even came from a family in London, England. Soon, there was enough money for clothes and toys for thousands of children.

Ana and the soccer team went to a toy store, filled ten shopping carts with toys, and bought them all. Then they packed and sent them to the flood victims in the nine states.

After Project Flood was finished, Ana did not stop. She heard about children who had traveled on a boat from Haiti to the United States and needed food and clothing. Project Flood collected food and clothing to help the Haitian children.

Every day, Ana read the newspaper and listened to the news. She wanted to help everyone she could. She was always looking for people whom her organization could help.

One afternoon, Ana and several students were wrapping boxes of clothes for Project Flood. Justin walked into the garage. He watched for a few minutes. Then he came over to Ana. "I'd like to help, too," he said.

RECALLING FACTS

Identifying setting

1. What are the settings in this story?

The setting are a soccer field, Ana's home, Ana's garage, Parton's store, and the shopping mall.

Recognizing sequence of events

2. What are the two things that Ana did to help Justin and the other children who could not play soccer?

First, she met with Mrs. Eisen, and they organized a bake sale. Then they held a raffle to earn even more money.

Recalling details

3. What is Project Flood?

It is a nonprofit organization that sends clothing and toys to needy families.

Recalling details

4. How did Ana's father help her?

He helped her set up Project Flood and go on-line.

Identifying cause and effect

5. What effect did Ana's fund-raising have on the flood victims?

They received money, clothes, and toys.

Using context clues

6. Draw a line to match each word to its correct meaning.

drive	contributed
donated	group effort
on-line	connected to other computers by a modem

(Answer: drive — group effort; donated — contributed; on-line — connected to other computers by a modem)

Interpreting facts

Inferring comparisons and contrasts

1. Do you think that Ana feels differently about helping others at the end of the story than she did at the beginning? Explain.

Answers may vary. By the end of the story, Ana realizes that she can help people by reaching out to others.

Making inferences

2. How do you thing Ana's parents feel about what their daughter did?

Answers may vary. They are very proud of her.

Inferring theme

3. What do you think is the theme, or the main idea, of this story?

Answers may vary. If you want to put out the effort, you can help those who need help.

Inferring cause and effect

4. Why do you think Justin wants to help Ana's group?

Answers may vary. He wants to help others because he was helped himself.

Inferring cause and effect

5. Why do you think so many people gave clothes and money to Project Flood?

Answers may vary. The people wanted to help those in need in any way that they could.

Applying information

6. What projects could you start to help people in your community?

Answers may vary.

Skill focus

Understanding the main character's actions will help you appreciate the story.

1. Who is the main character?

Ana is the main character.

2. What is Ana's first goal?

She wants to raise money so that ten children can play soccer.

3. What problem first concerns Ana?

Not all the children can afford to pay the soccer fees.

4. How does Ana solve this problem?

She raises money by organizing a bake sale and a raffle.

5. What is Ana's second goal?

She wants to raise money and send clothes and toys to the flood victims.

6. How does Ana solve her second problem?

She collects clothes and money locally. Then she goes on-line to collect more money and clothes from people all over the world.

7. How does Ana change as a result of her experiences?

Answers may vary. She learns that when she has a problem to solve, she can reach out to others for help. She also learns that just one person can do a lot to help people in need.

▶ Real Life Connections What do you think of Ana's decision to start Project Flood?

Lesson 21

Fact and Opinion

Reading a Social Studies Selection

Background Information

Between 1200 and 1500 C.E., the Incas, a wealthy and enlightened people, thrived in South America. This civilization of Indians lived in what is now known as Peru, Bolivia, and Chilé in South America. Every year, many Incas would make a pilgrimage. They hiked through the mountains and jungles of the Andes Mountains on the Inca Trail to Machu Picchu, the City of Light.

In 1911, an explorer and writer named Hiram Bingham "discovered" the royal city of Machu Picchu as he cut his way through the Peruvian jungle. Ever since, millions of people have been drawn to the ruins of this beautiful and ancient city.

In this selection, sixteen-year-old Kristen writes diary entries about her travels on this ancient trail. Kristen, her brother, Victor, and her parents begin their hike near the village of Ollantaytambo (OH lan tay TAM bo), Peru.

They travel along the same route as the Incas did over five hundred years ago.

Skill Focus

In your reading, you will often find statements of **fact** and statements of **opinion**. A fact is information that can be proved or checked. An opinion is information that is difficult to prove or check.

First, sort facts from opinions. Then look in the selection for conclusions that the author may have drawn. Check to see whether the conclusions are based on fact or opinion. A conclusion based on fact is always stronger than one that is based on opinion. You do not have to agree with the author's conclusion. But reading and thinking about facts and other people's opinions will help you dra' your own conclusions.

Sometimes authors do r draw conclusions about w they write. When authors not draw conclusions, you must do so.

Remember, facts and opinions are both importa When you read, try to distinguish facts from opinions. If the author has drawn a conclusion, try to identify the source of that conclusion.

Word Clues

Read the sentences below. Look for context clues that explain the underlined word.

> Anthropology is a science that studies human beings. An anthropologist will sometimes travel great distances to study a culture firsthand. The scientist focuses on the culture's customs, origins, and development.

The word *anthropologist* is explained in all three sentences, but the third sentence gives the most detail. Use **detail** context clues to find the meaning of the three underlined words in the selection.

Strategy Tip

As you read "Hiking the Inca Trail," look for facts and opinions expressed by the author. Also study the maps and track the trip as the author travels the route. It will give you information not found in the author's diary.

Hiking the Inca Trail

August 6, Day 1: So much has happened in the past few days! On Sunday, we took an airplane to Lima, Peru. Monday, we drove to Cusco (koos KO) and walked around the city. It was difficult to walk uphill. Dad said that was because Cusco is about 11,000 feet above sea level, and we needed to get used to the altitude. Even Victor was panting!

I've hiked a lot with my family, but none of us has ever hiked in the Andes Mountains! This trip was Mom's idea, because she's an anthropologist. Anthropology is a science that studies human beings. An anthropologist will sometimes travel great distances to study a culture firsthand. The scientist focuses on the culture's customs, origins, and development. Mom says this trip will be an education—a trip we'll never forget.

Today we started hiking a little past the village of Ollantaytambo. We followed the Urubamba River for a few miles and watched a red and yellow train passing below us.

It's winter in South America. Although it's the dry season, it's really warm today. Dad says that's because Peru is so near the equator. The sun is really strong, so we have to wear sunglasses and put on plenty of sunscreen.

We walked past small villages, and I bought a soft drink for two soles (SO lehs), or about 85 cents. As I was walking, I looked at my dirty shorts and felt a blister starting on my left heel. But I didn't stop for long, because Victor was way ahead. I didn't want him to think I couldn't keep up.

After hiking for about seven miles, we camped beside a stream and had dinner. As I write, I am wondering what my friend Dawn is doing tonight. She's probably going to the movies with Sophia. Suddenly, I feel very homesick.

August 7, Day 2: What a surprise this morning! We woke up, broke camp, hiked for about a mile, and came to the Temple of the Hummingbird, which is an ancient Inca ruin. Outside the temple, a little boy asked me for candy, and I gave him a piece of butterscotch. Then Victor and I explored the temple and found a place where Mom said they used to tie up condors. The Incas used condors to send and receive messages across long distances, just as people today use falcons and pigeons. Mom also says that when the Incas began their journey to Machu Picchu, they had to pass through the Temple of the Hummingbird before they could begin their pilgrimage.

Inside the ruins, I found a piece of paper that had *u*'s and *w*'s written on it. Some boy or girl had been practicing handwriting and had left this page behind. I picked it up. Then I realized that the little boy who had asked me for candy goes to school just as I do. Except he's a little kid, and Spanish is his first language.

The rest of the day was awful. We had to hike and hike, all uphill. Victor walked ahead, as usual, trying to show me how strong he is. Big brothers! They always show off!

I'm still not used to the altitude, so I had to take about twenty steps and rest for a few seconds. Sometimes, my heart felt as though it was going to explode. I think I have two blisters now.

When we reached the second campsite, I helped Victor put up the tent, but I was exhausted. Dad had a headache and felt weak, so he went to bed right after supper. Mom says that he has altitude sickness.

We are camping on a mountainside that looks straight at the snow-covered peaks of Mount Veronica. It's so beautiful, I'm glad we're all so exhausted and can't walk any farther. It's cold tonight, and I had to put on my sweater and down vest. I feel lucky to be here in the Andes Mountains, overlooking Mount Veronica. I'm beginning to understand why the Incas liked to walk the Inca Trail to Machu Picchu.

August 8, Day 3: Today we climbed and climbed and finally reached the Pass of the Eternal Woman! This pass is also called Warmiwañusca. It's the first pass on the Inca Trail, and it is almost 14,000 feet high. That's almost three miles above sea level! By the time we reached the top of the pass, there were about 30 people waiting for us. I met a boy named Mario. He is my age, and he lives in Lima, but he didn't know very much

English. I don't know much Spanish, so it was difficult to talk to him.

✔ I made an important decision today. I'm going to study Spanish next year. And I'm going to be serious about it this time! There was so much I wanted to talk to Mario about. All I could say was, *Como se llama?* He answered my question and said, "Mario." That's how I know his name.

After crossing the pass, we started hiking downhill through the Valley of the Rainbows. Just before lunch, we reached a place called Runkuracay (ROON kur rah KAY). The trail had turned into stone steps, and from here on, the Royal Road was clearly defined. We looked back and saw the valley that we had walked through and the Pass of the Eternal Woman.

We climbed over the second pass, and I started to get hungry. But Mom said that we had to wait until we reached Sayacmarca (SAY yah MARK ah). I asked why there were so many ruins on the trail to Machu Picchu. Mom said that the priests and Incas needed somewhere to stay at night along the way, so the buildings were placed exactly one day's walk from one another.

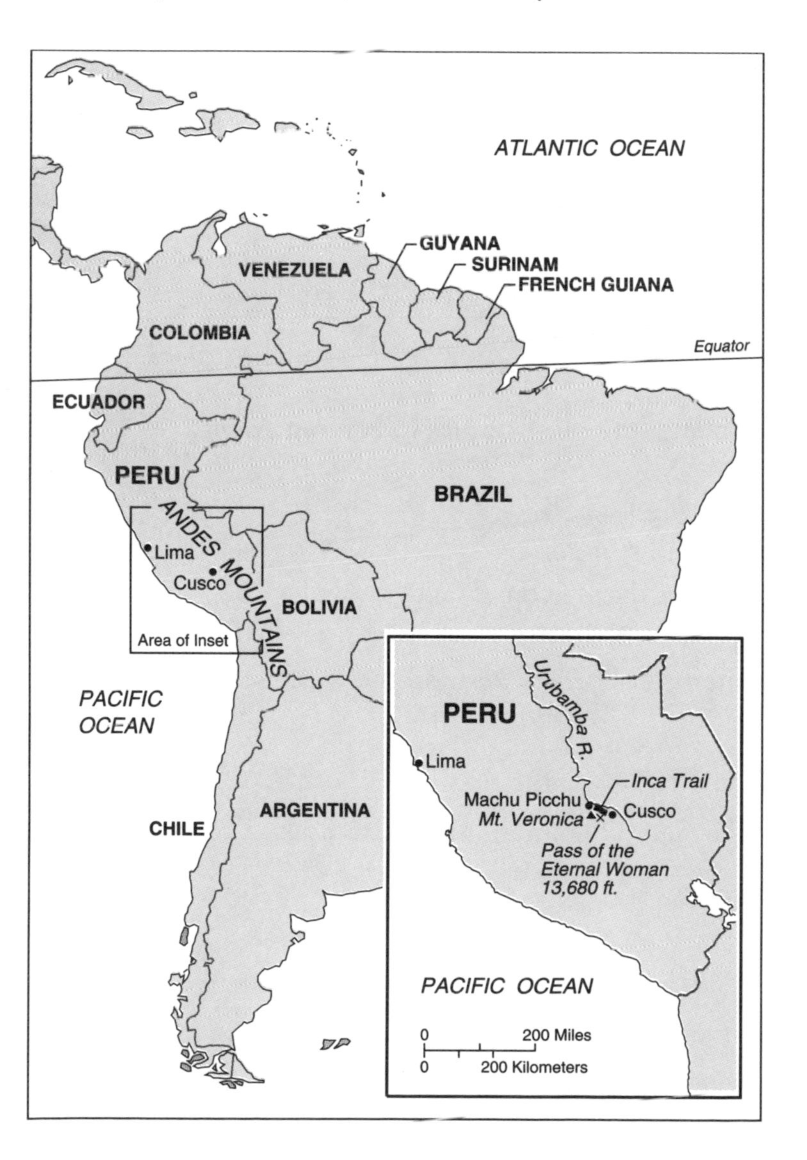

When we finally reached the circular structure, I groaned when I saw how high it was on the mountainside. My legs screamed for mercy as I climbed the hundred steps up the side. My legs forgave me after we feasted on slices of cantaloupe and peanut butter and jelly sandwiches.

After lunch we began to walk through dense jungle. The trail is pretty flat and built of smooth stones that are built into the hillside. I knew that if I took one false step, I would fall into the jungle below and never be heard of again. I walked very carefully. I almost forgot! We passed through a very dark cave made naturally by two large rocks. Victor and I stopped and leaned against the side and felt the cold earth against our backs. For just a moment, I felt glad to have him as a brother—and I don't get those feelings often!

It's funny. With every step I took today, I felt stronger and stronger. We must have hiked over 12 or 13 miles before we stopped at the last pass to camp. As I looked at the mountains, or what the Peruvians call the *apus*, (AP poos), I forgot that tomorrow we will reach Machu Picchu.

August 9, Day 4: The descent from the pass is really quite steep, but the Incas constructed a series of steps that helped us. Within minutes, we stood at the site of the Temple in the Clouds and looked at the valley below. Mom said that we were at 12,000 feet, but we will descend about 4,000 feet to Machu Picchu.

We stopped for lunch at Wiñay Wayna, another temple built on the side of a mountain. Looking down, we could see the Urubamba River far away, probably a mile below us. Behind the temple, there are two fountains, where we washed our hands and face. The Incas believed that if you bathed in this water, you could heal parts of you that are sick and stay young forever. That's why this temple has the English name of the Temple of Eternal Youth.

After lunch, we began our final descent. The slope was more gentle, and we moved at a pretty rapid pace, eager to find the royal city below. We passed through more dense jungle. We passed purple orchids, and I picked up a thick, pulpy white flower on the ground. I looked up, trying to find the tree from where it had fallen. But it was so tall, I couldn't find it. I began to walk slower to enjoy the walk. I do not know when I might make this walk again.

We reached the entrance of Machu Picchu by midafternoon. The door of the city is open now. But long ago, only the Incas could pass through and enter the city. We walked quietly through the entrance and thought about how the city must have looked over 500 years ago, long before it was abandoned.

We walked through the quarry, where the stones were cut for the buildings and sculptures. Mom showed us the temple, where the priests performed ceremonies. She pointed out how the buildings were made to lean inward, to protect them from earthquakes. She led us to the place where the people lived. We could still see the terraces where the farmers grew food and crops.

Most of the structures still proudly stand in the Royal City. Llamas graze on the grass, and tourists walk the streets and explore the temples and tombs.

I thought that a few hundred years ago, a teenaged girl just like me had probably lived here. What did she do all day? What clothes did she wear? What was important to her? Who were her friends? What was her family like? Did she go to school?

There is so much about the Incas I don't know, so much I don't understand. I remind myself that there is tomorrow. I have plenty of time to learn more!

RECALLING FACTS

Recalling details

1. Which explorer discovered Machu Picchu in the early twentieth century? Hiram Bingham discovered Machu Picchu.

Identifying cause and effect

2. Why did the Incas construct the Inca Trail?

They built the trail so that priests and the royal Incas could have a clear path to make a pilgrimage to Machu Picchu.

Recalling details/reading a map

3. Based on the selection and the map on page 69, match the place names in column A with the descriptions in column B.

A	B
b Bolivia, Chilé, Ecuador, Colombia, and Brazil	**a.** the mountains of Peru
a Andes	**b.** the countries that surround Peru
c Lima	**c.** the capital of Peru
d Pacific Ocean	**d.** the water that borders Peru on the west

Recalling details/reading a map

4. a. Based on the map of the Inca Trail, exactly how high was the first pass? 13,680 feet

b. What river passes below Machu Picchu and through Ollantaytambo? Urubamba River

Using context clues

5. Complete each sentence with the correct word below.

altitude **condors** **descent**

a. The descent down the mountain was gradual and well marked.

b. If you are at sea level in a coastal city, you are at a very low altitude.

c. Condors are very large birds that were used by the Incas to carry messages over long distances.

Interpreting Facts

Making inferences

1. How did Kristen change from the first day to the fourth day of the hike?

Answers may vary. At first, she was homesick and wanted to be at home with her friends. By the end of the trip, she was enjoying herself and eager to learn Spanish and find out more about the Incas.

Inferring unstated main idea

2. Which sentence tells the main idea of the paragraph with a check mark next to it?

○ a. Kristen doesn't understand Spanish.

○ b. Kristen is glad to be at the top of the first pass.

● c. Kristen wants to study Spanish so that she can speak to Spanish-speaking people.

Drawing conclusions

3. How did Kristen's visit to Machu Picchu affect her?

Answers may vary. She was captivated by the city and wants to learn more about the people who lived there.

Drawing conclusions

4. Based on what you read about Kristen's trip, how would you describe the Incas?

Answers may vary. The Incas were great builders. They had a very advanced society.

Making inferences

5. Think about Kristen's diary entries. How would you describe her character?

She is adventurous and curious. She is very observant.

Skill Focus

Identify each of the following statements as fact or opinion by writing *F* or *O* on the line. Then read the conclusion following each group of statements.

F The Incas lived between 1200 and 1500 C.E.

F The Incas built a city in the Andes called Machu Picchu.

F The Incas built a Royal Road for pilgrims to walk on that led to Machu Picchu.

Conclusion: The Incas built a Royal Road through the Andes that led to Machu Picchu.

O If you walk the Inca Trail, which was created over five centuries ago, you can tell that the Incas were great builders and engineers.

O The Incas thought a pilgrimage through the Andes was very important.

O Few ruins are as impressive as the ones at Machu Picchu.

Conclusion: The Incas built a Royal Road that led to Machu Picchu over five hundred years ago.

The same conclusion can be reached using facts or opinions as support. Is the conclusion based on fact stronger than the conclusion based on opinion? Explain.

The conclusion based on facts is stronger because each fact can be proved. The conclusion supported by opinions is based on information that is difficult to check or prove. It is based on someone's ideas, feelings, or beliefs.

▶ **Real Life Connections** Picture yourself hiking the Inca Trail. Which part would interest you most? Explain.

Lesson 22

Cause and Effect

Reading a Science Selection

Background Information

Pollution can harm our environment in many ways. For example, badly polluted air can cause serious diseases and reduce the air's ability to filter out harmful ultraviolet rays from the sun. As a result, scientists believe that climates around the world have begun to change. Water pollution also endangers many plants and animals that live in the oceans and in other bodies of water. Because of water and soil pollution, many farmers cannot grow enough food.

Now countries around the world are finally working together to limit the pollution that affects our air and water. Nations have even signed treaties to stop dumping waste into the oceans and to stop producing certain chemicals. On a community level, people are learning to work together to conserve water and energy.

The following selection describes four kinds of pollution: air, water, land, and noise pollution.

Skill Focus

The **cause** of something is the reason it happens. The **effect** is what happens as a result of the cause.

Some words signal cause and effect, such as *cause, effect, because, result,* and *affect.*

Think about cause and effect relationships as you read. For example, if a person won first prize in a contest, he or she would feel happy. The cause is winning first prize. The effect is feeling happy.

Sometimes many causes can produce a single effect. Read the following sentences.

> Jim didn't do well on his science test today. He didn't study last night. He went to bed late. He wasn't feeling well during the test.

The effect is that Jim didn't do well on his science test today. It is stated in the first sentence. The causes are stated in the next three sentences.

Causes
1. Jim didn't study.
2. Jim went to bed late.
3 Jim didn't feel well.

↓

Effect
Jim didn't do well on his science test.

Word Clues

Read the sentence that follows. Look for context clues that explain the underlined word.

> Air pollutants can irritate the respiratory, or breathing, tracts of people and animals.

If you do not know the meaning of the word *respiratory,* the phrase *or breathing* can help you. The meaning of the describing word *respiratory is* given in an appositive phrase.

Use **appositive phrases** to find the meaning of the three underlined words in the selection.

Strategy Tip

Preview "What Do We Need for Life?" Look for the headings that name the four types of pollution. Each of these is an effect. When you read the section that follows each heading, look for the causes of each type of pollution.

What Do We Need for Life?

We usually don't think about the air we breathe, the water we drink, the land we live on, or the noises we hear. These things are part of our **environment** (en VY rən mənt). The environment includes the land, air, and water around us. Each of these three parts of the environment is important to our lives and to our planet. Due to the growth of industries and population, many changes have taken place in our environment.

Each of us breathes about 4,000 gallons of air each day.

Air Pollution

The earth is surrounded by an ocean. There are no fish in this ocean. It is an ocean of air, almost 6,000 trillion tons of it. Each of us breathes about 4,000 gallons of air each day. Air has no smell, no taste, and no color. It is a mixture of several gases. The two most important gases in air are nitrogen and oxygen. These gases make up over 98 percent of the air we breathe.

Substances that make air dirty are known as air **pollutants** (pə LOOT ənts). Air pollutants are caused by many things. When fuel is burned, poisonous gases and smoke are released into the air. Automobile exhaust, factory fumes, and smoke from household chimneys are examples of air pollutants caused by the burning of fuel. Pollutants from the burning of fuel are the main cause of air pollution. Other air pollutants include smoke from burning garbage, smoke from forest fires, and chemical sprays.

Air pollutants can irritate the respiratory, or breathing, tracts of people and animals. **Carbon monoxide** (KAR bən mə NAK syd) and lead fumes from automobile exhaust affect respiration. Poisonous gases and soot from factory fumes weaken livestock, affect vegetable crops, dirty the area around the factory, and cause acid rain. Chemical pollutants can ruin buildings, as well as threaten people's health. Whatever the causes of air pollution, the results are always bad.

Water Pollution

Water can become polluted in many ways. Chemicals from factories, untreated sewage, crop sprays, oil spills, and wastes from mines all pollute water. This makes the water unfit for drinking, swimming, and bathing. The damage doesn't end there. Polluted water is also unfit for water animals. Water animals that are not killed by pollutants may hold pollutants in their bodies and then pass them along food chains. The people and other animals who are the final consumers in food chains are affected by the pollutants.

Detergents and agricultural fertilizers are two common pollutants in the water supply. Some water plants thrive, or grow well, on the substances found in these two pollutants. As a result, these plants grow rapidly and use up most of the available nutrients in the water environment. Then the plants begin to die and decay. The oxygen in the water supply is used up as a result of this decay. Thus, less oxygen is available for fish and other animals living in the water, and they may die.

Power plants cause another kind of water pollution. Some power plants use water to cool their generators, machines that make electricity. As the generators cool, they warm the water. This water, much warmer now, is returned to the lake or river, causing thermal, or heat, pollution. Plants and fish living in the water may be affected by the increase in water temperature. Water pollution caused by radiation is also dangerous to living things. Nuclear power plants give off radioactive materials that warm the water and endanger sea life. Whatever the causes of water pollution, the results are always bad.

Land Pollution

One cause of land pollution is the dumping of litter, or unwanted materials. Cans, bottles, papers, and plastics are just a few kinds of litter. Though some materials may decay, or break down, many factory-made substances, such as plastics, glass, and metals, do not decay. Instead, they remain in the environment, often poisoning it.

Another important land pollutant is toxic waste, which is chemicals or materials that can injure or kill living things. In the past, factories often dumped or buried their deadly waste products in unprotected landfills. Such waste can leak out into the soil or into drinking water. Whatever the cause of land pollution, the results are dangerous.

Noise Pollution

With the invention of machines to make life easier and more enjoyable, the sound levels around us have increased. Some of the machines are hair dryers, air conditioners, stereos, telephones, and lawn mowers. Unwanted or disturbing sounds are usually called noise pollution.

Noise pollution can have harmful effects on the human body. It can affect hearing, and the ability to concentrate, to sleep, and to speak. It can create tension and cause headaches.

Noise pollution can also affect animals. Animals affected by noise pollution may migrate to quieter areas. This can affect the natural balance in the environment. Whatever the causes of noise pollution, the results can be dangerous.

All living things have certain needs, such as food, oxygen, water, and a certain stable temperature. The survival of all living things depends on meeting these needs. The questions for the future are these: How long will our environment be able to meet our future needs? How can we protect our environment?

Recalling Facts

Recalling details

1. What is the environment?

The environment includes the land, air, and water around us.

Recalling details

2. What are the two most important gases found in air?

Nitrogen and oxygen are found in the air.

Recalling details

3. What are air pollutants?

Air pollutants are substances that make air dirty.

Recalling details

4. What is carbon monoxide?

Carbon monoxide is an air pollutant caused by automobile exhaust.

Recalling details

5. What is thermal pollution?

It is pollution caused by heat.

Identifying cause and effect

6. What causes land pollution?

The dumping of litter and toxic waste causes land pollution.

Identifying cause and effect

7. What can cause some water plants to thrive and use up the nutrients in the water environment?

The dumping of detergents and agricultural fertilizers into water can cause this situation.

Using context clues

8. Decide if each statement is true or false. Write *true* or *false* on the line provided.

a. Flowers thrive on sunlight and water.

true

b. A thermal blanket would keep a person cool. false

c. If a car's generator is not working, you cannot use the lights. true

INTERPRETING FACTS

Inferring cause and effect

1. How can the dumping of chemicals on land affect the water that people drink?

Answers may vary. The chemicals can seep into the water supply and pollute the water.

Making inferences

2. Where do power plants get the water that they use to cool their generators?

Answers may vary. They get the water from nearby lakes and rivers.

Inferring cause and effect

3. Think of a city street today and the same street a hundred years ago. What is one cause of noise pollution today that wasn't mentioned in the selection?

The automobile is one cause of modern air pollution.

Making inferences

4. In what ways have modern industry and scientific advances improved our lives?

Cures for disease, better crop production, and work-saving appliances have all improved our lives.

SKILL FOCUS

On the lines, write the causes for each effect. You may look back at the selection.

	Causes	Effect
1.	a. the burning of fuel	***Air Pollution***
	b. automobile exhaust	
	c. factory fumes	
	d. smoke from household chimneys	
2.	a. chemicals from factories	***Water Pollution***
	b. untreated sewage	
	c. crop sprays	
	d. oil spills	
	e. wastes from mines	
3.	a. hair dryers	***Noise Pollution***
	b. air conditioners	
	c. telephones	
	d. lawn mowers	

▶ Real Life Connections Find out what your community does with toxic waste. Is it deposited in a protected landfill? If not, are there plans to do this in the near future? Explain.

Lesson 23

Word Problems

Reading a Mathematics Selection

Background Information

A word problem is a mathematical problem that is written out in words, rather than in numbers. Think of a word problem as a puzzle that requires you to use reading and math skills at the same time. You might not be aware of it, but there are many times when you must solve word problems in your daily life. For example, when you follow a recipe, you are reading a word problem that requires you to add different amounts of ingredients. If you only want to make half the food that the recipe will make, then the word problem becomes more complicated.

Can you think of other kinds of word problems that you solve at home or school or at your job?

In the following selection, you will use the five steps to solve two word problems. Work through each step carefully. If you understand how to use each step, you can solve most word problems.

Skill Focus

Use the following five steps when solving word problems.

1. Read the problem. Be sure that you are familiar with all the words, especially the labels that are used with each number. Think about what question is being asked. Try to picture in your mind the information that is given. If you are not sure that you understand the question, reread the problem.
2. Decide how to find the answer. It may be helpful to draw a picture of the information that is given. Should you add, subtract, multiply, or divide? Use key words in the last sentence to help you decide which operation to use. Then write the mathematical sentence that will solve the problem.
3. Estimate the answer. When you estimate, you make a judgment or opinion about the value of something. Use rounded numbers to make an estimate.
4. Carry out the plan. Solve the mathematical sentence.
5. Reread the problem.Then write the complete answer. Is the answer logical? How close is it to your estimate? If your answer is not close to your estimate, start all over again with Step 1.

Word Clues

Some words can help you find the answer in a word problem. Such phrases as *how many more* and *how much greater* usually are signals to subtract. The word *together* is usually a signal to add. Look for key words in the last sentence of a problem.

Strategy Tip

In the following selection, you will read about and solve word problems. Remember, if you have difficulty completing any one of the five steps when solving a problem, redo all the steps that come before it.

Solving Word Problems

Facts on supercities are always being collected. Many of the facts are reported in the form of numbers. Suppose the following facts are known.

> In 1993, New York had a population of 18.2 million.
> In 1993, Georgia had 6.92 million people.

These facts can be put together to answer this question: "How many more people lived in New York than in Georgia in 1993?"

READ THE PROBLEM

New York had a population of 18.2 million. Georgia had a population of 6.92 million. How many more people lived in New York than in Georgia?

Be sure that you know the label that is used with each number fact. Are there any words that you do not know? If so, look them up to find their meanings. What question does the problem ask? Often the question is asked in the last sentence. *How many more people lived in New York than in Georgia?* Read the problem again.

DECIDE HOW TO FIND THE ANSWER

You need to decide how to put the facts together to answer the question. Facts can be put together in the following four ways:

1. Add to combine groups.
2. Subtract to compare groups.
3. Multiply to combine many small groups of the same size.
4. Divide to break down one big group into smaller groups.

Which way should you put the facts together to answer the question? The word *more* is a key word that tells you to compare information. Because the question asks you to compare, you need to subtract.

Now you can write a mathematical sentence to help you answer the question. You know two things: 18.2 million people lived in New York, and 6.92 million people lived in Georgia. This is your mathematical sentence:

$$18.2 - 6.92 = n$$

The letter n stands for the number you are trying to find.

ESTIMATE THE ANSWER

Round 18.2 million to 18 million. Round 6.92 million to 7 million. Subtract 7 million from 18 million.

$$18 - 7 = 11$$

Your estimate is 11 million.

CARRY OUT THE PLAN

$$18.2 - 6.92 = 11.28$$

REREAD THE PROBLEM

New York had 11.28 million more people than Georgia. Does this answer make sense? How close is this answer to your estimate?

Use the five steps to solve the following problem.

Read: In 1993, New York had a population of 18.2 million. The average family had 2.6 people. About how many families lived in New York?

Decide: Use division to break down one big group into smaller groups. Write a mathematical sentence to answer the question.

$$18.2 \div 2.6 = n$$

Estimate: Round 18.2 million to 18 million. Round 2.6 to 3. Divide 18 million by 3.

$$18 \div 3 = 6$$

Your estimate is 6 million.

Carry Out: $18.2 \div 2.6 = 7$

Reread: About 7 million families lived in New York.

Recalling Facts

Recalling details
1. In which sentence of a word problem is the question usually asked? the last sentence

Recalling details
2. You add to combine groups, subtract to compare groups, multiply to combine many small groups of the same size, and divide to break down one big group into smaller groups.

Recalling details
3. What label is used in the first problem? people

   In the second problem? families

Interpreting Facts

Making inferences
1. Which mathematical operation is similar to addition?

   multiplication

Making inferences
2. Which mathematical operation is similar to subtraction?

   division

Making inferences
3. Which two mathematical operations produce an answer that is greater than all the numbers in a problem?

   addition and multiplication

Making inferences
4. Which two mathematical operations produce an answer that is smaller than at least one of the numbers in a problem?

   subtraction and division

Skill Focus

Use the five steps to solve these problems. Write a mathematical sentence in the *decide* step.

1. Read: New Haven and Bridgeport are two Connecticut cities. They have areas of 48.9 square kilometers and 41.4 square kilometers. What is the area of the two cities together?

Decide: Add to put two groups together. $48.9 + 41.4 = n$

Estimate: Round 48.9 to 49. Round 41.4 to 40. $49 + 40 = 89$

Carry Out: $48.9 + 41.4 = 90.3$

Reread: The total area is 90.3 square kilometers.

2. Read: In Maryland, 2,100,000 people were employed in 1993. There were just over $2\frac{1}{3}$ times as many people living in the state. What was the population of Maryland?

Decide: Multiply to combine many groups of the same size. $2{,}100{,}000 \times 2\frac{1}{3} = n$

Estimate: Round 2,100,000 to 2,000,000. Round $2\frac{1}{3}$ to 2. $2{,}000{,}000 \times 2 = 4{,}000{,}000$

Carry Out: $2{,}100{,}000 \times 2\frac{1}{3} = 4{,}893{,}000$

Reread: The population of Maryland was over 4,893,000.

3. Read: In 1992, the average household income in Pennsylvania was $29,985. The average household income in Delaware was $35,739. How much greater was the Delaware income?

Decide: Subtract to compare the two groups. $35,739 – $29,985 = *n*

Estimate: Round $35,739 to $36,000. Round $29,985 to $30,000. $36,000 – $30,000 = $6,000

Carry Out: $35,739 – $29,985 = $5,754

Reread: The average household income in Delaware was greater by $5,754.

4. Read: The New York City seaport handled 127,145 million kilograms of cargo in 1990. There are 1,000 kilograms in a metric ton. About how many tons of cargo did New York City handle?

Decide: Divide to break down one group into smaller groups. $127{,}145 \div 1{,}000 = n$

Estimate: Round 127,145 to 127,000. $127{,}000 \div 1{,}000 = 127$

Carry Out: $127{,}145 \div 1{,}000 = 127.145$

Reread: New York City handled 127.145 metric tons of cargo in 1990.

5. Read: In 1994, Buffalo, New York, had a population of 328,123. Dunkirk, New York, had a population of 13,989. How many more people lived in Buffalo than in Dunkirk?

Decide: Subtract to compare the two groups. $328{,}123 - 13{,}989 = n$

Estimate: Round 328,123 to 328,000. Round 13,989 to 14,000. $328{,}000 - 14{,}000 = 314{,}000$

Carry Out: $328{,}123 - 13{,}989 = 314{,}134$

Reread: There were 314,134 more people in Buffalo than in Dunkirk.

Real Life Connections Research the population of your community ten years ago. How many more people live there today? Then use the information to make up a word problem to solve.

Syllables

To help you pronounce a long word, divide the word into syllables. Then pronounce each syllable until you can say the whole word. There are several different ways of deciding how a word should be divided.

Compound Words

One of the easiest guides to use in dividing words is the one that is used with a compound word. Because a compound word is made up of two words, it must have at least two syllables. Always divide a compound word into syllables by separating it between the two smaller words first. If these smaller words have more than one syllable, it may be necessary to use another guide. However, you can pronounce most compound words if you first divide them into two smaller words.

Read each of the following compound words. Divide the word into two syllables by writing each of the two smaller words separately on the line to the right of the compound word.

1. homesick ____home sick____
2. raincoat ____rain coat____
3. outline ____out line____
4. steamship ____steam ship____
5. snowfall ____snow fall____
6. footprint ____foot print____
7. doorway ____door way____
8. textbook ____text book____
9. someone ____some one____
10. farmhouse ____farm house____

Fill in the words necessary to complete the following guide.

Guide 1: A compound word is divided into ____syllables____ between the ____two____ smaller words.

Words with Double Consonants

Use another guide for words with double consonants. Divide the word into two syllables between the two consonants. Then read each syllable.

Use this guide to divide the following two-syllable words into syllables. Write each syllable separately on the line to the right of the word.

1. supper ____sup per____
2. happen ____hap pen____
3. sudden ____sud den____
4. command ____com mand____
5. quarrel ____quar rel____
6. suggest ____sug gest____
7. cotton ____cot ton____
8. sapphire ____sap phire____

Fill in the words necessary to complete the following guide.

Guide 2: A word that has a ____double____ consonant is divided into syllables between the ____two____ consonants.

Lesson 25

Syllables

Words with a Prefix or Suffix

A prefix always has at least one sounded vowel. This means that a prefix always contains at least one syllable. You can divide a word that has a prefix between the prefix and the root word.

Divide each word below into two syllables between the prefix and root word. Write each syllable separately on the line to the right of the word.

1. transport trans port
2. return re turn
3. precook pre cook
4. displace dis place
5. refill re fill
6. preview pre view
7. distrust dis trust
8. untrue un true
9. distaste dis taste
10 inside in side
11. replant re plant
12. disprove dis prove
13. undone un done
14. prepay pre pay

A suffix always has at least one sounded vowel. This means that a suffix always contains at least one syllable. You can divide a word that has a suffix between the root word and the suffix.

Divide each word below into two syllables between the root word and the suffix. Write each syllable separately on the line to the right of the word.

1. gladly glad ly
2. statement state ment
3. farmer farm er
4. helpful help ful
5. frighten fright en
6. breathless breath less
7. shortage short age
8. pitcher pitch er
9. brightly bright ly
10. careful care ful
11. beastly beast ly
12. broaden broad en
13. creamy cream y
14. handful hand ful

Fill in the word necessary to complete the following guide.

Guide 3: A word that has a prefix or suffix is divided into syllables between the prefix or suffix and the word.

Syllables

Words with Two Consonants Between Two Sounded Vowels

Below are some words that you already know. You can tell where to divide the words into syllables just by saying them to yourself. Say each word, listening to be sure that each syllable has only one vowel sound. Write each syllable separately on the line to the right of the word.

1. winter — win ter
2. order — or der
3. picture — pic ture
4. target — tar get
5. window — win dow
6. monkey — mon key

Fill in the words necessary to complete the following guide.

Guide 4: A word that has two consonants between two sounded vowels is divided into syllables between the two consonants.

You can use this guide to divide words that you do not know how to pronounce. Divide each word below into two syllables by writing each syllable separately on the line to the right of the word.

1. husband — hus band
2. wonder — won der
3. perhaps — per haps
4. garden — gar den
5. capture — cap ture
6. Denver — Den ver
7. convince — con vince
8. escape — es cape
9. expert — ex pert
10. signal — sig nal
11. enter — en ter
12. velvet — vel vet
13. carbon — car bon
14. former — for mer
15. tender — ten der
16. admit — ad mit
17. cactus — cac tus
18. doctor — doc tor
19. lantern — lan tern
20. canvas — can vas
21. picnic — pic nic
22. silver — sil ver
23. napkin — nap kin
24. helmet — hel met
25. circus — cir cus
26. basket — bas ket
27. shelter — shel ter
28. number — num ber

Lesson 27

Syllables

Words with One Consonant Between Two Sounded Vowels

Many words have only one consonant between two sounded vowels. This guide will help you in dividing such words. Guide 5a has to do with words in which the first vowel is long. Guide 5b has to do with words in which the first vowel is short.

You can tell where to divide the words below into syllables by saying them. Say the word. Listen to be sure that each syllable has only one vowel sound. Write each syllable separately on the line to the right of the word.

1. music ___mu sic___
2. climate ___cli mate___
3. bacon ___ba con___
4. locate ___lo cate___
5. notice ___no tice___
6. final ___fi nal___

Did one consonant come between two sounded vowels in each of these words? ___yes___

Was the first vowel long or short? ___long___

Did you divide before or after the consonant between the vowels? ___before___

Fill in the words necessary to complete the following guide.

Guide 5a: A word that has one ___consonant___ between two sounded ___vowels___, with the first ___vowel___ long, is usually divided into syllables before the ___consonant___.

You can use this guide to divide words you do not know how to pronounce. Divide each word below into two syllables by writing each syllable separately on the line to the right of the word.

1. later ___la ter___
2. nature ___na ture___
3. paper ___pa per___
4. hotel ___ho tel___
5. fever ___fe ver___
6. major ___ma jor___
7. native ___na tive___
8. motor ___mo tor___

Some words with a consonant between two sounded vowels do not follow the rule in the previous guide. They are divided after the consonant instead of before it. In these words, the first vowel is short instead of long.

Say each of the words below. Decide whether the first vowel is long or short. If it is short, divide the word into syllables after the consonant. Write each syllable separately on the line to the right of the word.

1. rapid ___rap id___
2. travel ___trav el___
3. topic ___top ic___
4. wagon ___wag on___
5. petal ___pet al___
6. relish ___rel ish___

Did one consonant come between two sounded vowels in each of these words? yes

Was the first vowel long or short? short

Did you divide before or after the consonant between the vowels? after

Fill in the words necessary to complete the following guide.

Guide 5b: A word that has one consonant between two sounded vowels, with the first vowel short, is usually divided into syllables after the consonant.

You can use this guide to divide words you do not know how to pronounce. Divide each word below into syllables by writing each syllable separately on the line to the right of the word.

1. digit dig it
2. magic mag ic
3. profit prof it
4. seven sev en
5. solid sol id
6. medal med al
7. river riv er
8. salad sal ad
9. visit vis it
10. petal pet al

Words with Blends

The word *subtract* has three consonants between two sounded vowels. Because the blend *tr* makes one sound, it is treated in the same way that a single consonant is treated. Divide the word between the consonant and the consonant blend: *sub tract.*

With a word that has three or more consonants between two vowels, find the blend and treat it as one consonant.

Circle the blend in each of the words below. Divide each word into two syllables by writing each syllable separately on the line to the right of the word.

1. children chil dren
2. congress con gress
3. substance sub stance
4. purchase pur chase
5. hindrance hin drance
6. bolster bol ster

When a word ends in *-le,* the *-le* and the consonant before it make up a syllable, as in *cra dle* or *a ble.* Divide these words into syllables by writing each syllable on the line to the right of the word.

1. bundle bun dle
2. jungle jun gle
3. gentle gen tle
4. bugle bu gle
5. tremble trem ble
6. candle can dle
7. whistle whis tle
8. staple sta ple

Fill in the words necessary to complete the following guide.

Guide 6: Do not split a consonant blend or a consonant and *-le*. Treat a consonant blend or consonant and *-le* as if it were one consonant.

Lesson 28

Word Origins

Roots, prefixes, and suffixes are word parts. You can often figure out the meaning of an unknown word if you know the meaning of each of its word parts.

Example: **philosopher**

This word comes from the Greek roots *philos,* which means "loving," and *sophos,* which means "wise." *Philosopher* means "someone who loves wisdom."

Latin Roots

Latin has been an important language since the days of the Roman Empire. During the Middle Ages, it became the language of scholars, or learned people. By using Latin, scholars from different lands could easily communicate with one another. Most books from the Middle Ages were written in Latin, too. Today over half the words in the English language can be traced back to Latin. Many of these words are related to law, government, and religion.

Example: **legislator, legislate**

Legislator means "one who brings the law," and *legislate* means "to make laws." Both are from the Latin root *leges,* which means "laws."

Greek Roots

Twenty-five hundred years ago, Greece was the center of learning for the entire Western world. Greece had the best government and the finest artists and writers. Once the Romans conquered Greece, they began to enjoy Greek art and writing so much that they made Greek words part of their own language. Some of these words are now part of the English language.

Example: **govern**

The Greek word *kybernan,* which means "to steer or rule," became *gubernare* in Latin because it was easier for the Romans to pronounce. The English word *govern* comes from the Latin word.

More English words came from these Latin words of Greek origin. About six hundred years ago, the people in Italy became more interested in learning than they had ever been before. They turned to the books, art, and language of ancient Greece. Gradually, more Greek words became part of the Latin language. Soon, scholars all over the Western world were using Greek words that they had changed to fit into their own language.

Example: **telescope**

The word *telescope* is formed by combining the root *tele* and the root *scope.* If you know that *tele* means "far away" and *scope* means an "instrument for observing," you can figure out that *telescope* means "an instrument for observing things far away."

Knowing the meaning of *scope* helps you with the meaning of such words as *stethoscope, microscope,* and *kaleidoscope.* Knowing the meaning of *tele* helps you with the meaning of such words as *telegraph, television,* and *telephone.*

A. The word *port* comes from the Latin root *portare,* which means "to carry." Read each sentence below and underline the word with the root *port.*

1. Rowboats transport visitors from the mainland to the island.
2. Many American blue jeans are made for export to foreign countries.
3. José took the portable television set from the bedroom to the kitchen.
4. The porter put the suitcases into the trunk of the car.
5. We import much of our coffee from South American countries.

Write the underlined words from the sentences on the lines below. Then match each one with its meaning. Write the letter of the correct meaning on the line after the word.

6. transport ___a___ a. carry out of
7. export ___b___ b. carry across
8. portable ___d___ c. one who carries
9. porter ___c___ d. able to be carried
10. import ___e___ e. carry into

B. Read the Latin and Greek word parts and their meanings.

Root	Meaning	Prefix	Meaning	Suffix	Meaning
aud (Latin)	to hear	bi (Latin)	two	logy (Greek)	study of
vis (Latin)	to see			phobia (Greek)	fear of

Underline the Latin or Greek word part from the chart in each of the following words.

1. audible
2. biceps
3. vision
4. zoology
5. claustrophobia
6. bicycle
7. audition
8. invisible

Complete each sentence by writing one of the eight words above on the line.

9. Some people are afraid of being in enclosed places. They have claustrophobia.

10. People who are interested in animals study animal life. The study of animal life is zoology.

11. To get a part in a play, an actor or actress performs at a hearing. There, his or her acting ability is tested. This is called an audition.

12. Some movies have ghosts you cannot see. You cannot see invisible ghosts.

13. A large muscle in the front of the upper arm and at the back of the thigh with two beginning points is the biceps.

C. Read the Greek word parts and their meanings.

Root	Meaning	Prefix	Meaning	Suffix	Meaning
scope	a device for seeing	auto	self	cracy	government
		demo	people		
phone	sound	micro	very small		
graph	writing				

Combine two of the word parts above to make a word that will complete each sentence. Write the word on the line.

1. A hair viewed under a microscope will appear larger than it really is.
2. The quiet man used a microphone so that everybody in the room heard his speech.
3. The type of government in which one person rules is an autocracy.
4. The type of government of, for, and by the people is a democracy.
5. Jenny hoped that the famous pitcher would autograph her baseball.

Reading a Bus Schedule

Have you ever taken a bus? If so, you may have checked a **bus schedule**. A bus schedule lists the times the buses run and tells where the buses make stops. In most cities, the busiest time for buses is rush hour, when most people go to and from work. More buses run during these hours, since the need for the buses is much greater at that time.

The bus schedule shows where a bus on route 44 stops. The times below each place show when a bus stops there. Read from left to right across each line to find out what time the bus going from Mount Vernon Place to North Shore Apartments makes each stop.

BUS ROUTE 44 — Northbound from Downtown

Monday through Friday

	MOUNT VERNON PLACE	RUXTON ROAD	GREEN-SPRING AVENUE	STEVENS VILLAGE MALL	PARK CREST ROAD	NORTH SHORE APARTMENTS
A.M.	7:30	7:45	7:49	7:52	7:55	7:59
	8:20	8:35	8:39	8:42	8:45	8:49
	9:30	9:45	9:49	9:52	9:55	9:59
	10:30	10:45	10:49	10:52	10:55	10:59
	11:30	11:45	11:49	11:52	11:55	11:59
P.M.	12:20	12:35	12:39	12:42	12:45	12:49
	2:10	2:25	2:29	2:32	—	2:39
	2:40	2:55	2:59	3:02	3:05	3:09
	3:10	3:25	3:29	3:32	—	3:39
	4:15	4:30	4:34	4:37	4:40	4:44
	4:40	5:01	5:05	5:08	5:11	5:15
	4:55	5:16	5:20	5:23	5:26	5:30
	5:05	5:26	5:30	5:33	5:36	5:40
	5:10	5:31	5:35	5:38	5:41	5:45
	5:15	5:36	5:40	5:43	5:46	5:50
	5:20	5:41	5:45	5:48	5:51	5:55
	5:30	5:51	5:55	5:58	6:01	6:05
	5:40	6:01	6:05	6:08	6:11	6:15
	5:50	6:11	6:15	6:18	6:21	6:25
	6:05	6:20	6:24	6:27	6:30	6:34
	6:30	6:45	6:49	6:52	6:55	6:59
	7:30	7:45	7:49	7:52	7:55	7:59
	8:30	8:45	8:49	8:52	8:55	8:59
	9:30	9:45	9:49	9:52	9:55	9:59

Saturday

	MOUNT VERNON PLACE	RUXTON ROAD	GREEN-SPRING AVENUE	STEVENS VILLAGE MALL	PARK CREST ROAD	NORTH SHORE APARTMENTS
A.M.	8:30	8:45	8:49	8:52	8:55	8:59
	11:30	11:45	11:49	11:52	11:55	11:59
P.M.	1:20	1:35	1:39	1:42	1:45	1:49
	2:40	2:55	2:59	3:02	3:05	3:09
	3:40	3:55	3:59	4:02	4:05	4:09
	4:15	4:30	4:34	4:37	4:40	4:44
	4:45	5:00	5:04	5:07	5:10	5:14
	5:15	5:30	5:34	5:37	5:40	5:44
	6:15	6:30	6:34	6:37	6:40	6:44
	7:15	7:30	7:34	7:37	7:40	7:44
	8:15	8:30	8:34	8:37	8:40	8:44
	9:15	9:30	9:34	9:37	9:40	9:44

Sunday & Holidays

	MOUNT VERNON PLACE	RUXTON ROAD	GREEN-SPRING AVENUE	STEVENS VILLAGE MALL	PARK CREST ROAD	NORTH SHORE APARTMENTS
A.M.	8:30	8:45	8:49	8:52	8:55	8:59
	11:30	11:45	11:49	11:52	11:55	11:59
P.M.	1:30	1:45	1:49	1:52	1:55	1:59
	3:30	3:45	3:49	3:52	3:55	3:59
	5:30	5:45	5:49	5:52	5:55	5:59

A. Use the information on the bus schedule to complete each sentence.

1. The name of the place where bus route 44 begins is Mount Vernon Place.
2. The name of the place where bus route 44 ends is North Shore Apartments.
3. The first bus leaves Mount Vernon Place at 7:30 A.M. each weekday morning.
4. The last bus leaves Mount Vernon Place at 9:15 P.M. every Saturday evening.
5. It takes three minutes to go from Greenspring Avenue to Stevens Village Mall.
6. The buses leaving Mount Vernon Place at 2:10 P.M. and 3:10 P.M. on weekdays do not make a stop at Park Crest Road.
7. If you leave Mount Vernon Place by 4:15 P.M. any weekday, it takes fifteen minutes to arrive at Ruxton Road. But if you leave at 5:50 P.M., it takes 21 minutes. It takes longer at these times probably because they are the rush hours.
8. If you take the 3:55 P.M. bus on Saturday from Ruxton Road, you will arrive at Park Crest Road at 4:05 P.M.
9. The 5:05 P.M. bus from Greenspring Avenue arrives at North Shore Apartments at 5:15 P.M.
10. The days that the bus leaves Stevens Village Mall at 1:52 P.M. are Sundays and holidays.

B. Fill in the circle next to the answer to each question.

1. On Saturdays, when does the 8:15 P.M. bus from Mount Vernon Place arrive at Park Crest Road?
   - ○ a. 8:44 P.M.
   - ● b. 8:40 P.M.
   - ○ c. 8:30 P.M.
2. If you leave Ruxton Road on the 11:45 A.M. bus on a Sunday, what time will you arrive at North Shore Apartments?
   - ● a. 11:59 A.M.
   - ○ b. 11:59 P.M.
   - ○ c. 11:49 P.M.
3. What time does the last bus leave Mount Vernon Place on holidays?
   - ○ a. 9:30 P.M.
   - ○ b. 9:44 P.M
   - ● c. 5:30 P.M.
4. On Saturdays, how many morning buses travel from Ruxton Road to the Stevens Village Mall?
   - ● a. two
   - ○ b. five
   - ○ c. twelve
5. How many days a week does a 4:30 P.M. bus go from Ruxton Road to Stevens Village Mall?
   - ○ a. five
   - ● b. six
   - ○ c. seven
6. How many buses travel route 44 between 4:00 P.M. and 6:00 P.M. on weekdays?
   - ○ a. three
   - ● b. ten
   - ○ c. eleven
7. How long does it take to get from Mount Vernon Place to Greenspring Avenue on a Sunday?
   - ○ a. 15 minutes
   - ○ b. 21 minutes
   - ● c. 19 minutes
8. To get to North Shore Apartments by 5:00 P.M. on Tuesday, when do you need to leave Stevens Village Mall?
   - ○ a. 4:15 P.M.
   - ● b. 4:37 P.M.
   - ○ c. 5:08 P.M.

UNIT 4

Seeing Both Sides

Lesson 30

Point of View

Reading a Literature Selection

Background Information

Segregation had been the law of the land in the South for many years. Segregation laws separated whites and African Americans. African American children attended separate schools. All African Americans had to use separate public facilities, including drinking fountains, swimming pools, and restrooms. In 1955, an African American woman courageously defied segregation laws on city buses. Rosa Parks, "the mother of the Civil Rights Movement," put a movement into motion that would last over a decade. The Civil Rights Movement in the United States in the 1950s and 1960s changed the lives of all Americans. More importantly, however, the Civil Rights Movement reversed segregation laws in the South.

The following selection is a short biography of Rosa Parks, an African American seamstress, who helped bring to public attention the unjust laws regarding the segregation of African Americans in the South.

Skill Focus

Many books are written about real people. In an autobiography, a person tells about his or her own life. The author writes from the **first-person point of view,** using the pronouns *I, me,* and *we.* Because the narrator tells the story from his or her perspective, readers see the story's events through the eyes of one character. In a biography, someone else tells a person's life story. The author, or narrator, writes from the **third-person point of view.** The author uses the pronouns *she, he,* and *they.* The third-person narrator knows what all the characters are thinking, feeling, and doing.

Word Clues

Read the sentence below. Look for the context clues that explain the underlined word.

> Parks had many skills that she had not been allowed to employ in jobs, but she got to use them now.

If you don't know the meaning of the word *employ,* the word *use* in the rest of the sentence can help you. To employ something is to use it.

Detail context clues are found in the same sentence, or in the sentence before or after the word they describe or explain. Look for **detail** context clues to find the meaning of the three underlined words in the selection.

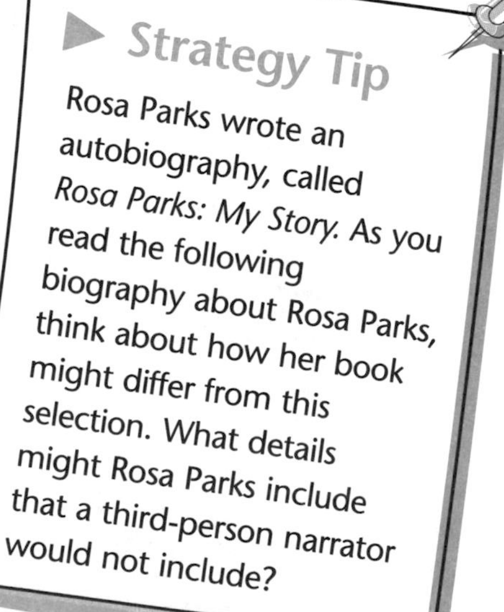

Rosa Parks

At 43, Rosa Parks sits at the front of a city bus after the Supreme Court ruling banned segregation on public buses and trains.

Rosa Parks often lay awake at night. She listened for the sound of galloping horses. When she was a little girl, many African Americans lay awake, listening fearfully.

Parks was born in 1913. Her name was Rosa McCauley then. When she was still a young child, her family moved to a small farm near Tuskegee, Alabama, where Parks lived with her mother, grandparents, and brother.

African Americans were afraid because white men rode horses in the night, firing guns to frighten them. These members of the Ku Klux Klan, dressed in white and wore hoods over their heads. They burned buildings and even killed people.

As Parks was growing up, she found that there were rules for African Americans. They could not drink from the same water fountains as white people. They could not eat at lunch counters in stores. African American children and white children could not go to the same school. And the schools for African American children were crowded and small. Some did not even have desks.

Schools were especially important to Parks and her family. Parks's mother had gone to college and had taught school for a while. Parks could read when she began school because her mother had taught her. When Parks was older, her mother returned to teaching. Her daughter was one of her students.

When Parks was eleven, her mother sent her to a private school for girls in Montgomery, Alabama. Her mother had saved money to pay for the school fees. Parks studied such subjects as English and science, but she learned something even more important. Her mother and grandparents had taught her to believe that she could do whatever she wanted to in life. And the teachers in this school, who were white, also helped Parks to believe in herself.

When the school was closed, Parks attended Booker T. Washington Junior High and then took some high school courses at a state college that offered courses for students of all ages. When her mother became ill, Parks had to drop out of school. Friends introduced her to Raymond Parks, a barber, whom she later married. With her husband's encouragement, Rosa Parks went back to school and received her high school diploma.

Parks took the jobs that she could find, including working in a hospital and sewing at home. But several years after graduation, she still had few choices of jobs. And there were separate rules that affected African Americans. Even the buses were segregated in Montgomery. African Americans could not sit in the front of the bus. They could sit only in the back. On a crowded bus, they had to give up their seats to white people. Also, African Americans had to pay their fare at the front of the bus. Then they had to get out of the bus, go to the door at the back, and get on again.

One day, Parks tried to break this rule. She got on at the front of the bus, paid her fare, and started down the aisle. The bus driver came toward her and grabbed her coat sleeve. He told her to get off the bus and use the back door to get back on. When she argued with him, he ordered her off the bus. She got off, and the bus left without her.

Parks then made a decision to do

something to help herself and all African Americans. She joined the National Association for the Advancement of Colored People. This group, the NAACP, helps African Americans in such areas as jobs, housing, and legal aid. Parks had many skills that she had not been allowed to employ in jobs, but she got to use them now. She became secretary of the Alabama NAACP. The president, Edgar Daniel Nixon, was very impressed with her work.

Parks and Nixon also worked together for the Montgomery Voters League. The goal of this organization was for all African Americans to vote. However, to do so, they had to pass a test and not make a single mistake. Parks visited homes, helping people learn how to take the test. Many white people did everything they could to keep African Americans from voting. Parks and Nixon were told that they would be in danger if they encouraged African Americans to vote. But this did not stop them from providing support to the people they wanted to help.

Slowly progress *was* being made in civil rights. Members of the NAACP went to the United States Supreme Court to argue that segregated schools were unfair to African American children. In 1954, the Supreme Court agreed. The justices decided that separate schools for African American and white children did not provide equal education. This was a great victory. But Parks looked for still more ways to end segregation.

The Montgomery boycott was led by Martin Luther King, Jr., who called for an end to segregation on buses.

Help came from Virginia Durr, a white woman for whom Parks worked. Durr convinced Parks to attend classes at the Highlander Folk School in Tennessee. People from all over the country attended this school, learning ways to fight segregation. Parks enjoyed attending Highlander with people of different races and backgrounds. When she returned home, she had a chance to use what she had learned.

Parks now had a job sewing at a department store in Montgomery. One day, she got on the bus to return home, and she recognized the driver. He was the same man who had ordered her off the bus several years ago and then had driven away. Now, in 1955, Parks took a seat in the middle of the bus. At the next stop, several white people got on, and a white man was left standing. The bus driver ordered the people in Parks's row to give up their seats. At first, no one stood up. Then everyone but Parks got up. She kept sitting. She was tired after working all day, but no more tired than usual. She was simply tired of giving in.

The bus driver told Parks he would have her arrested. She still did not move. Two policeman came and arrested her. She called home from the police station, and her mother called E. D. Nixon. He came to the station, along with Virginia and Clifford Durr. Virginia Durr was the first person Parks saw after she left her jail cell. After bail was paid, Parks was allowed to go home.

Then Nixon asked Parks an important question: Would she allow her case to be made a test case against segregation? Although Parks agreed, her husband was uncertain about her decision.

Meanwhile, Nixon talked with the African American ministers in Montgomery. He told them that he wanted all African Americans to stop riding the buses. One of the ministers was Martin Luther King, Jr. Nixon asked King to lead the boycott of the buses, and King agreed. Jo Ann Robinson, of the Political Women's Council, provided handbills urging African Americans to boycott the buses. A newspaper published a story about the boycott. Black ministers spoke about the boycott in church, urging people not to ride any buses.

Fred Gray, a lawyer, went to court with Parks on the day of her trial. He entered a plea of not guilty. But there was no effort to defend Parks against the charges. The plan was to allow her to be found guilty and then to appeal to a higher court. Local courts would not change the segregation laws. The only hope for change was appealing to the higher courts. Parks was found guilty, and she paid a fine of ten dollars, plus four dollars in court costs.

African Americans in Montgomery did not ride the buses for over a year. Some went to work in car pools, in wagons, and on horses or mules. But mostly they walked. The bus company lost money and had to cut back service, but no rules were changed. There were threats against African Americans and the Kings' home was bombed. The atmosphere of fear continued. While many white people blamed African Americans for all the problems, some white people did join the bus boycott.

The U.S. Supreme Court settled Parks's case thirteen months after the boycott began. The court ruled that segregated buses were unfair. From then on, African Americans could sit where they wished in buses or trains.

Parks had lost her job in the department store not long after the boycott started. Later, she and her family moved to Detroit, Michigan. There she continued to fight for civil rights. She worked in the office of John Conyers, an African American congressman, and was elected to the board of directors of the NAACP. In 1979, she won an award, the Spingarn Medal, for her civil rights work.

RECALLING FACTS

Identifying setting

1. Where do the main events in the biography take place?

They take place in Montgomery, Alabama.

Recalling details

2. In what year was Rosa Parks arrested?

She was arrested in 1955.

Identifying cause and effect

3. What did Parks do to cause her arrest?

She refused to give up her seat on a bus to a white man.

Recalling details

4. How did Virginia Durr help Rosa Parks?

She convinced her to attend Highlander Folk School. She also bailed Parks out of jail.

Recognizing sequence of events

5. Tell in order what E. D. Nixon did after Rosa Parks was released from jail.

He asked Parks if she would allow her case to be made a test case for segregation. He talked with African American ministers about a bus boycott. He then asked Martin Luther King, Jr., to lead the boycott.

Identifying cause and effect

6. How did the year-long bus boycott affect African Americans?

Because they did not ride the buses, African Americans had to get to work in other ways, such as walking, car pools, wagons, horses, or mules. There were also threats made against them.

Identifying cause and effect

7. What was the final effect of the bus boycott?

The U.S. Supreme Court ruled against segregated buses. As a result, African Americans could sit where they wished.

Using context clues

8. Decide if each statement is true or false. Write *true* or *false* on the line provided.

a. If a sick child is segregated from other children, she is put in the same room with them. false

b. A league could be a group of students who are raising money for citywide recycling bins. true

c. If you are encouraged to do a good job, you are being supported in your efforts. true

INTERPRETING FACTS

Making inferences

1. Rosa Parks was encouraged to believe in herself when she was growing up. How do you think this influenced her actions as an adult?

Answers may vary. Her self respect gave her the courage for her convictions. This led to her working for the civil rights of African Americans.

Inferring cause and effect

2. Why do you think E.D. Nixon wanted to use Parks's case as a test case against segregation?

Answers may vary. Nixon felt that a higher court ruling in Rosa Parks's favor could have an important effect on other civil rights issues.

Inferring cause and effect

3. Why do you think E.D. Nixon asked Martin Luther King, Jr., to lead the bus boycott?

Answers may vary. Nixon recognized King's outstanding leadership qualities and believed that people would follow him.

Making inferences

4. Some white people in Montgomery supported the bus boycott. What does this suggest about these people?

Answers may vary. It suggests that they realized that segregation was unjust.

Inferring cause and effect

5. Why do you think Rosa Parks lost her job in the department store?

Answers may vary. White people were angry about the boycott; the store was afraid of losing business if Parks continued to work there.

Drawing conclusions

6. Why is Rosa Parks called "the mother of the civil rights movement"?

Answers may vary. Her courage led to the bus boycott and the Supreme Court decision that ended segregation on buses.

SKILL FOCUS

As you answer these questions, think about how a writer's point of view affects what a reader learns.

1. From what point of view does the narrator tell the story of Rosa Parks' life?

The story is told from the third-person point of view.

2. What kinds of things might Rosa Parks include when writing her life story from the first-person point of view?

She might include many details about her life that someone else might not know; she could describe not only the events but also her feelings about them.

3. What might be a strength of a life story written from the third-person point of view?

Answers may vary. A third-person narrator can often be more objective than someone writing his or her own life story.

4. Imagine that you are a reporter who is writing a news story about the bus boycott. Write the lead sentence of your story. Use the third-person point of view.

Answers will vary.

▶ **Real Life Connections** Put yourself in Rosa Parks' shoes. What would you have done when the bus driver ordered you to give up your seat?

Lesson 31

Differences of Opinion

Reading a Social Studies Selection

Background Information

In the years before the Civil War in the United States, the North and the South did not agree on many issues. However, each side believed its opinion was right, and each side was willing to fight for what it believed.

The Civil War is also known as the War Between the States and the War of Succession. It started when Southern troops fired on Fort Sumter, a military post in Charleston, South Carolina, on April 12, 1861. It ended on April 8, 1865, when Confederate General Robert E. Lee surrendered to Union General Ulysses S. Grant at Appomattox Court House in Virginia. This conflict took more American lives than any other war in history.

The selection that follows discusses some of the major differences between the North and the South that led to the Civil War in 1861.

Skill Focus

People often do not agree with one another about certain issues or problems. Each person looks at the same issue or problem differently. Each has a different opinion.

There can be many opinions about one issue. Often opinions are based on what seems to be true. As a result, these opinions are debatable. Strong arguments can be presented to support any opinion.

It is important to examine **differences of opinion** before drawing conclusions. Ask yourself the following questions before drawing conclusions.

1. What is the issue about which there are differences of opinion?
2. How many different opinions are there?
3. How are the opinions different?
4. What are the reasons for the differences of opinion?
5. What, if anything, happens as a result of these different opinions?

Word Clues

When you read a selection, you may find words that you don't know because they are not part of your experience.

Read the following sentence.

> The disagreements between the North and the South centered on five major issues: slavery, tariffs, taxes, political power in the House of Representatives, and political power in the Senate.

This sentence gives no context clues that explain what tariffs are. You will have to look the word up in a dictionary.

When you come across a word that you don't know and there are no context clues, look up its meaning in a dictionary. You may find it more convenient to finish what you are reading before you look up the word.

Use a **dictionary** to find the meaning of the three underlined words in the selection.

Strategy Tip

The following selection focuses on five major issues on which Northerners and Southerners disagreed. Read the headings and the maps. As you read, identify the different opinions about each issue and look for the reasons for each opinion.

Conflict Between the North and South

The Civil War began as a result of many differences between the North and the South. These differences had their beginnings in the early 1800s. Tensions continued to grow for several decades. When the war started in 1861, most Americans believed the conflict would not last long. Instead, it stretched into four years of bloody fighting. In the end, more Americans died in the Civil War than in any other war in our nation's history.

The disagreements between the North and the South centered on five major issues: slavery, tariffs, taxes, political power in the House of Representatives, and political power in the Senate. People in the North had strong feelings about each of these issues. So did the people in the South. Each side had reasons for the way it felt.

Slavery

The North and the South had differing beliefs about slavery. The North, with its large population, had more factories than the South. As a result, manufacturing was important to the North's economy. There were enough people to work in these factories.

The South's economy, on the other hand, was based on plantation agriculture. The owners of large plantations depended on slave labor. They needed slaves to work in the fields.

Many people in the North did not believe in slavery. They thought the people of the South should not own slaves. Although some Southerners opposed slavery, most believed that they needed slaves to raise cotton and tobacco. They saw each attempt by the North to abolish slavery as a threat to their economy.

Tariffs

Ever since the nation's beginning, Congress has placed tariffs on European manufactured goods imported into the United States. Tariffs raise the price of foreign products, making them cost more than U.S. manufactured goods. The growing industries of the North approved of protective tariffs. Because of them, more people bought cheaper U.S. manufactured goods.

The Southern plantation owners bitterly objected to this protection for Northern manufacturers. Southerners, after all, exported cotton and other raw materials to Europe. In exchange, they had to buy many European manufactured goods. Because tariffs raised the prices of the foreign items that they bought, Southerners protested. They saw tariffs as an indirect tax on the South. Their representatives had argued in Congress against the tariffs since the early 1800s. But Congress continued to pass laws that raised the tariffs.

Taxes

Taxes for road building also emphasized differences between the North and the South. People in the North needed good roads so that they could send their manufactured goods to

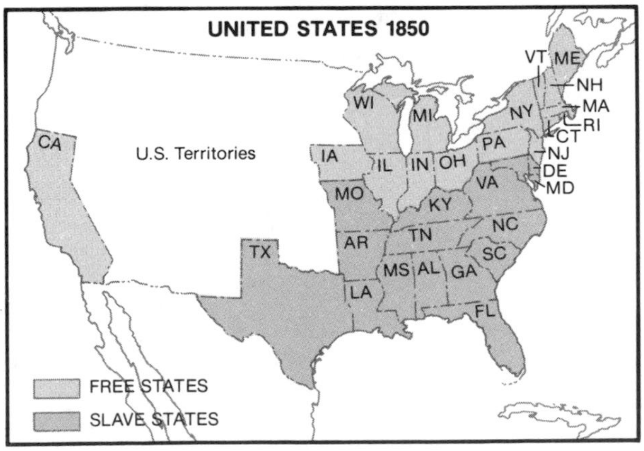

This map shows the United States in 1850, eleven years before the Civil War.

other parts of the country. Money to build these roads came from taxes paid by both Northerners and Southerners. The South, however, had many navigable rivers. Southerners used the steamboat as their chief means of transportation. Because they used rivers to ship their crops to the coast, Southerners didn't need as many roads. Therefore, they objected to paying the taxes needed to build roads. They thought that the states should have more say in how money from taxes was used.

Political Power in the House of Representatives

Another difference of opinion arose over control of the House of Representatives. In the North, the growing number of factories meant an increasing demand for labor. Many of the people coming from Europe settled in the North because of the jobs available there. As a result, the population of the North grew rapidly. The greater a state's population, the more House representatives it is entitled to. Soon, the North had more representatives in the House than the South did. This advantage gave Northerners more power to pass laws in the House of Representatives.

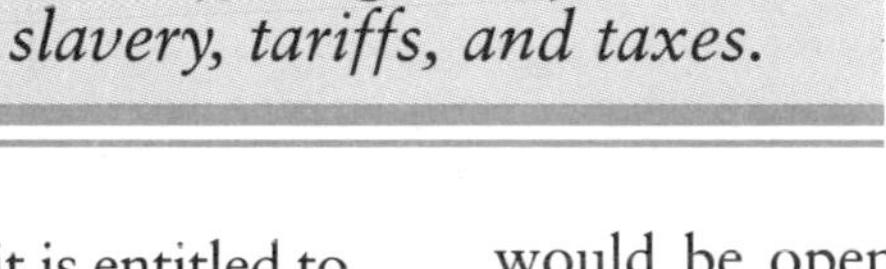

The South wanted to have more power in the House. However, its population was smaller than that of the North. Southerners argued for the right to count slaves as part of the population. This way, the South would get more representatives. The North believed that slaves should not be counted just to give the Southerners more representatives in the House. If the slaves were to be counted, the North argued, they should be freed first.

Political Power in the Senate

By 1819, there were fifteen Northern free states and fifteen Southern slave states. Each state had two senators. While the Southerners knew that they couldn't control the House, they struggled with the North for control of the Senate.

In 1850, the territory of California asked to join the Union as a free state. Northerners favored letting California join the Union; Southerners opposed California's admission. With sixteen free states, more senators would come from the North than from the South. If this happened, the free states would gain control of the Senate. After much heated debate, the Compromise of 1850 was reached. This compromise allowed California to be admitted as a free state. The remainder of the southwestern territory would be open to slavery if the people who settled there voted for it.

✔ Gradually, the tensions between the North and the South grew worse. The Southern states concluded that they had no future in the Union and withdrew from it. The country soon divided. In the Civil War that followed, Northerners fought against Southerners. After four years of fighting, the North won the war, and the Union was preserved. The task of reunion, however, proved to be long and difficult.

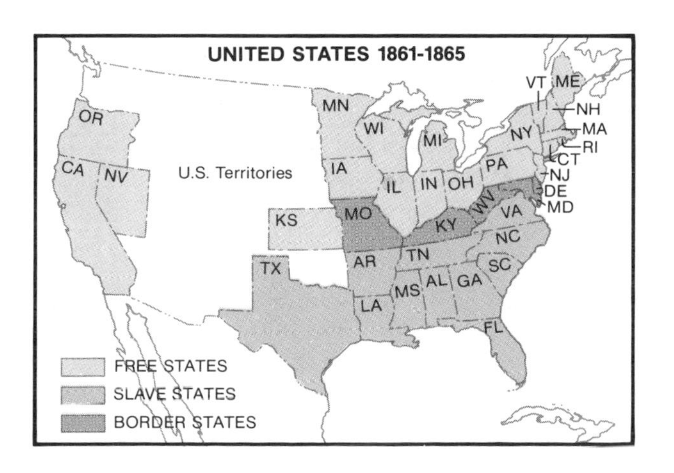

This map shows how the United States was divided during the Civil War.

RECALLING FACTS

Use the maps on pages 96 and 97 to answer questions 1 through 5.

Reading a map/comparing and contrasting

1. How many slave states were in the Union in 1850? 15 by 1865? 11

Reading a map/comparing and contrasting

2. How many free states were in the Union in 1850? 16 by 1865? 20

Reading a map

3. Which four states came into the Union after 1850 as free states? Oregon, Nevada, Kansas, Minnesota

Reading a map

4. How many states were in the Union before the war? 31 after the war? 36

Recalling details

5. What were the five major areas of disagreement between the North and the South?
Slavery, tariffs, taxes, political power in the House of Representatives and political power in the Senate.

Recalling details

6. Why did the North favor allowing California to enter the Union as a free state?
California's admission as a free state would give the North two more senators and more political power.

Identifying cause and effect

7. What was the result of the disagreements between the North and the South?
The result was the Civil War.

Using context clues

8. Write the letter of the correct meaning on the line next to each word.

b territory
c senators
a representatives

a. members of the lower house of Congress; number determined by state population
b. a part of the United States that is not a state
c. members of the upper house of Congress; two from each state

INTERPRETING FACTS

Making inferences

1. The map shows several states as border states. How might the conflict have been different here than in other states?
Answers may vary: (1) More battles were probably fought in the border states; (2) more family members and friends who lived near one another probably fought against one another.

Inferring the unstated main idea

2. Which sentence tells the main idea of the paragraph that has a check mark next to it?
   a. The Compromise of 1850 was the main cause of the Civil War.
   b. The disagreements between the North and South could easily have been resolved.
   (c.) The differences in interests and viewpoint between the North and South seemed too great to be settled, and a civil war resulted.

Making inferences

3. Why do you think most Americans didn't think the Civil War would last very long?
Answers will vary. People probably believed the war would be settled quickly because the country couldn't survive a conflict of this kind for a long peroid of time.

Making inferences

4. Why do you think that unifying the country after the war was difficult?
Answers will vary. It was difficult for people in the North and South to overcome their memories of the horrible war.

Skill Focus

Fill in the chart below by contrasting the opinions expressed in the selection you just read. First, read the middle column. It indentifies the issues on which the two sides had differences of opinion. Next, write *For* or *Against* to describe the opinion each side had about the issue. Then write the reason each side had the opinion it did. The first issue is completed for you.

North	Issue	South
Opinion: Against Reason: Northern factories had enough workers; they didn't need slaves.	**Slavery**	Opinion: For Reason: Cotton and tobacco were the basis of the South's agricultural economy; slaves were used to raise these crops.
Opinion: For Reason: Growing Northern industries benefitted from tariffs that made foreign goods more expensive than American-made goods.	**Tariffs on foreign goods**	Opinion: Against Reason: Southerners needed to buy foreign goods in exchange for the cotton and raw materials they exported to Europe. They felt these tariffs were an indirect tax on them.
Opinion: For Reason: Northerners needed good roads to distribute their manufactured goods. They wanted taxes to be used to build these roads.	**Taxes for road construction**	Opinion: Against Reason: Southerners used navigable rivers to transport their goods. They objected to their tax dollars being spent on roads that were of no use to them.
Opinion: Against Reason: The North didn't want to include slaves in the population count simply to give the South more representatives; the North would agree only if the slaves were freed.	**Inclusion of slaves in population count**	Opinion: For Reason: The South wanted its slaves counted to give it greater representation in the House of Representatives.
Opinion: For Reason: The North favored California's admission to the Union as a free state because it would give the North two more senators than the South.	**Admission of California as a free state**	Opinion: Against Reason: The South opposed California's admission because it would give the North more political power than the South.

Real Life Connections Imagine that you lived in the United States in 1861. How might you have been affected by the Civil War?

Lesson 32

Classifying

Reading a Science Selection

Background Information

Minerals are the most common solid materials found on the earth. In fact, the land and oceans rest on a layer of rock that is made out of minerals. They make up rocks on the earth's surface and are present in soil. Minerals are also found on the moon and on the planets Mercury, Venus, and Mars.

Minerals range from rock salt and pencil "lead" to gold, silver, and gems. Although there are about 3,000 different kinds of minerals, only about 100 of them are common. Most of the other minerals are much more difficult to find than gold.

Minerals serve many important uses. The mineral graphite, for example, is used to make pencil leads. Other products made from minerals include fertilizers for farming and chemicals for manufacturing.

The following selection discusses minerals. It describes how minerals are classified according to their color, texture, luster, and hardness.

Skill Focus

Sometimes information is organized by **classifying** similar objects or ideas into groups. It is then easier to see similarities and differences among these groups. Classifying is especially helpful for scientists who work with a great number of objects.

For example, scientists classify the many different kinds of gems and minerals into groups. The members of each group are classified together because they are similar in some way. The members of a group may be similar in how they look, in how hard they are, or in any of several other ways.

When reading information about groups of objects, ask yourself such questions as the following.

1. What is similar about the objects that scientists classify together in the same group?

2. How are the members of one group different from those of another group?

Word Clues

Read the sentences that follow. Look for context clues that explain the underlined word.

> However, mineralogists have identified all of these minerals and arranged them in an order based on their physical properties. A property is a quality or characteristic of a substance. Physical properties are qualities of a substance that can be identified by one of the five senses.

The word *properties* is explained in the sentences following it. These sentences give details to help you understand the meaning of the word *properties.*

Use **detail** context clues to find the meaning of the three underlined words in the selection.

Strategy Tip

When you read "Gems and Minerals," try to find the similarities and differences among the different gems and minerals. Also think about the similarities and differences among groups.

Gems and Minerals

For thousands of years, people have removed minerals from the ground. Minerals do not come from living things or from the remains of living things. Minerals are solid substances found on or in the ground.

Most gems are minerals. Diamonds, which are often colorless, are minerals. So are brightly colored gems, such as rubies, sapphires, and emeralds. These four are called **precious** stones because they are rare and valuable. They are the most costly gems. Other gems, such as garnets and turquoises, are not as rare or valuable. They are called **semiprecious** stones.

✔ Iron, copper, talc, gypsum, and aluminum are minerals, just as diamonds and rubies are. These minerals, however, are not cut, polished, and used in jewelry. Instead, they have many other important uses in construction and industry. For the most part, these useful minerals are not as valuable as gems.

Some nongem minerals are very valuable and have been used for centuries in jewelry and for other decorative purposes. Gold and silver are two examples of valuable nongem minerals.

The study of minerals is called mineralogy. There are over 2,000 different kinds of minerals. Many of them look alike. However, mineralogists have identified all of these minerals and arranged them into groups based on their physical properties. A property is a quality or characteristic of a substance. Physical properties are qualities of a substance that can be identified by one of the five senses. Physical properties, therefore, can be seen, tasted, felt, smelled, or heard. Color is an example of a physical property because

The Copperbelt of Zimbabwe in Africa is one of the world's main sources of copper. Mining is the chief industry in Zimbabwe. Here, African mine workers are drilling holes for blasting at one copper mine in Zimbabwe.

it can be seen. Texture is a physical property because it is a quality that can be felt.

The most obvious physical property of a mineral is its color. Many minerals can be identified by experts by color alone. For example, **malachite** (MAL ə kyt) is always green. **Azurite** (AZ ə ryt) is always blue.

Diamonds, rubies, sapphires, and emeralds are known as precious stones because they are rare and valuable.

Some minerals have the same color as other minerals. Rubies, for example, are red. So, too, are some kinds of **fluorite** (FLOR yt) and **quartz** (kworts). The trained eye of a mineralogist, however, is able to distinguish between the slight color differences of these three minerals.

If color is not enough to identify a mineral, scientists have to investigate further. The way minerals feel, or their texture, can be a clue to their identities. Talc and graphite are greasy to the touch. The clay minerals feel earthy.

Another physical property of minerals, luster, can be used to help identify them. Luster is the way a mineral reflects light. Some minerals have a dull, or matte, luster. Others are very shiny and are said to have a glassy luster. Silky, pearly, and brilliant are some other words used to describe a mineral's luster.

Hardness is based on which substances can scratch other substances. The blade of a pocketknife, for example, can scratch a penny. Scientists say that the knife blade is harder than the penny. The same knife blade, though, cannot scratch a diamond. The diamond is harder than the blade.

Mineralogists have made a scale to show how hard a gem or mineral is. The scale goes from 1 to 10. Talc is rated at 1. It is the softest mineral. Diamonds, the hardest mineral, are rated at 10. Scientists can scratch an unknown mineral sample with tools whose hardnesses are known. Scratching the unknown mineral helps scientists figure out where on the hardness scale the mineral belongs.

A mineral's color, texture, luster, and hardness, as well as other physical properties, determine how it is classified. By testing the properties of minerals, a mineralogist can distinguish between minerals that seem alike. Scientists have classified all known minerals.

The United States and Chilé have the largest sources of copper. This open pit copper mine in Utah is one of many that can be found in the United States today.

RECALLING FACTS

Recalling details

1. Where are minerals found?

Minerals are found in or on the ground.

Recalling details

2. What is the difference between precious gems and semiprecious gems?

Precious gems are rarer and more valuable than semiprecious gems.

Recalling details

3. What are most gems?

Most gems are minerals.

Recalling details

4. What is a physical property?

It is a quality or characteristic that can be seen, tasted, felt, smelled, or heard.

Recalling details

5. What are two nongem minerals that are very valuable?

gold and silver

Recalling details

6. What is the study of minerals called?

mineralogy

Recalling details

7. How many minerals are there?

over 2,000

Recalling details

8. What are two physical properties of minerals?

color, texture, luster, or hardness

Using context clues

9. Complete each sentence with the correct word below.

scale **texture** **luster**

a. The texture of a glass table is smooth.

b. How would you rate her acting on a scale of 1 to 10?

c. The wax gave the kitchen floor a bright luster.

Interpreting Facts

Making inferences

1. What are two nongem minerals that are precious and are used in jewelry?

gold and silver

Making inferences

2. Why might it be important for a mineralogist to distinguish between a ruby and a garnet?

Answers may vary. Rubies are very valuable. Garnets are not as valuable.

Inferring the unstated main idea

3. In the selection, the main idea of the paragraph with a check mark next to it is not stated. Underline the sentence below that states its main idea.

a. Some minerals are harder than others.

b. Some minerals are not gems.

c. All gems are not minerals.

Making inferences

4. Why do you think mineralogists have arranged minerals into groups based on their physical properties?

Answers may vary. This system helps scientists to classify the minerals according to similar characteristics. Scientists can also more easily identify minerals that are alike in important ways.

Skill Focus

A. The following chart includes the names of several minerals. Put check marks in the correct boxes to show which are gems and which are nongems.

Minerals

	Diamond	Iron	Emerald	Garnet	Gypsum	Copper	Talc
Gem	✔		✔	✔			
Nongem		✔			✔	✔	✔

B. Complete the following chart by filling in the top row with the names of six of the gems that were mentioned in the selection. Put check marks in the correct boxes to show which are precious and which are semiprecious.

Gems

	Diamond	Garnet	Sapphire	Emerald	Turquoise	Ruby
Precious	✔		✔	✔		✔
Semiprecious		✔			✔	

C. Use the following chart to answer the questions below it.

Properties of Precious Gems

	Diamond	Sapphire	Ruby	Emerald
Hardness	10	9	9	8
Color	usually colorless	usually blue	red	green

1. Which is harder, a diamond or a sapphire? a diamond
2. Which is harder, a sapphire or an emerald? a sapphire
3. What color is a ruby? red

D. Use the following chart to answer the questions below it.

Mohs Hardness Scale

Mineral	Talc	Gypsum	Calcite	Fluorite	Apatite	Feldspar	Quartz	Topaz	Corundum	Diamond
Hardness	1	2	3	4	5	6	7	8	9	10

1. Which mineral is hardest? diamond
2. Which mineral is softest? talc
3. Which is harder, feldspar or quartz? quartz
4. Which is harder, topaz or corundum? corundum
5. Which is harder, calcite or fluorite? fluorite

▶ **Real Life Connections** Which gems or minerals can you identify at home, around your community, or in a jewelry store?

Lesson 33

Word Problems

Reading a Mathematics Selection

Background Information

You will be using five steps to solve word problems in this selection. Word problems are math problems that are described using complete sentences. They include the information you will need to find the answer to the problem. Sometimes more than one arithmetic operation is needed to solve the problem.

Skill Focus

Use the following five steps when solving word problems.

1. Read the problem. Be sure you are familiar with all the words, especially the labels. Think about what question is being asked. Try to picture in your mind the information that is given. Read the problem again to be sure you understand the question. It may be helpful to draw a picture of the information that is given.
2. Decide how to find the answer. Then decide if you should add, subtract, multiply, or divide. In solving some problems, you may need to do two arithmetic operations. If so, you will need to write two mathematical sentences to find the answer. Look for key words in the last sentence of the problem to help you decide.
3. Estimate the answer. When you estimate an answer, you must make an educated guess based on information that is provided. Use rounded numbers to make an estimate. If two operations are necessary, estimate both.
4. Carry out the plan. Do the arithmetic that will give you the answer.
5. Reread the problem. Then write the complete answer. Is the answer logical? How close is it to your estimate?

Word Clues

When you read word problems, look for the key words that will help you find the answer. In problems in which two operations are needed, you should look for key words for both operations. Words, such as *and, total, all together,* and *twice as much,* tell you that the answer will be larger than the other numbers in the problem. Often you will either add or multiply to find the answer.

Words, such as *how much more, left, each,* and *divided,* tell you that your answer will be less than at least one of the numbers in the problem. Often you will either subtract or divide to find the answer.

Strategy Tip

Read each problem in the following selection carefully to decide if two operations are needed. Remember to look for word clues as you read each problem.

Solving Word Problems with Two Operations

These are the five steps that you can use to solve word problems.

1. Read the problem.
2. Decide how to find the answer.
3. Estimate the answer.
4. Carry out the plan.
5. Reread the problem.

When working with problems that require two operations, you will need to decide which two operations are necessary to find the answer. It may help to draw a diagram. When you estimate, you will need to estimate both arithmetic operations. When you carry out the plan, you will need to do two arithmetic operations to solve the problem.

Use the five steps to solve this problem.

READ THE PROBLEM

Before the Battle of Fort Sumter in 1861, Major Anderson reported that this much food was left: 6 barrels of flour, 3 barrels of sugar, and 24 barrels of salt pork. How many more barrels of salt pork were there than barrels of flour and sugar?

Read the problem again. Be sure that you know the label that is used with each number fact. Are there any words that you do not know? If so, look them up to find their meanings. What question does the problem ask? Often the question is asked in the last sentence. *How many more barrels of salt pork were there than barrels of flour and sugar?*

DECIDE HOW TO FIND THE ANSWER

You will need to do two arithmetic operations to find the answer. The problem tells you that there are 24 barrels of salt pork. You need to first find out how much flour and sugar there are combined. For the first operation, you must add because you are combining amounts. The key word *and* in the last sentence of the problem is the clue to add. The following is your mathematical sentence.

$$6 + 3 = n$$

For the second operation, you must subtract because you are comparing the number of barrels of salt pork with the number of barrels of flour and sugar taken together. The key words *how many more* give the clue to subtract. The following is your mathematical sentence.

$$24 - n = b$$

In this mathematical sentence, the letter n stands for the answer to the first operation. When you need to use another letter, you can choose the first letter of the label in the problem. The letter b stands for the difference between the number of *barrels* of flour and sugar combined and the number of *barrels* of salt pork.

ESTIMATE THE ANSWER

Use rounded numbers to help make an estimate. Round to the nearest ten, first adding and then subtracting.

First operation: $6 + 3 = 9$ Round to 10
Second operation: $20 - 10 = 10$
Your estimate is 10.

CARRY OUT THE PLAN

Do the arithmetic.
First operation: $6 + 3 = 9$
Second operation: $24 - 9 = 15$

REREAD THE PROBLEM

After rereading the problem, write the complete answer. There were 15 more barrels of salt pork than there were barrels of flour and sugar. Does the answer make sense? How close is your answer to your estimate? If the answer is not close to your estimate, you should start all over.

Use the five steps to solve this problem.

Read: General Sherman commanded 80,000 soldiers. He divided them into two equal groups. Then 12,500 more soldiers joined one of the groups. What was the total number of soldiers in the larger group?

Decide: You will need to do two operations to solve this problem. The problem describes a large group: 80,000. For the first operation, you must break this group into two smaller groups. The key word *divided* is a clue to divide. For the second operation, you must combine two number facts. The word *total* is a clue to add. Write a mathematical sentence for each step.

$$80{,}000 \div 2 = n$$
$$n + 12{,}500 = s$$

The letter s stands for the total number of soldiers in the larger group.

Estimate: Round the two larger numbers to the nearest ten thousand. Then divide and add.

$$80{,}000 \div 2 = 40{,}000$$
$$40{,}000 + 10{,}000 = 50{,}000$$

Carry Out:

$$80{,}000 \div 2 = 40{,}000$$
$$40{,}000 + 12{,}500 = 52{,}500$$

Reread: After rereading the question, write the complete answer. There were 52,500 soldiers in the larger group. Does this answer make sense? How close is it to your estimate?

RECALLING FACTS

Recognizing sequence of events

1. Write the five steps for solving word problems.
   a. Read
   b. Decide
   c. Estimate
   d. Carry out
   e. Reread

Recalling details

2. Sometimes two operations are needed to solve a problem. List the three steps in which you would have to do the two operations.
   a. Decidc
   b. Estimate
   c. Carry out

Recalling details

3. What label is used in the first problem?
   barrels

   What label is used in the second problem?
   soldiers

INTERPRETING FACTS

Making inferences

1. Why should you start all over if your answer is not close to your estimate?
   Your answer may be wrong, and you don't know in which step the mistake was made.

Making inferences

2. How can drawing a picture of the information that is given help you solve a word problem?
   Answers may vary. It can help you organize and see the information. As a result, you will understand the word problem better.

Making inferences

3. In a problem that requires two operations, why can't you do the second operation first?
   You need the answer from the first operation in order to do the second operation.

Making inferences

4. Why do you use two different letters to stand for the numbers you are looking for?
   You are looking for a different number in each operation.

SKILL FOCUS

Use the five steps to solve these word problems.

1. **Read:** The soldiers at Fort Sumter had 6 barrels of flour and 2 barrels of vinegar. A shipment of food to the fort contained twice as much food as they already had. What was the total number of barrels brought to the fort?

   Decide: Add to combine two groups. Multiply many small groups of the same size. $6 + 2 = n$ $n \times 2 = b$

   Estimate: $6 + 2 = 8$ Round to 10. $10 \times 2 = 20$

   Carry Out: $6 + 2 = 8$ $8 \times 2 = 16$

   Reread: The total number of barrels brought to the fort was 16.

2. **Read:** During one battle, General McClellan of the Union Army commanded 24,348 men. The Confederate Army had 65,197 men. Only $\frac{2}{3}$ of McClellan's men were ready for battle. How many more soldiers did the Confederates have ready for battle than the Union did?

   Decide: Multiply many small groups of the same size. Subtract to compare. $24{,}348 \times \frac{2}{3} = n$ $65{,}197 - n = c$

   Estimate: $24{,}000 \times \frac{2}{3} = 16{,}000$ $65{,}000 - 16{,}000 = 49{,}000$

   Carry Out: $24{,}348 \times \frac{2}{3} = 16{,}232$ $65{,}197 - 16{,}232 = 48{,}965$

   Reread: The Confederates had 48,965 more soldiers ready for battle than the Union did.

3. **Read:** General Schofield marched 18 miles with his soldiers. It took them 6 hours. About how many hours would it take to march 24 miles?

   Decide: Divide one large group into smaller groups. Divide other into smaller groups. $18 \div 6 = n$ $24 \div n = h$

   Estimate: $20 \div 10 = 2$ $20 \div 2 = 10$

   Carry Out: $18 \div 6 = 3$ $24 \div 3 = 8$

   Reread: It would take them about 8 hours to march 24 miles.

4. **Read:** The Union had 105 million acres of farmland. The Confederacy had 57 million acres of farmland. Each acre had to be worked by 3 people. How many people all together in the Union and the Confederacy had to work farms and could not be soldiers?

   Decide: Add to find the total number of acres. Divide large group by smaller group. $105 + 57 = n$ $n \div 3 = p$

   Estimate: $100 + 60 = 160$ $160 \div 3 = 53\frac{1}{3}$

   Carry Out: $105 + 57 = 162$ $162 \div 3 = 54$

   Reread: 54 million people in the Union and the Confederacy had to work farms.

▶ **Real Life Connections** Name two occasions when you have had to use two mathematical operations to solve a problem.

Syllables

Following is a summary of some guides to help you divide words into syllables.

Guide 1. In a compound word, divide between the two smaller words.

Guide 2. In words with double consonants, divide between the double consonants.

Guide 3. In words with a prefix or suffix, divide between a root word and its prefix or suffix.

Guide 4. In words with two consonants between two sounded vowels, divide between the two consonants.

Guide 5a. In words with one consonant between two sounded vowels with the first vowel long, you usually divide before the consonant.

Guide 5b. In words with one consonant between two sounded vowels with the first vowel short, you usually divide after the consonant.

Guide 6. Do not divide between consonant blends or consonant and *-le*. Consider a consonant blend as if it were one consonant.

Divide each of the words below into two syllables. Write the syllables separately on the line to the right of the word. Then write the number of the guide or guides that you used on the line to the left of the word. If two or more different guides apply to the same word, write all the guide numbers that you used for the word. The first word is done for you.

No.	Guide(s)	Word	Syllables
1.	1, 4, 6	gangplank	gang plank
2.	2, 4	luggage	lug gage
3.	1, 4	rainfall	rain fall
4.	4	market	mar ket
5.	1	doorway	door way
6.	5b	chemist	chem ist
7.	4	shoulder	shoul der
8.	2, 6	cobble	cob ble
9.	5a	polar	po lar
10.	3	coastal	coast al
11.	3	careful	care ful
12.	3	unkind	un kind
13.	5a	fever	fe ver
14.	2, 4	carriage	car riage
15.	6	candle	can dle
16.	4	fertile	fer tile
17.	5a	cyclone	cy clone
18.	4	enter	en ter
19.	1, 4, 6	moonstone	moon stone
20.	1, 6	limestone	lime stone
21.	4	turkey	tur key
22.	5b	linen	lin en
23.	3	steamer	steam er
24.	3	yearly	year ly
25.	2, 6	battle	bat tle
26.	4	carbon	car bon
27.	5a	motion	mo tion
28.	4	captain	cap tain

Lesson 35

Fact and Opinion

If someone told you that Muscles Malone was the greatest wrestler in history, what would you think? You might agree with the statement or you might not agree. But in either case, the statement is an opinion. It is not a statement of fact.

There is a big difference between fact and opinion. A **statement of fact** can be checked and proven. If you hear or read that city hall has just been painted, you can look at city hall to see the new coat of paint. If you heard or read that the New York Jets won all their games in 1995, you can check a record book. A statement of fact can be proved by checking other sources.

A **statement of opinion** tells what someone believes or thinks is true. Such statements as "The Peanuts are the best team in the state" or "Dancing Danny is a better wrestler than Muscles Malone" are opinions. It is difficult to prove or disprove statements of opinion. Words, such as *better, best, worse,* and *worst,* are sometimes found in opinions. These words do not mean the same thing to everyone.

There is nothing wrong with opinions. Everyone has them, and it's interesting to share your opinions with other people. Look at these two statements.

1. The Cubs are the best baseball team in the league.
2. The Cubs have won 25 out of 30 games this year.

Which statement would you accept as a fact? The second one is a fact because it is based on information that can be checked.

When you hear or read statements such as these, you need to decide whether they are facts or opinions.

Read the following statements. Some are statements of facts. Others are statements of opinions. On the line before each statement, write **F** if it is a statement of fact or **O** if it is an opinion.

O 1. The Somerset Street team has the best swimmers.

F 2. The Somerset Street team won first place in 3 races.

F 3. Long Tall Harry ran the mile in 3 minutes, 59 seconds.

O 4. Bill Boxer is better looking than Sam Soccer.

F 5. Pam Pacer jogs every morning from six o'clock to eight o'clock.

F 6. Leaping Larry is taller than Charlie Charger.

F 7. The next world champion will be chosen on December 15.

F 8. Carla threw her tennis racket to the ground.

O 9. Mike is a poor loser.

O 10. Sahar is the best tennis player on the team.

F 11. The first team to score five points wins the match.

O 12. The Wildcats are a better team than the Cougars.

O 13. It is wrong to have ball games on Saturday nights.

F 14. The Strawtown Champions play the Tor Terrors every other Saturday.

O 15. Surely there are better ways to spend a Saturday night.

F 16. Tracy has been on the Tor Terrors team for three years.

F 17. The Lions have a four-game winning streak.

O 18. The Woodcut Lakers will win the championship this year.

O 19. Nothing could be further from the truth.

F 20. The final score was Woodcut Lakers 6 and Sandpiper Flyers 8.

Lesson 36

Similes and Metaphors

Somctimes an author compares two things that are not really alike at all. An author does this to draw a sharp picture in the reader's mind. These comparisons make what you are reading more interesting and colorful.

Read the following sentences.

Heather looks good in her new coat.
Heather looks like a million dollars in her new coat.

Which of the two sentences above gives a clearer, more interesting picture of how Heather looks? If you said the second one, you are right. In this sentence, a girl is being compared to a million dollars. Comparing two things using the word *like* or *as* is called a **simile.**

Read the following sentences.

During August, the room was an oven.
During August, the room was hot.

Which sentence gives a better idea of how hot the room was? The first sentence does. This sentence contains a **metaphor.** A metaphor, like a simile, compares two things, but neither *like* nor *as* is used. A metaphor compares two things by suggesting that one thing is really another. A room and an oven are not usually alike, except in this special way—both are hot.

To understand a sentence that uses either a simile or a metaphor, you need to decide which two things are being compared. Then you can use context clues to figure out the way in which the two unlike things are similar.

Underline the two things being compared in each sentence. Fill in the circle next to the sentence that explains the meaning of the simile or metaphor.

1. Sitting by the campfire, I felt as snug as a bug in a rug.
   ○ A bug was in my clothes.
   ● I felt warm and comfortable.
2. Mr. Filbert's living room is a greenhouse.
   ● The living room is filled with plants.
   ○ The living room is painted green.
3. The baby is growing like a weed.
   ● The baby is growing quickly.
   ○ The weeds in the garden are small.
4. Doctor Rodriquez is as gentle as a lamb.
   ○ Doctor Rodriquez takes care of lambs.
   ● Doctor Rodriquez is calm and patient.
5. Clouds are cotton balls in the sky.
   ● Clouds look soft and white.
   ○ Cotton balls are in the sky.
6. Steven eats like a horse.
   ● Steven eats a lot of food.
   ○ Steven eats hay.
7. Amy ran as fast as a deer.
   ○ Amy likes to run with deer.
   ● Amy runs at a fast pace.
8. Dewdrops sparkled like diamonds on the grass.
   ○ Dewdrops and diamonds were on the grass.
   ● The grass was shiny from dew.
9. Jack's father told him to stop working like a horse.
   ● Jack was working too hard.
   ○ Jack was working in a field of grass.
10. At high noon, the desert is like an oven.
    ○ The desert is used for cooking.
    ● The desert is very hot.
11. The news spread around school like wildfire.
    ● The news spread with great speed.
    ○ The news made the school catch fire.

Lesson 37

Table of Contents

Using a table of contents saves you time when you want to find out what kind of information is in a book. The table of contents gives you a quick overview of the topics in the book. This is especially true if you are interested in reading about a general subject.

The **table of contents** lists the titles of the chapters and gives the page on which each chapter begins. Sometimes a table of contents gives the most important topics included in each chapter. It may also give the page on which each topic begins.

To use a table of contents, glance through the chapter titles and topics until you find your subject. Then turn to the page number given next to the chapter title or topic. Read this section until you find the information you need on your subject.

Below is a table of contents from a science book. To answer the questions that follow it, use two steps.

1. Look at the chapter titles to find out under which one you might find the information asked for.
2. Read through the topics under that title to find out on which page that particular topic begins.

Contents

Page

1. You need to find information about trout.
   a. Under which chapter title would you look? Animal Life
   b. Under which topic would you look? Fish
   c. On which page would you start to read? 45
2. You need to find information about thunderstorms.
   a. Under which chapter title would you look? Weather and Its Changes
   b. Under which topic would you look? Thunderstorms and Electricity
   c. On which page would you start to read? 152
3. You need to find information about how to improve garden soil.
   a. Under which chapter title would you look? Soil, the Basis of Growing Things
   b. Under which topic would you look? How to Improve Soil
   c. On which page would you start to read? 182
4. You need to find information about how minerals are formed.
   a. Under which chapter title would you look? Minerals, the Earth's Treasure House
   b. Under which topic would you look? How Mineral Deposits Are Formed
   c. On which page would you start to read? 231
5. You need to find information about the use of calcium.
   a. Under which chapter title would you look? Minerals, the Earth's Treasure House
   b. Under which topic would you look? Uses of Minerals
   c. On which page would you start to read? 246
6. You need to find information about air pressure.
   a. Under which chapter title would you look? The Air Around Us
   b. Under which topic would you look? Properties of Air
   c. On which page would you start to read? 111
7. You need to find information about reptiles.
   a. Under which chapter title would you look? Animal Life
   b. Under which topic would you look? Reptiles
   c. On which page would you start to read? 63
8. You need to find information about the causes of snow.
   a. Under which chapter title would you look? Weather and Its Changes
   b. Under which topic would you look? Why Do We Have Snow?
   c. On which page would you start to read? 151

Alphabetical Order

In a dictionary, you often find several pages of words that all begin with the same two letters. To find a word on these pages, you will need to use the third letter of the word. For example, the word *fabric is* listed before the word *face* because *b* comes before *c* in the alphabet. When words begin with the same two letters, they are arranged in alphabetical order according to the third letter in the words.

On the numbered lines, write each set of words below in alphabetical order according to the first three letters in each word. Cross out each word in the list after you write it.

Word		Answer	Word		Answer
lodge	1.	loan	seize	1.	seal
long	2.	lock	serve	2.	secret
loan	3.	lodge	self	3.	seed
love	4.	loft	sew	4.	seize
loft	5.	log	set	5.	self
loom	6.	long	secret	6.	senior
lock	7.	loom	seven	7.	serve
log	8.	lose	senior	8.	set
lose	9.	love	seal	9.	seven
low	10.	low	seed	10.	sew

Sometimes you will need to use the fourth letter of a word in order to find the word in the dictionary. The word *honey* is listed before the word *honor* because *e* comes before *o* in the alphabet. When words begin with the same three letters, they are arranged in alphabetical order according to the fourth letter in the words.

On the numbered lines, write each set of words below in alphabetical order according to the first four letters in each word. Cross out each word in the list after you write it.

Word		Answer	Word		Answer
collar	1.	cold	merge	1.	mercy
column	2.	collar	merry	2.	mere
color	3.	color	mercy	3.	merge
cold	4.	colt	merit	4.	merit
colt	5.	column	mere	5.	merry

Lesson 39

The Dewey Decimal System

Call numbers on library books indicate exactly where each nonfiction book is kept in the library. A call number is found on the spine, or narrow back edge, of the book, and on each card in the card catalog or each entry in the computer catalog.

The call number is determined by the subject of the book. Books on the same subject have similar call numbers and are kept in the same section of the library.

In most libraries, nonfiction books are classified according to the **Dewey Decimal** system. It is called a decimal system because books are classified according to ten general subject areas.

Study the numbers and subjects of the Dewey Decimal system.

Main Classes of the Dewey Decimal System

Numbers	Subject	Examples of Types of Books
000–099	General Reference Works	encyclopedia, bibliographies
100–199	Philosophy and Behavior	conduct, morals
200–299	Religion	myths, Bible
300–399	Social Science	law, customs
400–499	Languages	dictionaries, English and foreign language
500–599	Pure Science	astronomy, chemistry
600–699	Applied Science	engineering, radio
700–799	Arts and Recreation	music, sports
800–899	Literature	plays, poems
900–999	History	geography, biography

Suppose you are studying the Civil War. In which number category would you find books on this subject? Since the Civil War is classified as history, Civil War books are found in the 900s. After locating the subject card in the card catalog, you see that the call number for Civil War books is 973. Libraries usually label each section of shelves so you can find a book easily.

On the line to the right of the type of book, write the number category where you would find each of the following books.

1. a book that teaches French 400–499
2. a book explaining how to ski 700–799
3. an encyclopedia article on Mexico 000–099
4. a book comparing religions 200–299
5. a book describing discoveries in astronomy, such as quasars and black holes 500–599
6. the plays of Shakespeare 800–899
7. a book about how infants behave 100–199
8. a book about United States laws 300–399
9. a book explaining how rocket engines work 600–699
10. a book about Viking explorers 900–999

Reading a Television Schedule

What is the easiest way to find out what shows are on television? Check a newspaper schedule or a local program guide. A **television schedule** shows what time each program begins and what channel it is on. The schedule may give a brief summary of some programs, as well as other information. Many schedules list programs on cable television. These programs are listed after the regular television shows.

Examine the following television schedule.

Wednesday Evening

7:00 **2** NEWS UPDATE
4 NIGHTLY NEWS
5 ALL AROUND THE U.S.A. — Variety
Singer Mary Aruba entertains in Southern cities, including Charleston, Atlanta, and New Orleans.
7 LOCAL NEWS REPORT
9 MOVIE — Drama
"Soldier Boys." (1988) Three boys leave their homes for the first time to enlist in the Civil War. Mark Simon, Carl Bianco, Alan Peters. (90 min.)
11 DERECHO DE NACER
13 BUSINESS NEWS
WAT PEOPLE ON THE MOVE — Travel

7:05 **2** BASEBALL
Kansas City Royals at New York Yankees. (Live)

7:30 **4** MOPPETS — Children
7 WORLDWIDE NEWS
11 LUIS AND FRIENDS — Interview
Host Luis Raphael talks to basketball star Kirk Stratton and 12-year-old actress Lindsay Gray.
13 BLUEGRASS FESTIVAL — Music
performances by Smokey Mountain Singers, Billy Joe Flynn, Rita Murray.
HPO BIG JOE DANIELS — Country Music
ESN SPORTS — Pro Volleyball

8:00 **4** AUTO RACING
The French Grand Prix, taped April 20 in Monte Carlo. (30 min.)
5 TV MAGAZINE
Tips on hair care; a group of students model Civil War fashions they created.
7 MOVIE — Drama
"Attack." (1982) When President Lincoln (Spencer Flack) sends troops to Fort Sumter, they are forced to surrender, and the Confederate flag is raised. (2 hrs.)
11 ONE COUPLE — Comedy
Guest Sandy Newman plays a nervous runner in her first marathon.
13 DANCE TODAY
The Philadelphia Ballet Company performs "Pas de Deux," "Fancy Free," and "Cakewalk."
WLM MOVIE — Musical
"High School Prom." (1972) Oldie but goody. Todd Michaels at his best.

8:30 **4** GYMNASTICS
National High School Tournament, taped May 1 in Chicago. (60 min.)
5 NORTH AND SOUTH — Drama
During the second battle of Bull Run, Union General Pope (Frank Courtney) is outwitted by Generals Lee and Jackson.
11 INCREDIBLE DAYS — Drama
Roger (Jeff Lynch) plays an astronaut captured by the inhabitants of an alien planet. (Repeat; 60 min.)
13 GUESS WHAT — Game
HPO MOVIE — Drama
"Office Politics." (1993) Modern-day drama about two women who want the same job.

A. Use the information on the television schedule to complete the following sentences. Circle the letter of the phrase that completes each sentence.

1. Two programs scheduled at 7:00 include
   (a.) "News Update" on channel 2 and "Nightly News" on channel 4.
   b. "Worldwide News" on channel 7 and "All Around the U.S.A." on channel 5.
   c. "Worldwide News" on channel 7 and "Auto Racing" on channel 4.

2. On "TV Magazine," you learn about
   (a.) hair care and clothing worn during the Civil War period.
   b. a basketball star and a 12-year-old actress.
   c. Charleston, Atlanta, and New Orleans.

3. The baseball game between the Royals and Yankees
   a. begins at 7:05 and ends at 8:30.
   (b.) begins at 7:05 and ends after 8:30.
   c. begins at 7:00 and ends after 8:30.

4. The number *1988* following the title of the 7:00 movie means that
   a. this will be the one thousand, nine hundred eighty-eighth time this movie is being aired.
   b. this movie was last shown on television in 1988.
   (c.) this movie was made in 1988.

5. If you want to see a movie and laugh and sing, you should watch
   a. "Soldier Boys."
   b. "Office Politics."
   (c.) "High School Prom."

6. The only sports show on cable television between 7:00 and 8:30 is
   a. baseball.
   b. gymnastics.
   (c.) volleyball.

7. "All Around the U.S.A." begins at 7:00. You can tell that this program is an hour long because
   a. the words *one hour* follow the description of the show.
   b. the same program is listed for channel 5 at 7:30.
   (c.) no other program is listed on channel 5 until 8:00.

8. You know that the episode of "Incredible Days" has been shown before because
   (a.) the schedule indicates that it is a repeat.
   b. the schedule indicates that it lasts for 60 minutes.
   c. the schedule indicates that three guest stars will appear on the show.

9. You can tell that "North and South" deals with the Civil War because
   a. the episode is about the Union surrendering Fort Sumter to the Confederacy.
   (b.) the episode is about the battle of Bull Run and Generals Lee and Jackson.
   c. it takes place in the Southern cities of Charleston, Atlanta, and New Orleans.

B. Decide if each of the following questions can be answered using the television schedule. Write *yes* or *no* on each line.

1. Which programs are on at 6:00 P.M.? no
2. At what time is "One Couple" over? yes
3. Does Spencer Flack star in the movie "Attack"? yes
4. On what channel is "Business News"? yes
5. On what date did the Grand Prix auto race take place? yes
6. Who are the finalists in the gymnastics tournament? no
7. What is "Derecho de Nacer" about? no
8. Are any programs for children scheduled on Wednesday night? yes
9. Is "Luis and Friends" a live or a taped program? no
10. What is the name of the game show host on "Guess What"? no
11. How many news programs are on between 7:00 and 8:00? yes
12. Where is the baseball game being played? yes

UNIT 5

Mexico

Lesson 41

Theme

Reading a Literature Selection

Background Information

People everywhere have dreams and goals. Some people, afraid of being misunderstood or laughed at, let their dreams die. Others hold on to their dreams, determined to make them come true. In this story, a young Mexican boy struggles to hold on to his dream while helping to solve the problem his family faces.

Skill Focus

Theme is the meaning or message in a story. Most authors do not directly state the theme of their stories. Instead, the reader must think about the characters and events in the story to infer, or figure out, the theme.

Often a story's title tells you in very few words what the story is about. Use the title as a clue to help you infer the story's theme.

Not all stories have a theme, however. An author sometimes writes a story simply to entertain readers. This kind of story may not have a message. A story has a theme only when the author uses the characters and events to make a comment about life, society, or individuals.

The following questions will help you figure out the theme of a story.

1. What does the title of the story mean?
2. What does the main character learn about himself, herself, or others by the end of the story?
3. What is the author's purpose for writing the story? Is the author writing a story simply to entertain or is the author trying to convey a message?
4. What is the author's message?

Word Clues

Read the sentences that follow. Look for context clues that explain the underlined word.

> He liked to look at the posters of the bullfighters on the wall. These people went into the ring alone with the angry bull. The bullfighters had to be brave and talented. It was their job both to kill the bull and to entertain the crowd.

The word *bullfighters* in the first sentence is explained in the sentences following it. These sentences give details about bullfighters. They help you to understand the meaning of the word *bullfighters.*

Detail context clues are often found in the sentences surrounding the underlined word. Use **detail** context clues to find the meaning of the three underlined words in the selection.

Strategy Tip

As you read "A Different Sort of Dream," think about what the author is saying about people like Luis. What message do you think the author wants to tell you by the end of the story? Use the questions in the Skill Focus to help you figure out the story's theme.

A Different Sort of Dream

Luis usually looked forward to market day. The marketplace in town became alive with color and excitement. The streets were lined with people selling things and calling out to each other. Their voices made a kind of song.

Today, however, Luis and his family were in low spirits. There had been no rain for weeks. Without water, the corn crop was small. They did not have even one sack of corn to sell today.

Luis's mother found a good spot in the marketplace, out of the hot sun. Luis helped her spread out the few vegetables that they had brought to sell.

"Even if we sell all these vegetables, we won't have enough money for the things we need," Mother said.

"If only it would rain," said Father. There were lines of worry between his eyes.

"I'm sure it will rain soon," Antonio said. Luis's brother always tried to look on the bright side.

Only Luis's little sister Rosa was not worried. She was too excited by all the people and noise to think about rain or corn or money.

Father parked the truck and then went to talk to some of the other farmers. Antonio rushed to the gate of the bullfighting ring. He liked to look at the posters of the bullfighters on the wall. These people went into the ring alone with the angry bull. The bullfighters had to be brave and talented. It was their job both to kill the bull and to entertain the crowd. Antonio wanted to be a bullfighter himself some day. Father said that was a fine dream.

Luis had a different dream. He wanted to be an artist. He had told no one of his wish. Once, Father had seen him drawing and had become angry.

"Drawing will not help you feed the family. It does not bring you money," he had said.

So Luis kept his dream to himself. He spoke very little for fear that others might laugh at him. He put all his feelings into the pictures that he drew in secret.

"Go and sell some peppers," Mother told him now.

Luis took the basket of peppers and started down the street. "Peppers!" he called. "Fresh peppers!" Rosa followed along behind him.

The morning sun was already very hot. Still, Luis enjoyed walking up and down the busy street. The colors of the fruits and vegetables, the woven rugs, and the bright clay pots made a picture in his mind. He thought about how he would draw the marketplace.

"Look, Luis!" Rosa called. She pulled him over to a man who was selling wooden dolls. Each doll had been perfectly carved out of a block of wood. What beautiful work the man had done! Luis wished he had a knife so that he could try to carve something.

Just then, Luis heard his father's voice. "What are you doing, Luis? It's time to go."

As they walked toward the truck, Antonio rushed up. "Father!" he cried. "You should see the pictures of the new bullfighter. He looks so brave!"

Father smiled at Antonio. "Yes," he said. "The bullfighter is a great man."

Antonio pulled himself up tall, and his eyes glowed. "I will be a great bullfighter one day!"

"That would be wonderful," Father said proudly. He glanced at Luis. He said nothing, but Luis could guess his thoughts. Father was wishing that Luis, too, had a brave dream.

Luis felt very sad. It was all right for his sister Rosa to look at dolls. Antonio could admire bullfighters. But Luis knew Father did not understand his wish to be an artist.

On the way home, Luis forgot his sadness. The mountains shone in the afternoon sun. How beautiful they were! Luis's fingers were eager to draw them, but he had little time to draw that week.

There was much work to be done on the farm. It still had not rained, and the well had gone dry. Every morning, Luis walked for miles to get water from a deeper well. In the afternoon, he chopped weeds in the cornfields. Luis did not mind the hard work. He liked the smell and feel of the earth. While he worked, he thought about what he would draw.

Each day, the sun seemed to grow hotter. The worry lines in Father's face deepened. One morning, he stared across the dusty cornfields.

"If it doesn't rain soon, we won't have any crop," Father said. "We'll have to eat our seed corn, and then we won't have any seed to plant in the spring."

"Where will we get the money to buy seed?" Mother asked.

Father shook his head. There was no answer.

"It's no use going to market tomorrow," Mother said. "We have so few things to sell."

"Even a few pesos will help," said Father. "We'll send Luis to the market. He can sell some peppers while the rest of us stay and work in the fields."

. . . Luis knew Father did not understand his wish to be an artist.

So it was decided. Luis was so excited that he could hardly sleep that night. He had never been to the market alone before.

The next morning, Luis was ready before the first rooster's crowed. Father put the peppers into the basket. Luis was all set to go when he suddenly had an idea. He ran inside and took some sheets of paper from under his bed. He hid them among the peppers.

The walk to town was very long and uncomfortable. When Luis arrived at the market, he was hot and dusty. He found a spot in the noisy marketplace and spread his serape on the ground. Luis, like other people in his country, often wore the brightly colored woolen blanket around his shoulders. Today, however, he put the peppers on it. Then he took out the sheets of paper. They were all the pictures that he had drawn. He spread his drawings out on the serape, too. A short time later, a man asked him about his drawings.

"I'd like to buy this one," the man said as he admired one particular drawing. "You are a good artist. I have friends who may want to buy some of your drawings. Will you be here all day?"

"Yes," said Luis. "I will be here until the market closes." Luis was so excited that it took him several minutes to tell the man how many centavos to pay for the drawing. The man gave Luis many copper coins. There were at least a hundred. That meant that Luis had more than a peso.

Before the end of the day, three more people bought Luis's drawings. Each person told Luis how wonderful his drawings were. It was the most exciting day Luis had ever had. As he prepared to leave, Luis counted all the centavos. There was enough money to buy food. There might even be some money left over.

Luis's face showed nothing. He had learned to hide his feelings. But joy burst inside him as wild and bright as the fireworks on fiesta day. Even that holiday celebration had never made him feel this happy!

When Luis arrived home, he gave the money to his father.

"What is this?" Father asked. "You did not get so much money by selling those few peppers."

Shyly, Luis told him what had happened.

"Someday Luis will be a great artist!" Mother said. She hugged Luis as she heard the story.

Father walked over to Luis. He smiled as he often did when Antonio talked about becoming a bullfighter.

"My son Luis—always doing something for the family. This time we will do something for you. Here, my son. Here is the extra money." Father put his arm around Luis. "Our artist must use it to buy himself more paper and pencils."

Recalling Facts

Identifying setting

1. Where and when does the story take place?

The story takes place in a small town in Mexico in the present.

Identifying cause and effect

2. There had been no rain for weeks. How did this affect Luis and his family?

With little to sell at the market, they do not have enough money to buy food and other things that they need.

Recalling detail

3. How does Luis help his family?

The money from selling his drawings buys food for the family.

Comparing and contrasting

4. a. How does Luis's father react to seeing Luis draw?

Luis's father becomes angry.

b. How does Luis's father react when Antonio shows an interest in becoming a bullfighter?

Luis's father is proud of Antonio's dream.

Recalling details

5. Why does Luis's father give his son extra money at the end of the story?

He wants Luis to buy more paper and pencils.

Using context clues

6. Fill the circle next to the word that correctly completes each sentence.

a. A brightly colored woolen blanket is a

○ fiesta. ○ peso. ● serape.

b. Centavos are Mexican

● coins. ○ peppers. ○ drawings.

c. A fiesta is a

○ vegetable. ● celebration. ○ bull.

Interpreting Facts

Understanding character

1. How does Luis show that he is responsible?

Answers may vary. He weeds the cornfields and sells peppers at the market. He is responsible for getting water every day. He also goes to the market alone.

Making inferences

2. Why does the marketplace have a special appeal to Luis the artist?

Answers may vary. Luis enjoys the marketplace because of its bright colors and the fine handicrafts sold there. It appeals to Luis the artist.

Inferring comparisons and contrasts

3. a. Why is Luis's father proud of Antonio's dream?

Answers may vary. Becoming a bullfighter is an acceptable, traditional dream for a young boy.

b. Why is Luis's father not proud of Luis's dream?

Answers may vary. Becoming an artist is seen as impractical and unusual.

c. Why does Luis's father respond differently to the two dreams?

Answers may vary. Luis's father is concerned with providing for his family. He knows a bullfighter can earn a living. He is not sure an artist can.

Understanding character

4. By the end of the story, how has Luis's father changed?

Answers may vary. Luis's father sees that an artist can earn a living and provide food for the family. He changes his mind about Luis's dream and supports his son.

Skill Focus

1. What is the title of the story? A Different Sort of Dream

2. On whose dream does the story focus? Luis's dream

3. What is Luis's dream? to be an artist

4. Why is Luis's dream "a different sort of dream"? Luis's dream to be an artist is unusual. To be an artist requires special talents. Because Luis has these skills, he can have "a different sort of dream" from the dreams of the people around him.

5. Why does Luis not talk about his dream? Luis thinks that his father and others will not understand his desire to be an artist. He also fears that they might laugh at him.

6. Does Luis let his dream die? Explain. No. Luis secretly holds on to his dream. Then, one day, he sells his drawings. The money that he earns helps buy food for his family. His family is proud of him. Luis no longer has to keep his dream secret.

7. What does Luis discover about himself? Luis discovers that others think his drawings are good. He discovers that artistic talent is valuable.

8. What does Luis's family discover about Luis? The family realizes that Luis is a talented artist. They are proud of his dream.

9. What is the author's message? Answers may vary. His theme is that individuals should believe in their dreams even if they are different from the dreams of other people. It's important not to give up on your dreams.

▶ **Real Life Connections** Put yourself in Luis's shoes. How would you feel about your dream? How would you feel after selling your drawings?

Lesson 42
Reading a Map

Reading a Social Studies Selection

Background Information

The following selection tells how rainfall and natural resources play an important role in the development of a country's cities and industries. Mexico's largest industrial areas are near rich mineral deposits, fertile farmlands, and dense forests.

Skill Focus

When reading textbooks, you will often find maps. Not all maps are alike. Different maps show different kinds of information.

A **population** map tells you how many people live in an area. Symbols on the map show where people live. The map key tells the number of people that each symbol represents.

A **rainfall** map shows the average amount of rain that falls in an area. The amount of rain is shown in inches and centimeters. Usually the map shows the rainfall for an entire year.

A **product** map shows the mineral, farm, and forest products of an area. Symbols show the specific areas in which the products are produced in large amounts. The product names, pictures of the products, or both, are used as symbols.

Be sure to study the maps that accompany selections in a textbook. The following questions will help you read different kinds of maps.

1. What kind of map is this? population? rainfall? product?
2. What information does this kind of map give?
3. What do the symbols on the map represent?

Maps, together with the facts in a selection, give you more information about a place than either one could alone.

Word Clues

Read the sentence below. Look for context clues that explain the underlined word.

> Mexico is rich in fertile soil, thick forests, and deposits of minerals—those substances in the earth that are not animal or vegetable.

If you do not know the meaning of the word *minerals*, the phrase, *those substances in the earth that are not animal or vegetable,* can help you. The word *minerals* is explained in this phrase. A phrase that explains a word coming before or after it is an appositive phrase. An appositive phrase may be introduced by such words as *or* or *that is* or by punctuation, such as a dash or a colon.

Use **appositive phrases** to find the meaning of the three underlined words in the selection.

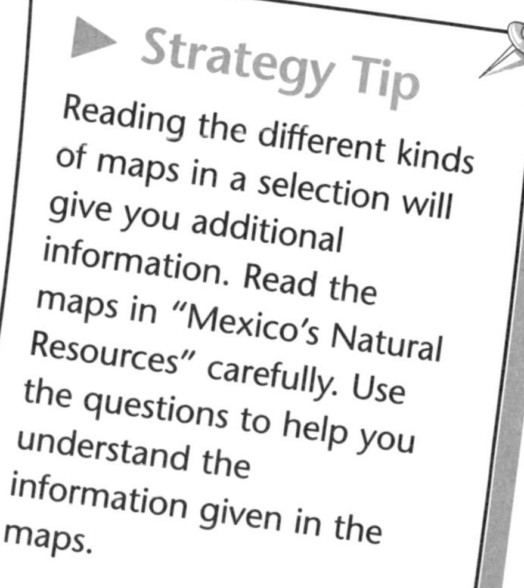

Mexico's Natural Resources

Mexico is the northernmost country of Latin America. It lies directly south of the United States. Mountains and plateaus cover about two-thirds of Mexico. Forests, deserts, and valleys are also found in the country. Mexico is rich in fertile soil, thick forests, and deposits of minerals—those substances in the earth that are not animal or vegetable. These natural resources are used in manufacturing, farming, mining, and other industries. The products that come from these natural resources are important to Mexico's economy, or Mexico's system of making, distributing, and using goods. Many of these products are made in Mexico's largest cities and major manufacturing centers and then exported for use in other countries.

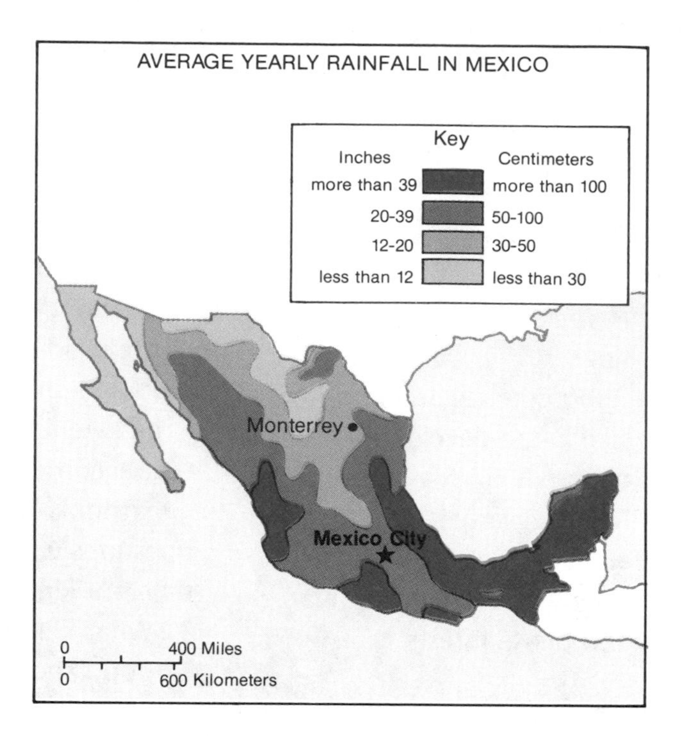

Rich Mineral and Fossil Fuel Deposits

✔ As early as the 1500s, Mexico's rich silver deposits attracted Spanish explorers. Since then, Mexico has become one of the world's

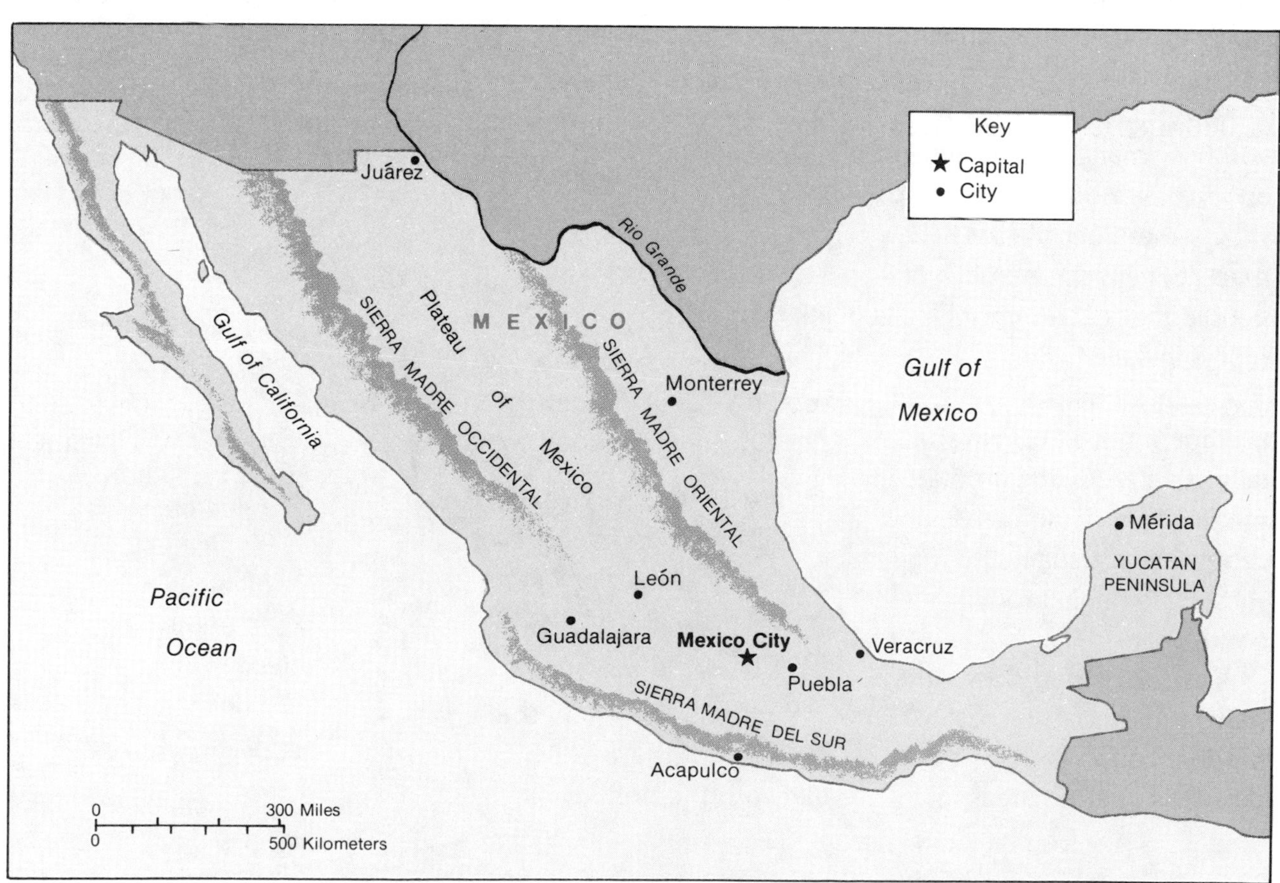

This map shows Mexico's major river, mountain ranges, and cities.

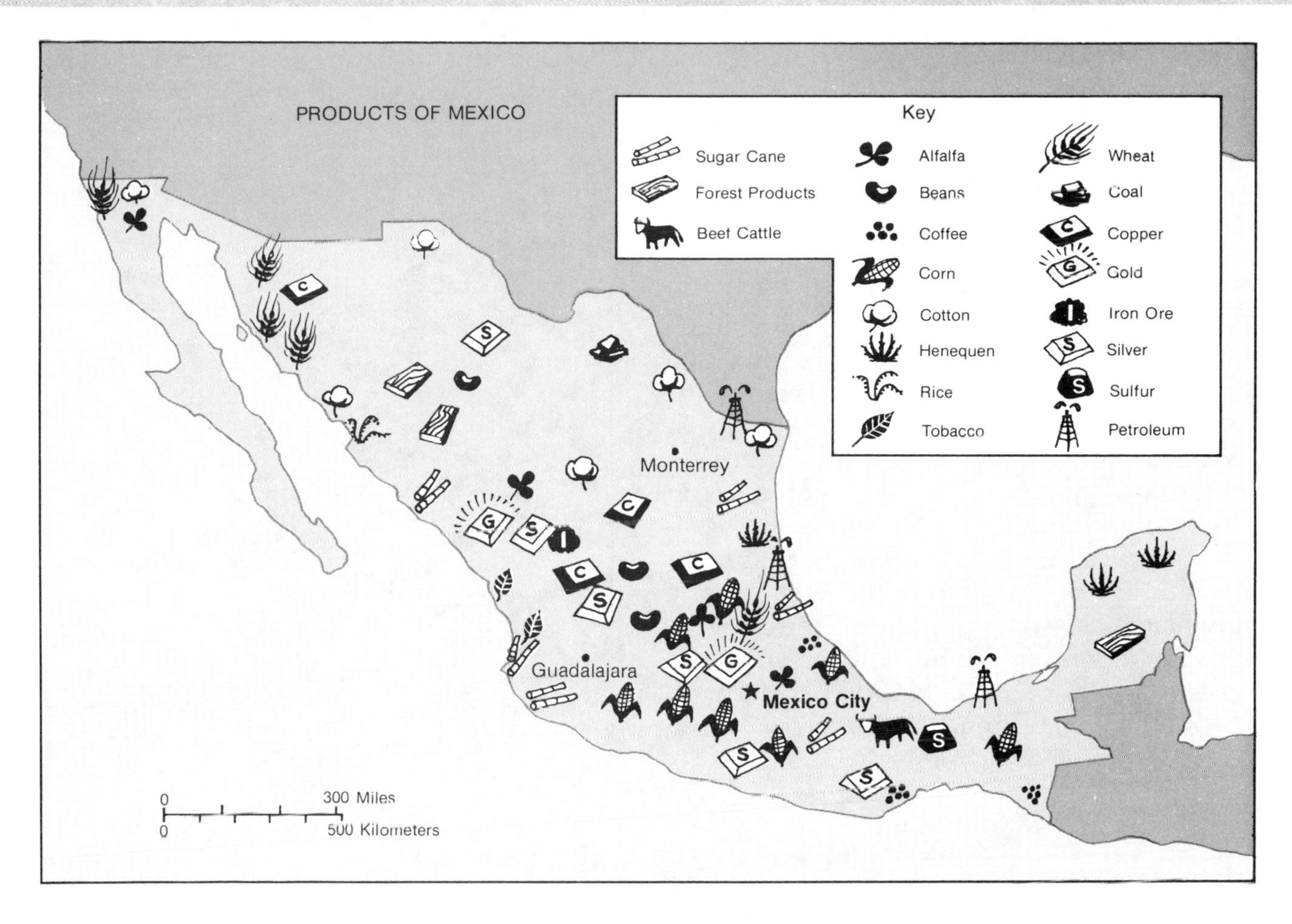

leading silver producers. Silver mining is one of Mexico's chief industries today. Mexico mines about 1,200 tons (1,080 metric tons) of silver a year. Mexico also has large quantities of zinc, lead, gold, and sulfur. Large deposits of iron ore and coal support Mexico's growing steel industry.

Q.: Mexico City has the second largest population of all the cities in the world. Which city has the largest population?
A.: Tokyo

In the 1970s, vast deposits of petroleum were discovered along Mexico's east coast and in the Gulf of Mexico. These deposits greatly increased the importance of Mexico's petroleum industry. Oil is Mexico's leading export.

Fertile Soil

Many kinds of crops are grown in Mexico. This is possible because of the different kinds of soil and because rainfall varies so greatly across the country. The best farmlands are found in the central part of the country where the soil is rich and where there is sufficient, or enough, rainfall. This central region is called the Central Plateau of Mexico.

Rich soil is also found in rainy, hot, southern Mexico and along the eastern coastal plains. More farmland is used for corn than for any other crop. Other leading crops include beans, wheat, cotton, sugarcane, and coffee.

Also important are alfalfa, rice, tobacco, and henequen. Henequen is a plant with swordlike leaves. Its valuable ropelike fibers are used in making twine.

Thick Forests

Dense forests cover about one-fifth of Mexico. The largest forests are in the northwest and central mountains and in the rainy south and southeast. From these forests comes timber used for furniture, for paper, and in the construction industry. The hardwoods used include ebony, mahogany, and rosewood. From the pine forests comes the wood that supplies Mexico's pulp (material from which paper is made) and paper industry. Sapodilla trees grown in the south provide chicle. Chicle is used in making chewing gum. This rubberlike substance is obtained by boiling down the milky juice of the sapodilla tree.

Economic and Urban Growth

Most of Mexico's mining, agriculture, and manufacturing takes place within 300 miles (480 kilometers) of Mexico City. Mexico City, the capital and largest city in Mexico, is one of the largest urban areas in the world. Almost 25 million people live in Mexico Ctiy and its surrounding area.

Each year more and more Mexicans move from the countryside to these densely populated cities. More than two-thirds of the people of Mexico live in the large cities and nearby towns of Mexico City, Guadalajara, León, Puebla, and Monterrey. The development of natural resources is helping Mexico's economic and urban growth.

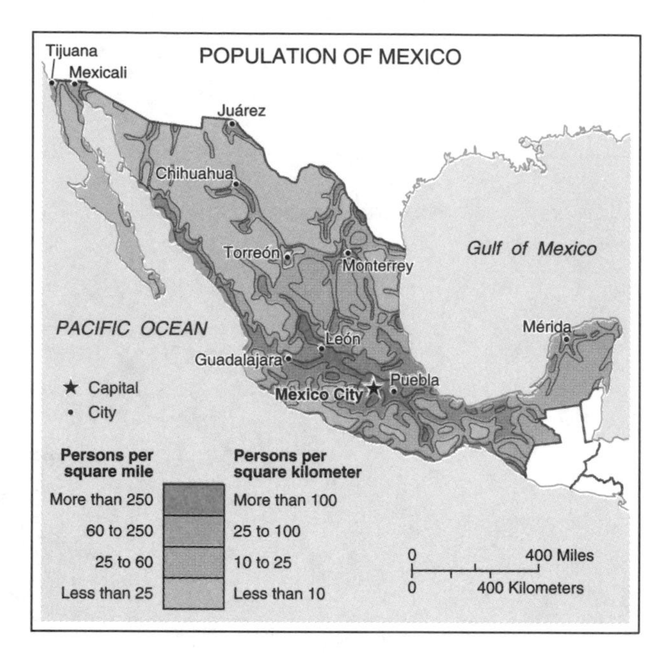

RECALLING FACTS

Identifying cause and effect

1. What was the result of finding petroleum deposits along Mexico's east coast and in the Gulf of Mexico?
Oil is Mexico's leading export.

Identifying cause and effect

2. Give two reasons why Mexico is able to grow so many kinds of crops.
Different kinds of soil and varied rainfall make possible the growth of many kinds of crops.

Recalling details

3. How are sapodilla trees important?
They provide chicle, a substance used in making chewing gum.

Recalling details

4. Why is henequen an important crop?
It is important because its ropelike fibers are used in making twine.

Recalling details

5. Where is most of Mexico's petroleum industry located?
within 300 miles (480 kilometers) of Mexico City

Identifying cause and effect

6. What is responsible for Mexico's economic and urban growth?
the development of natural resources

Recalling detail

7. Where are Mexico's forests?
Mexico's forests are in the northwest and central mountains and in the south and southeast.

Using context clues

8. Circle the correct meaning of the underlined word or words in each sentence.

   a. If you are full after eating lunch, then you have had enough food.
      no **(sufficient)** **some**

   b. Paper is made from a mixture of ground-up wood and rags.
      petroleum **copper** **(pulp)**

   c. Coffee is one product important to Brazil's system of making, distributing, and using goods.
      (economy) **minerals** **resources**

INTERPRETING FACTS

Making inferences

1. What is one reason that Mexico City is the largest city in Mexico?
Answers may vary. It is the largest city because most of Mexico's industries are close to it.

Making inferences

2. Why does two-thirds of Mexico's population live in large cities and nearby towns?
Answers may vary. More jobs and housing are available in large cities. There is also more manufacturing there.

Inferring the unstated main idea

3. Reread the paragraph with a check mark next to it. Which of the following sentences states the main idea?

 a. Mexico is one of the world's leading silver producers.

 (b.) Many valuable minerals are mined in Mexico.

 c. Mexico's steel industry uses a great deal of coal.

Inferring cause and effect

4. Why were early Spanish explorers attracted to Mexico's silver deposits?
Answers may vary. Early explorers were attracted to Mexico's silver deposits because of the wealth and power such a discovery would bring. Silver was very valuable.

Inferring cause and effect

5. What effect will Mexico's growing petroleum industry have on the country's future economy?
Answers may vary. Because oil is so important today, Mexico's growing petroleum industry will probably have a positive effect on the country's economy.

Drawing conclusions

6. Do you think the development of natural resources will continue to help Mexico's economic and urban growth? Explain.
Answers will vary. As more natural resources are developed, Mexico will prosper and its cities will grow.

SKILL FOCUS

Use the appropriate map to answer the questions that follow.

A. The population map of Mexico on page 126 shows where most of the people in Mexico live. The cities on the map are the largest in Mexico.

Study the map. Decide whether the following statements are true or false. Then write *T* or *F* on the line next to each statement. If you cannot tell from the map whether the statement is true or false, write *N*.

F 1. The northwest is the most densely populated part of Mexico.

F 2. The central part of Mexico is sparsely populated.

F 3. More Mexicans live along the seacoast than in the interior of the country.

T 4. The greatest population density is in and around Mexico City.

N 5. Most people live in the parts of the country with the driest climate.

T 6. Many areas in Mexico have fewer than 25,000 persons.

B. The rainfall map of Mexico appears on page 124. It shows how much rain falls in each part of Mexico in a normal year. The key tells you how many inches or centimeters each shade of color represents. Use the key and the map to decide whether the following statements are true or false. Write *T* or *F* on the line next to each statement.

T 1. Some parts of Mexico receive fewer than 12 inches (30 centimeters) of rain in a year.

F 2. Northern Mexico receives more rain than southern Mexico.

T 3. Most of southern Mexico receives more than 39 inches (97.5 centimeters) of rain in a year.

F 4. Central Mexico receives some of the heaviest rain in the entire country.

T 5. The driest parts of the country are in the north.

T 6. If you wanted to live in an area that receives about 15 inches (37.5 centimeters) of rain a year, you would have to live in central Mexico.

T 7. The average rainfall in the most densely populated part of Mexico is about 30 inches (75 centimeters) a year. (Use both the rainfall map and the population map.)

C. The product map of Mexico appears on page 125. It shows where the leading mineral, farm, and forest products of Mexico are produced. Study the map. Be sure to read the key. Then write *T* or *F* next to each of the following statements.

T 1. Forest products are found in the north central and southeastern parts of Mexico.

F 2. The northwest is a densely populated mining region. (Use both the product map and the population map.)

T 3. Petroleum deposits are plentiful along the east coast and the Gulf of Mexico.

F 4. The heaviest concentration of mining and farming is in the central part of Mexico, around the city of Monterrey.

F 5. Henequen is grown primarily on the west coast.

T 6. Corn, alfalfa, and wheat are leading crops in Mexico.

Real Life Connections Research the natural resources in your geographic area. How do these natural resources affect the economy?

Lesson 43

Diagrams

Reading a Science Selection

▶ Background Information

Volcanoes are openings in the earth's surface through which lava, hot gases, and rock fragments erupt. Volcanic eruptions can be so violent that they blow the entire mountain apart. Most volcanic eruptions can't be predicted by scientists. However, some volcanoes, such as those in Hawaii, will expand slightly before they erupt. Scientists can use special instruments to predict when these particular volcanoes might erupt.

This selection is about volcanoes and how they are formed.

▶ Skill Focus

Diagrams are often used in textbooks to show readers what the words in the text explain. When reading a selection with diagrams, read the paragraphs first. These paragraphs usually discuss the information shown in the diagram. Sometimes a paragraph will include a reference to a diagram, such as "See Figure 1." You should stop reading and study the diagram at that point.

When you study a diagram, be sure to read the **labels** and the **caption.** It is often helpful to reread the paragraphs that refer to the diagram. Going back and forth from the text to the diagram will help you understand the ideas in the textbook, article, or selection.

When you read a selection that includes diagrams, follow these steps.

1. Read the paragraph before each diagram. Then study the diagram and read its labels and caption.
2. Slowly read the rest of the paragraphs. Look back at the diagrams whenever you think they will help you understand the selection.
3. After you have finished reading the paragraphs and studying the diagrams, look away from the selection. Try to picture what you have read and the details in the diagrams. If you are not able to do this, read the paragraphs and study the diagrams again.
4. Continue to work in this way until you understand all the ideas in the selection.

▶ Word Clues

Read the sentences that follow. Look for context clues that explain the underlined word.

> This molten rock often contains gases. Molten, or melted, rock is called **magma.**

If you do not know the meaning of the word *molten,* the word *melted* in the next sentence can help you. The words *molten* and *melted* are synonyms. Molten rock is melted rock.

Look for **synonym** context clues to find the meaning of the three underlined words in the selection.

▶ Strategy Tip

Before you read "Volcanoes," read all the headings and words in boldfaced type. Then look at the diagrams and pictures. Read the captions and labels to become familiar with the scientific terms that you will read about.

Volcanoes

A volcano is a mountain from which hot liquid rock, solid rocks, gases, and ashes are thrown from deep below the earth's surface. This outpouring is called an **eruption** (i RUP shən). Powerful forces below the earth's surface cause volcanic eruptions.

Scientists have theories that explain the eruption of volcanoes. Temperatures deep below the earth's surface are very high. The earth is so hot that some of the rock is melted. This molten rock often contains gases. Molten, or melted, rock is called **magma** (MAG mə).

Magma is lighter than solid rock because it is liquid. Because it is lighter, it slowly rises from deep below the surface and forms a pocket near the surface. This pocket is called a magma chamber.

The magma, which is under great pressure, moves from the magma chamber through any broken or weakened part of the solid rock above it. A volcanic eruption occurs when the magma is forced to the earth's surface. When the magma reaches the surface, it blasts or flows out an opening. Magma that reaches the surface is called **lava** (LAV ə).

Types of Lava

One type of lava is thick and contains very little water. During an eruption, this lava often dries and hardens as it reaches the earth's surface. If the lava plugs up the openings in the volcano, it becomes impossible for more lava and gases to escape. Pressure builds up again, causing another eruption. This type of lava usually erupts violently. The thick lava flows slowly and cools into rough, jagged sheets of rock. The edges of these sheets are uneven.

Another type of lava is thin and contains a great deal of water. It is highly fluid and flows rapidly down a volcano's slopes. The thin lava usually erupts quietly and spreads over a large area. It hardens into smooth, folded sheets of rock.

Types of Volcanoes

Volcanoes are formed by lava eruptions. The **cinder-cone** type of volcano is formed by violent eruptions of thick lava. Explosions blow lava, gases, and pieces of rock through an opening in the earth. This type of volcano is cone-shaped and has steep sides.

Shield volcanoes are formed by quiet eruptions of thin, highly fluid lava. The lava

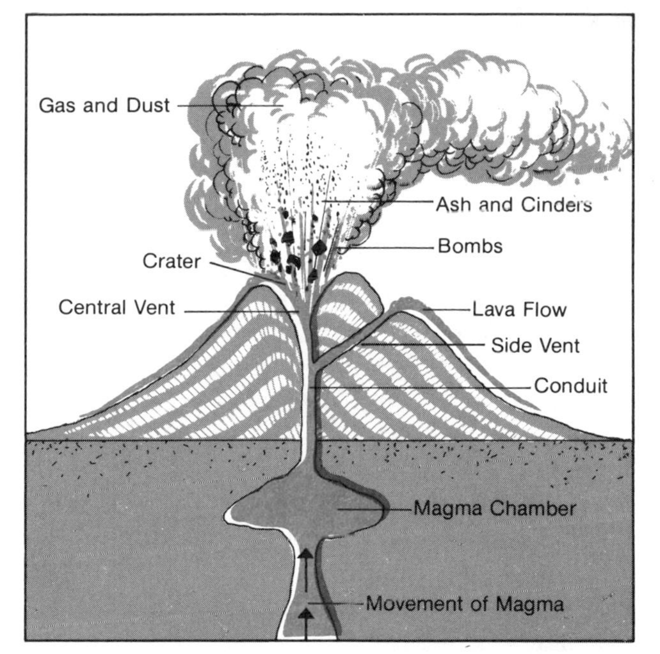

Figure 1. This diagram shows the parts of a volcano.

flow usually spreads over a low, wide area. Shield volcanoes have gently sloping sides.

Composite (kəm POZ it) volcanoes are created by eruptions of both thick and fluid lava. First, a violent eruption occurs. Thick lava bursts out of the earth. The lava hardens, and the ground is covered with pieces of rock. Then a quiet eruption occurs. Fluid lava covers the rocks. The two different types of eruptions continue and build up a composite volcano.

Parts of a Volcano

The long passageway through which lava flows is called a **conduit** (KAHN doo ət). The conduit runs from the magma chamber to the opening at the top of the volcano. The opening from which the lava erupts is called the **vent.** Volcanoes often have more than one vent. Cinder-cone volcanoes have a steep-sided pit at the top. This pit is called the **crater.**

Volcanic Rocks

During violent eruptions, pieces of hardened lava, or volcanic rock, are blown into the air. The smallest pieces are called volcanic dust. Slightly larger pieces are called volcanic ash. Soil that contains volcanic ash is usually good for raising crops. The largest pieces of volcanic rock are called cinders or volcanic bombs. Volcanic bombs can weigh several tons.

Where Volcanoes Occur

✓ One of the main areas where volcanoes occur extends all around the edge of the Pacific Ocean. This area is called the Ring of Fire. The ring includes New Zealand, the Philippines, Japan, and the west coast of North and South America. Volcanoes are also found along the coast of the Mediterranean Sea. Italy, Greece, and Turkey are three countries in that part of the world that have volcanoes. The Mid-Atlantic Ridge is another

Figure 2. Volcanoes are found in many parts of the world.

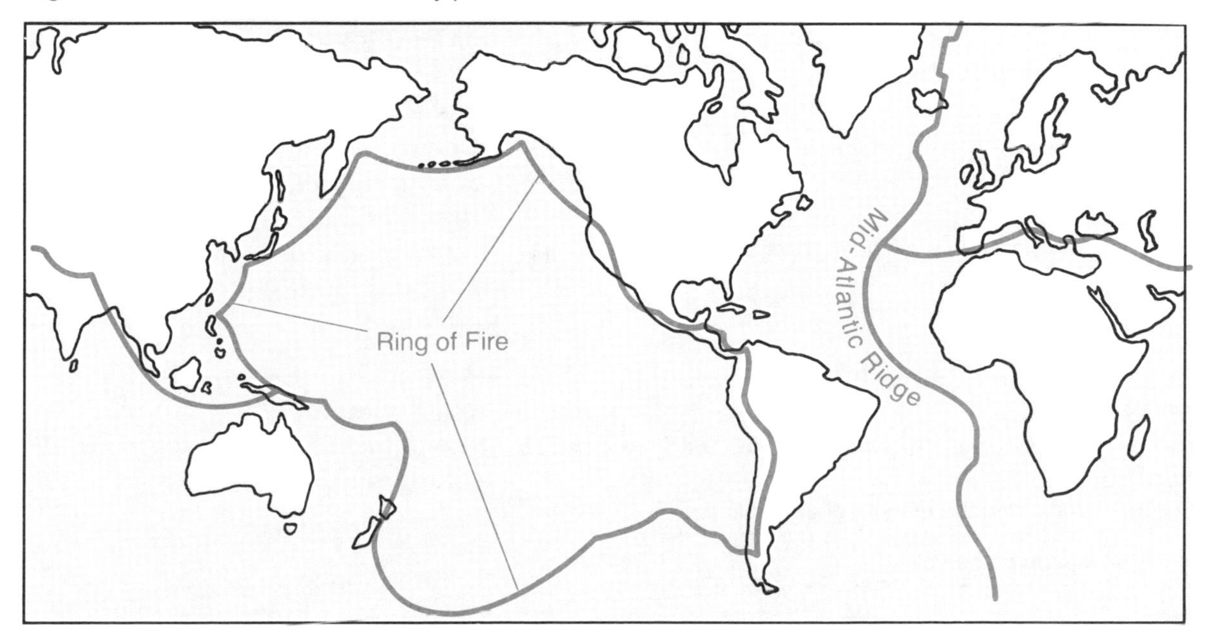

part of the world where volcanoes are found. This ridge extends from Iceland down the middle of the Atlantic Ocean.

In these parts of the world, people have always feared volcanoes. Eruptions have occurred throughout history. In 79 C.E., Mount Vesuvius in Italy erupted. This catastrophe destroyed several towns, including Pompeii. The disaster buried Pompeii under 12 to 15 feet of ashes and cinder. In 1883, Krakatoa, a volcano in Indonesia, erupted violently. The explosion was so loud that it was heard as far as 4,800 kilometers away. It caused huge waves in the surrounding ocean. In 1980, Mount St. Helens erupted in Washington state. Volcanoes are one of the most powerful and destructive forces of nature. Even modern science has found no way to control the harmful effects of volcanoes.

In 1980, Mount St. Helens erupted in Washington state.

Recalling Facts

Recalling details

1. What is a volcanic eruption?

A volcanic eruption is an outpouring of hot liquid rock, solid rocks, gases, and ashes from deep below the earth's surface.

Recalling details

2. What is magma?

Magma is molten rock.

Recalling details

3. What is lava?

Lava is magma that has reached the surface of the earth.

Recalling details

4. What are two types of lava?

Lava can be either thick or thin.

Recalling details

5. What are three types of volcanoes?

Three types of volcanoes are cinder-cone, shield, and composite.

Recalling details

6. Where does the conduit extend in the volcano?

The conduit runs from the magma chamber to the opening at the top of the volcano.

Recalling details

7. What is the crater in a volcano?

The crater is the steep-sided pit at the top of cinder-cone volcanoes.

Reading text with diagrams

8. In your own words, explain what happens during the eruption of a volcano. Be sure to use the names of the parts of the volcano.

Magma rises from deep below the earth's surface. It collects in a magma chamber. It then rises up through breaks in the rock and bursts out through the vent of the volcano.

Reading text with diagrams

9. Look at Figure 2. What does the label *Ring of Fire* mean?

It is one of the main areas where volcanoes are found.

Using context clues

10. Draw a line to match each word with its meaning.

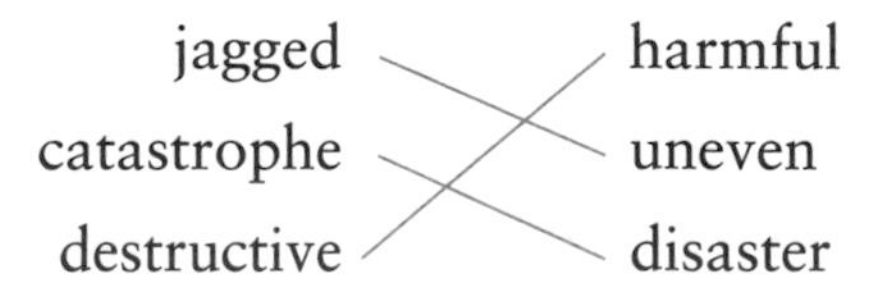

INTERPRETING FACTS

In questions 1-3, fill in the space between the lines next to the correct answer.

Making inferences

1. The temperature deep inside the earth's surface is
   - ▌ a. always hot.
   - || b. sometimes hot and sometimes cool.
   - || c. always cool.

Inferring cause and effect

2. Why have people living in areas where volcanoes erupt always feared volcanoes?

   Answers may vary. People had no way of predicting when volcanoes would erupt. They also couldn't protect themselves.

Inferring the unstated main idea

3. In the selection, the paragraph with a check mark next to it does not have a sentence that directly states the main idea. Choose the sentence below that states the main idea of the paragraph.
   - || a. Volcanoes can be found in the tropical regions of South America.
   - ▌ b. Volcanoes are found mainly in three areas of the world.
   - || c. Volcanoes are more common in the northern hemisphere.

Making inferences

4. Volcanoes occur in areas of the world where
   - ▌ a. there is shifting of sections of rock under the ground.
   - || b. the weather is always very hot.
   - || c. there is very little water.

SKILL FOCUS

1. Look at Figure 1. In your own words, explain what is happening.

   A volcano is erupting. Magma and volcanic rocks are bursting through the vents of the volcano.

2. What is the name of the long passageway through which the lava flows to the surface?

   conduit

3. What is the name of the pocket where the lava pools near the earth's surface?

   magma chamber

4. What is the name of the opening from which the lava flows?

   vent

5. What type of volcano is shown in Figure 1?

   a composite volcano or a cinder-cone volcano

▶ **Real Life Connections** What do you think local governments can do to help people living near volcanoes prepare for an eruption?

Lesson 44

Mathematical Terms and Symbols

Reading a Mathematics Selection

▶ Background Information

When you study geometry, you learn about the shape, size, and position of geometric figures. Some of these figures are flat, such as circles, triangles, and rectangles. Some of these figures are solid, such as cubes, cones, and spheres.

It is believed that the ancient Egyptians were the first people to use geometry extensively. Some of the earliest uses of geometry included measuring the lengths and areas of land. The word geometry comes from two Greek words that mean "earth" and "to measure."

It is important to understand geometry because the world is full of geometric shapes. Rectangular walls are used to build houses and other buildings. Triangular supports are used to build bridges. Many things from an earthworm to a pencil are shaped like cylinders.

When you read the following selection, pay close attention to the diagrams. They will help you understand the special meanings of certain words.

▶ Skill Focus

When reading many types of material in textbooks, you may come across words that are used in a special way. These words may have meanings that you know when they are used in an ordinary situation. However, when they are used in textbooks, they may have different meanings.

The following familiar words have special meanings when they appear in a mathematics textbook: *line, ray, angle,* and *point.* The meanings of these words in the context of mathematics are as follows: A **line** goes on forever. It never ends. A **ray** is a part of a line. It has only one end point. An **angle** is formed when two rays meet. A **point** has no dimensions. It cannot be seen.

Be sure also to pay special attention to the diagrams in math textbooks. They show how the figures described in the textbooks look. Diagrams can help you understand the meanings of new terms.

▶ Word Clues

When reading the following selection, look for these important words: *point, line, line segment, end point, ray, angle, vertex, side.* The diagrams should help you understand these words as they apply to mathematics. Also study the symbols that are used to represent each word.

▶ Strategy Tip

If you're still having difficulty with the special meaning of a word, look it up in a dictionary. Also, study the symbols that stand for some of the ideas described in the selection. These symbols are shortened ways of writing mathematical ideas.

Reading Mathematical Terms and Symbols

The study of geometry begins with the word **point.** A point has no size. It has neither length nor width. It is usually shown by a dot. The point is named using a capital letter. This is how point S is written.

S

Many, many points that go on forever can be placed next to each other. This is called a **line.** A line has length but no width. A line extends on and on in both directions. It never ends. Arrows on a line show that it never ends. A line can be named using any two points on the line. This is line ST. It is written $\overleftrightarrow{ST}$.

A line can also be named using a small letter. This is line k. It is written *line k*.

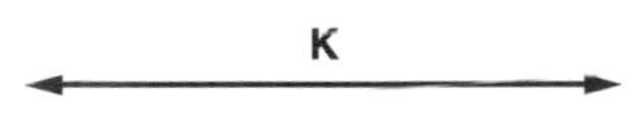

A part of a line is called a **line segment.** A line segment has a beginning and an end. This is line segment $\overline{ST}$. The points S and T are fixed. These are called **end points.** The symbol for line segment ST is $\overline{ST}$. The symbol over the letters has no arrows. This tells you that ST is part of a line with two end points.

Another part of a line is called a **ray.** A ray starts at one point and extends on and on in one direction. A ray is named by using two points. The end point comes first, followed by a point nearer the tip of the arrow. The symbol for ray ST is $\overrightarrow{ST}$.

This is ray TS. The symbol for ray TS is $\overrightarrow{TS}$.

When two rays have the same end point, they form an **angle.** This is an angle formed by rays SR and ST.

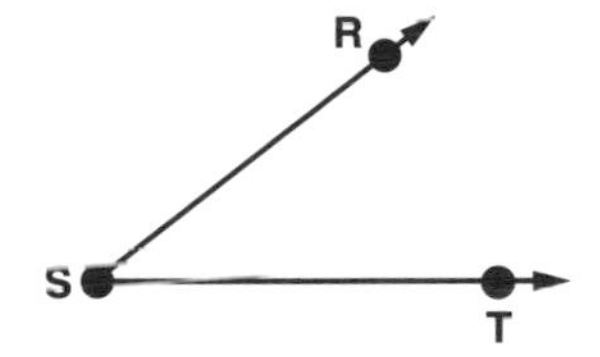

An angle has a **vertex.** The vertex is the common end point of the two rays. Point S is the vertex of the angle above. The angle also has sides. The sides are the two rays that form the angle. The sides of the angle are $\overrightarrow{ST}$ and $\overrightarrow{SR}$. An angle is named and written using the three points and the symbol for angle: $\angle RST$ or $\angle TSR$. The point of the vertex is always named in the middle. An angle can also be named using just the point of the vertex: $\angle S$.

$\angle RST$ $\angle TSR$ $\angle S$

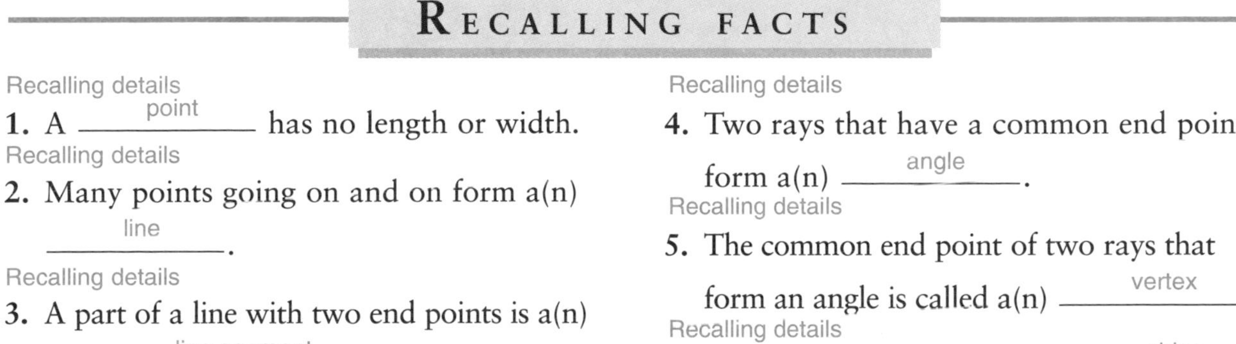

RECALLING FACTS

Recalling details
1. A point has no length or width.

Recalling details
2. Many points going on and on form a(n) line.

Recalling details
3. A part of a line with two end points is a(n) line segment.

Recalling details
4. Two rays that have a common end point form a(n) angle.

Recalling details
5. The common end point of two rays that form an angle is called a(n) vertex.

Recalling details
6. The rays of an angle are its sides.

INTERPRETING FACTS

Inferring cause and effect

1. Why is this ray named *AB* and not *BA*?

It is named *AB* because it starts at *A* and extends through *B*. *BA* would mean the ray starts at *B* and goes through *A*.

Making inferences

2. Why can't you name angle *XCY* angle *C*?

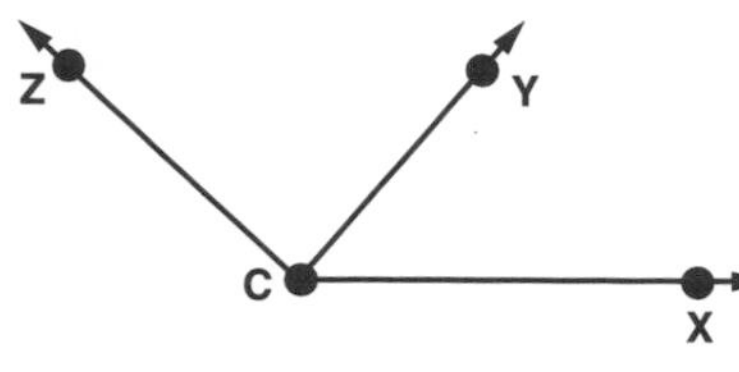

Angle *C* could be any of these angles: ∠*YCZ*, ∠*XCY*, or ∠*XCZ*.

SKILL FOCUS

Following is a map of part of downtown Mexico City. Notice that when roads meet, they form angles. The streets and avenues form rays and line segments. The locations of some buildings look like points.

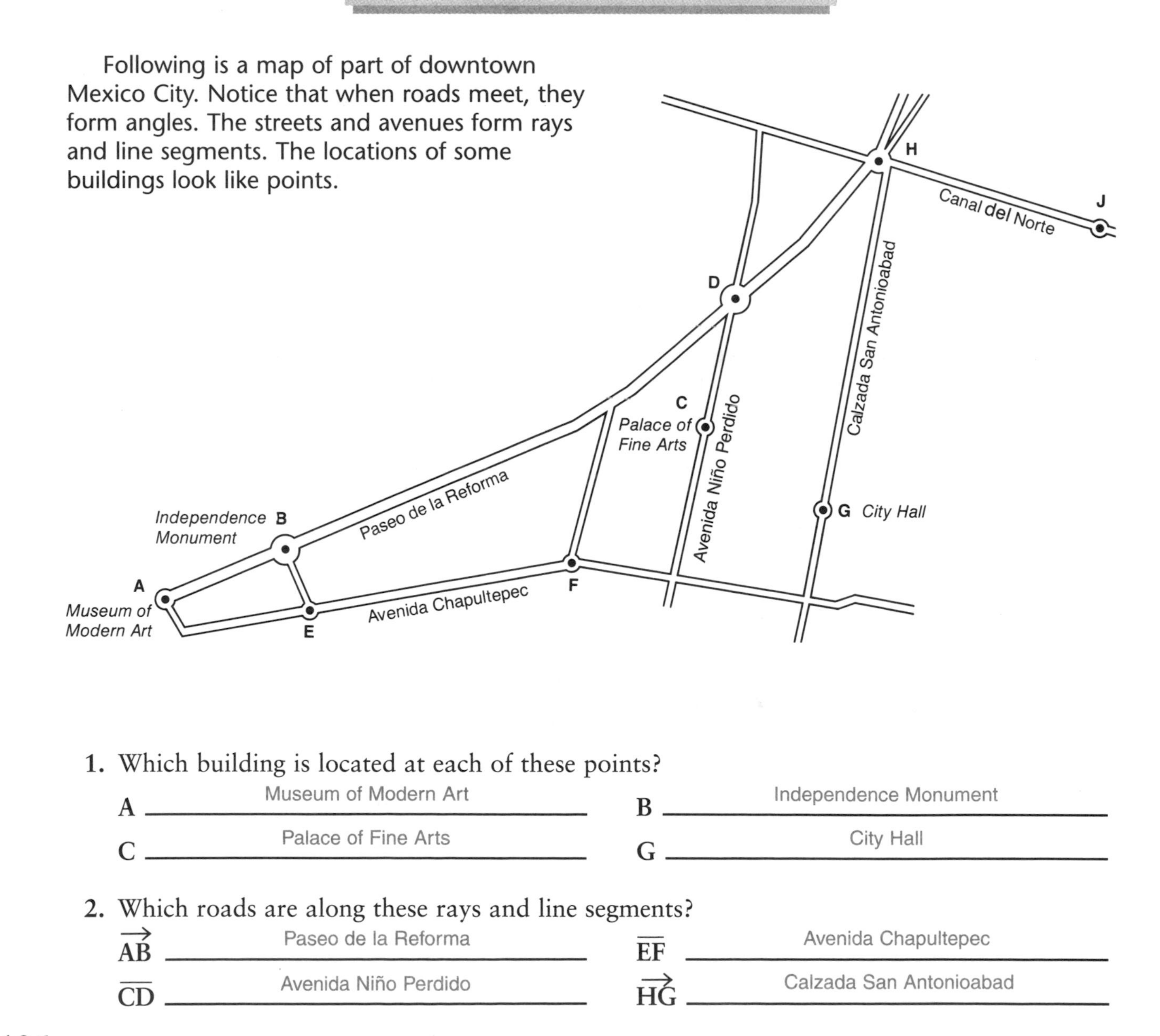

1. Which building is located at each of these points?

A Museum of Modern Art

B Independence Monument

C Palace of Fine Arts

G City Hall

2. Which roads are along these rays and line segments?

$\overrightarrow{AB}$ Paseo de la Reforma

$\overline{EF}$ Avenida Chapultepec

$\overline{CD}$ Avenida Niño Perdido

$\overrightarrow{HG}$ Calzada San Antonioabad

3. Which roads are along these angles?

$\angle$GHJ Calzada San Antonioabad and Canal del Norte

$\angle$CDH Avenida Niño Perdido and Paseo de la Reforma

4. Draw and label four points.

Possible answer: Q, O, R, P

5. Name three different segments on this line.

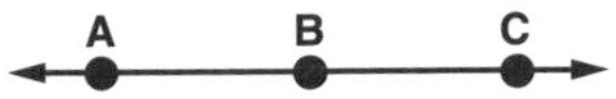

$\overline{AB}$, $\overline{BC}$, $\overline{AC}$

A B C

6. Draw line segments connecting points *A*, *B*, *C*, and *D*.

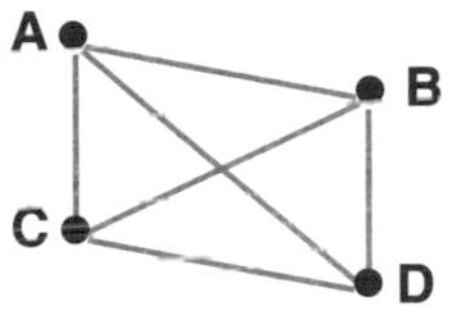

How many segments can you draw? 6

Name each segment. $\overline{AB}$, $\overline{BD}$, $\overline{AC}$, $\overline{CD}$, $\overline{CB}$, $\overline{AD}$

A B C D

7. Draw and name two rays.

Possible answer: $\overrightarrow{QR}$, $\overrightarrow{UV}$

R Q U V

8. Draw two rays with a common end point. Possible answer:

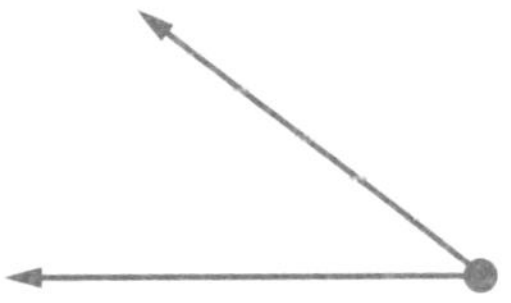

9. Draw an angle. Name it three different ways.

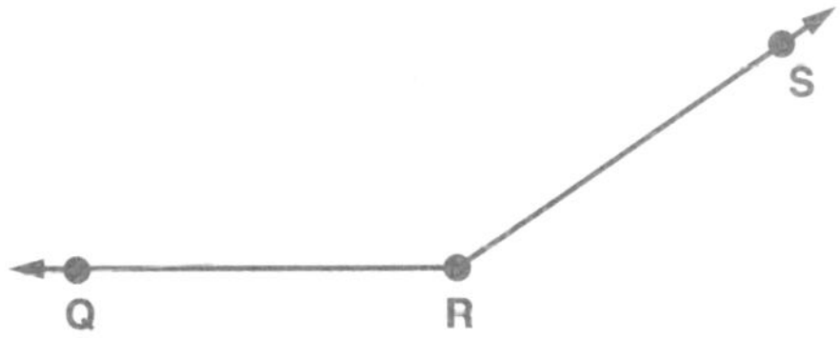

Possible answer: $\angle$QRS, $\angle$SRQ, $\angle$R

S Q R

10. Name the sides of this angle.

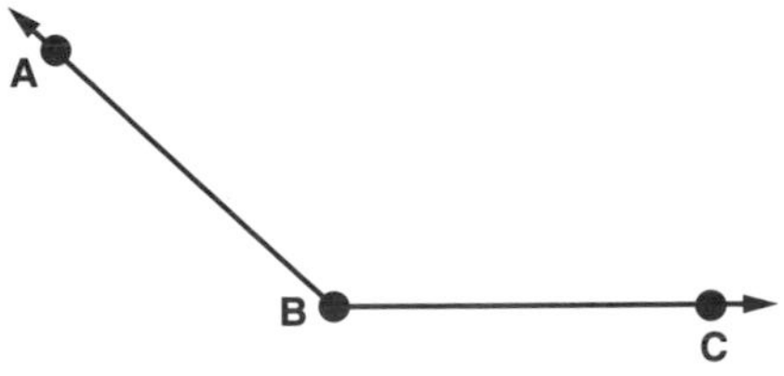

$\overrightarrow{BA}$, $\overrightarrow{BC}$

A B C

11. Name the vertex of the angle in question 10. B

Real Life Connections An angle is formed when two lines meet. Identify an angle in your classroom.

Main Idea and Supporting Details

In reading for details, the first step is to find the main idea of the paragraph. The second step is to find the details that give more information about the main idea.

The following paragraph is about Columbus. The main idea and supporting details are listed after the paragraph. Read them.

Columbus thought that he had reached India when he landed in this part of the world. When he left Spain, his purpose was to find a westward water route for ships sailing to India. When he saw land after his ten weeks of sailing, he thought that he had found the sought-after water route. He gave the name *Indians* to the people he met on the islands that he visited. It was not until some time later that Columbus realized he had not landed on the shores of India.

Main Idea Columbus thought that he reached India when he landed in this part of the world.

Supporting Details

a. Columbus wanted to find a water route to India when he sailed from Spain.

b. When Columbus saw land after sailing for a long time, he thought that he had reached India.

c. He called the people *Indians.*

d. Later, Columbus realized that he had not found India.

For each paragraph, write the sentence that states the main idea. Then write the major details in your own words.

1. American Indians lived in different kinds of houses. Indians near the Great Lakes lived in wigwams. Plains Indians lived in tipis. In Eastern Woodland tribes, several families lived together in longhouses. Southwest Indians lived in houses made of adobe brick.

2. American Indians also traveled a variety of ways, depending upon where they lived. Those who lived near water made canoes. Some of these canoes were made out of tree bark and were easy to carry; others were large dugout canoes that carried as many as 60 people. Some Indians made light boats of reeds. Indians who did not live near water traveled by other means. For example, the Plains and Southwest Indians traveled by foot or on horseback.

3. The daily diet of most Indians came from the crops and animals where they lived. Plains Indians killed wild animals, such as buffalo and elk, for food. Pueblo Indians raised corn, beans, and squash. Potatoes were an important crop among the Incas. Many Indian groups also caught fish in nearby streams.

4. The Indians made many things they needed. They made hatchets from stone. Their arrowheads were made of flint. Their bows were made of wood. Many also used clay to make pottery.

5. Almost all Indians played athletic games. Footracing was popular in many areas. Different kinds of ball games were played by many Indians. Usually only women played shinny, a kind of field hockey that was common in North America. Northern Indians enjoyed a game called snow snake, in which each player tried to slide a dart or spear farthest on the snow or ice.

Paragraph 1

Main Idea American Indians lived in different kinds of houses.

Supporting Details

a. Near the Great Lakes, Indians lived in wigwams.

b. Indians in the Plains lived in tipis.

c. Eastern Woodlands Indians lived in longhouses.

d. Southwest Indians lived in houses made of adobe brick.

Paragraph 2

Main Idea Native Americans used a variety of methods of transportation.

Supporting Details

a. Those who lived near water traveled in canoes.

b. The Plains and Southwest Indians traveled by foot or on horseback.

Paragraph 3

Main Idea The daily diet of most Indians came from the crops and animals where they lived.

Supporting Details

a. Plains Indians mainly ate wild animals, such as buffalo and elk.

b. Pueblo Indians ate corn, beans, and squash.

c. The Incas raised potatoes.

d. Many also ate fish caught in nearby streams.

Paragraph 4

Main Idea The Indians made many things that they needed.

Supporting Details

a. Hatchets were made from stone.

b. Arrowheads were made of flint.

c. Bows were made of wood.

d. Pottery was made of clay.

Paragraph 5

Main Idea Almost all Indians played athletic games.

Supporting Details

a. Many Indians enjoyed footracing.

b. Ball games were also popular.

c. Women played shinny, a type of field hockey.

d. Snow snake was played by northern Indians on snow or ice.

Lesson 46

Outlining

Making an outline is one way to help you remember what you read. An **outline** is a listing of the important ideas from a selection. A good outline shows how the main ideas and supporting details in a selection are organized.

The most important ideas, or main ideas, in a selection are written next to Roman numerals: I, II, III, IV, V, and so on. The supporting details that give more information about each of the important ideas are written next to capital letters: A, B, C, D, and so on. This is called a **two-step outline**. The Roman numerals and capital letters are arranged so that you can easily see the information.

Following is a paragraph and an outline of the paragraph.

American Indians lived in different kinds of houses. The Great Lakes Indians lived in wigwams. Plains Indians lived in tipis. In Eastern Woodland tribes, several families lived together in longhouses. Southwest Indians lived in houses made of adobe brick.

American Indians

I. Different kinds of homes
- **A.** Wigwams—Great Lakes
- **B.** Tipis—Plains
- **C.** Longhouses—Eastern Woodlands
- **D.** Adobe brick—Southwest

Notice that *Different kinds of homes* is written next to Roman numeral I. These words state the main idea of the paragraph. *Wigwams—Great Lakes* is written next to capital letter A. This phrase is the first detail about Indian homes in the paragraph. The other details are written next to capital letters B, C, and D.

An outline gives only key words. Each phrase begins with a capital letter.

Several other things are important to know about outlining. Every outline should have a title. When you outline a selection, remember to include at least two important main ideas from what you have read. An outline of a selection can never have a Roman numeral I without a Roman numeral II. Likewise, at least two supporting details should come under each Roman numeral. An A should always be followed by a B.

Below is more of the selection on American Indians. You have already found the main ideas and details for each paragraph in the last lesson. Now use the two-step outline form to outline the paragraphs. Do this the same way as the sample on page 140.

American Indians also traveled a variety of ways, depending upon where they lived. Those who lived near water made canoes. Some of these canoes were made out of tree bark and were easy to carry; others were large dugout canoes that carried as many as 60 people. Some Indians made light boats of reeds. Indians who did not live near water traveled by other means. For example, the Plains and Southwest Indians traveled by foot or on horseback.

The daily diet of most Indians came from the crops and animals where they lived. Plains Indians killed wild animals, such as buffalo and elk, for food. Pueblo Indians raised corn, beans, and squash. Potatoes were an important crop among the Incas. Many Indian groups also caught fish in nearby streams.

The Indians made many things they needed. They made hatchets from stone. Their arrowheads were made of flint. Their bows were made of wood. Many also used clay to make pottery.

Almost all Indians played athletic games. Footracing was popular in many areas. Different kinds of ball games were played by many Indians. Usually only women played shinny, a kind of field hockey that was common in North America. Northern Indians enjoyed a game called snow snake, in which each player tried to slide a dart or spear farthest on the snow or ice.

II. Means of travel
  A. Water travel – canoes
  B. Land travel – horses and on foot
III. Daily diet
  A. Wild animals—Plains
  B. Corn, beans, squash—Pueblo
  C. Potatoes—Incas
  D. Fish—Many Indians
IV. Handmade items
  A. Hatchets from stone
  B. Arrowheads of flint
  C. Bows from wood
  D. Pottery from clay
V. Games
  A. Footracing
  B. Ball games
  C. Shinny
  D. Snow snake

Now look back at Lesson 45 and compare the list of main ideas and supporting details there with your outline. Do they both give the same information? Which one gives more details? Which one is shorter?

Lesson 47

Guide Words

At the top of each dictionary page are two words in boldfaced type. These words are called **guide words.** Guide words help you find entry words easily and quickly. They tell you the first entry word on the page and the last entry word on the page. All the other entry words on the page come between these two words in alphabetical order.

Following are some guide words that might appear at the top of some pages in a dictionary.

Page 97: **bird/bite**	Page 537: **miracle/misery**
Page 120: **camp/candle**	Page 653: **poker/polite**
Page 205: **clock/cloud**	Page 797: **slip/slouch**
Page 310: **figured/filter**	Page 900: **trade/trap**
Page 403: **hummock/hurry**	Page 942: **ward/wary**

Underline the words that you would find on the following pages.

1. Page 97

birth	bitter	Bible	biscuit	beach	baboon	bison	bomb

2. Page 120

cane	cacao	cancel	canvas	chain	canal	clay	campus

3. Page 205

crude	clip	clog	camera	comb	court	clot	cactus

4. Page 310

flood	film	fortress	file	finger	faction	filbert	fawn

5. Page 403

hulk	humus	hydra	hoof	hurdle	humid	hygiene	hovel

6. Page 537

minor	Mars	mildew	mirth	motor	middy	mustard	miser

7. Page 653

poise	poke	polar	pliant	policy	portal	prattle	pungent

8. Page 797

slope	screen	slot	slug	sleuth	smug	snipe	slew

9. Page 900

trace	traffic	tragic	track	train	tramp	tropic	trail

10. Page 942

ware	want	warm	wart	wall	warn	wash	warrant

Lesson 48

The Dictionary

In a dictionary, the entry word and all the information about it is the **entry**. The entry word always appears in boldfaced type. If the word has more than one syllable, it is divided into syllables to show where the word can be divided at the end of a line of writing. The entry word is followed by a **respelling** of the word in parentheses. The respelling shows you how to pronounce the word. The part-of-speech label follows the respelling. The labels are usually abbreviated as follows: ***adj.*** for adjective, ***adv.*** for adverb, ***conj.*** for conjunction, ***interj.*** for interjection, ***n.*** for noun, ***prep.*** for preposition, ***pron.*** for pronoun, and ***v.*** for verb.

The meanings are arranged according to parts of speech. For example, if an entry has noun meanings, all the noun meanings are grouped together and numbered following the label ***n.*** Any meanings that the word may have for any other part of speech are numbered and placed after the proper label. When an entry has only one meaning for any part of speech, the definition is not numbered. At the end of some entries are phrases or idioms. An **idiom** is a group of words that has a meaning different from the meaning the words have by themselves. In some dictionaries, idioms have a dash in front of them and appear in boldfaced type.

nose (nōz) ***n.*** **1** the part of the head that sticks out between the mouth and the eyes and has two openings for breathing and smelling. The nose is part of the muzzle or snout in animals. **2** the sense of smell [a dog with a good *nose*]. **3** the ability to find out things [a reporter with a *nose* for news]. **4** anything like a nose in shape or in the way it is placed, as the front of an airplane or the bow of a ship. ◆ ***v.*** **1** to move with the front end forward [The ship *nosed* into the harbor.] **2** to meddle in another's affairs. **3** to smell with the nose. **4** to rub with the nose. **—nosed, nos'ing** **— by a nose,** by just a little bit [to win *by a nose*]. **— look down one's nose at,** to be scornful of: *used only in everyday speech.* **—nose out,** to win by just a little bit. **—on the nose,** exactly; precisely: *a slang phrase* [You guessed the score *on the nose*.] **—pay through the nose,** to pay more than something is worth. **—turn up one's nose at,** to sneer at; scorn. **—under one's nose,** in plain view.

Use the dictionary entry above to answer the following questions.

1. What is the entry word? nose
2. Write the respelling. nōz
3. How many noun meanings follow the part-of-speech label ***n***? 4
4. Write the second verb meaning. to meddle in another's affairs
5. Write the third noun meaning the ability to find out things
6. How many idioms are given following the meanings? 7
7. Write the first idiom. by a nose
8. Write the idiom that you would use only in everyday speech. look down one's nose at
9. Write the slang idiom that means *exactly*? on the nose
10. How do you spell the past tense of *nose*? nosed

Lesson 49

Reading a Menu

How do you know what to order when you go to a restaurant? The best thing to do is to look at the menu. A menu lists all of the different foods that the restaurant serves and gives the price of each item.

The following menu is from a Mexican restaurant, so most of the dishes on the menu have Spanish names. As you read the menu, notice the headings, which identify the types of foods served in the restaurant.

TACO JOE'S RESTAURANT

6116 First Avenue

Open Seven Days a Week

APPETIZERS

NACHOS melted cheese on tortilla chips with jalapeño pepper	2.50
GUACAMOLE mashed avocados, onions, tomatoes, with tortilla chips	2.50
ENSALADA lettuce, onions, tomatoes, egg, and avocado (regular)	3.50
(small)	2.50

SOUPS

SOPA DE POLLO chicken soup	2.25
SOPA DE FRIJOL NEGRO black bean soup	2.50

ENTRÉES

TACOS 3 crisp folded corn tortillas* stuffed with ground beef or chicken	5.25
ENCHILADAS 3 tortillas stuffed with cheese, beef, or chicken, topped with melted cheese and red hot Mexican sauce	5.50
BURRITOS 3 rolled flour tortillas stuffed with chunks of beef	5.50
TOSTADOS 3 open crisp tortillas topped with beans, ground beef, and lettuce	5.50
JOE'S COMBINATION chicken taco, cheese enchilada, and burrito	5.75
POLLO A LA MEXICANA chicken with tomatoes, onions, and green peppers	7.25
STEAK RANCHERO sliced steak with tomatoes, onions, and peppers	7.95
CAMARONES VERACRUZANA shrimp with tomatoes and peppers in a deep-fried flour shell	9.25

*a very thin, round pancake

SIDE ORDERS

Refried beans topped with cheese	2.00
Vegetable of the day	1.50
Basket of tortilla chips	1.25

DESSERTS

FLAN caramel custard	2.50
MANGO tropical fruit topped with whipped cream	3.25
ICE CREAM vanilla or strawberry	2.00
NATILLA Spanish cream and pudding	2.50

BEVERAGES

Coffee	1.00
Tea	1.00
Milk	.85
Juice	.85

A. Use the information on the menu to answer each question on the line provided.

1. Which three entrées cost the same? enchiladas, burritos, tostados
2. What is the most expensive entrée on the menu? Camarones Veracruzana
3. Which three different stuffings can you order in enchiladas? cheese, beef, or chicken
4. Which two entrées do you choose between if you want to eat both chicken and cheese? enchiladas or Joe's combination
5. Which dessert is a kind of fruit? mango
6. If you do not want to eat onion, which appetizer must you choose? nachos

7. Why won't a vegetarian order Joe's Combination?

because the taco is made with chicken and the burrito is made with beef

8. How are the tortillas used for tacos different from those used for burritos?

Tacos use crisp folded corn tortillas, while burritos use rolled flour tortillas.

9. How are the tortillas used for tacos similar to those used for tostados?

Both are crisp.

10. You have $8.25 to spend on dinner. You have already ordered tacos and milk. Which dessert can you afford? ice cream

11. Figure the cost of the following meals.

guacamole	$ 2.50	sopa de pollo	$ 2.25	small ensalada	$ 2.50
sopa de frijol negro	2.50	steak ranchero	7.95	beef enchiladas	5.50
tacos	5.25	broccoli	1.50	beans with cheese	2.00
tea	1.00	juice	.85	flan	2.50
	$ 11.25		$ 12.55		$ 12.50

12. Find the least expensive meal in question 11. List the menu heading for each item in that meal.

appetizers, soups, entrées, beverages

13. Why doesn't Taco Joe's menu list spaghetti or veal parmesan?

They are Italian foods; Taco Joe's has Mexican food only.

B. Read the statements about the menu and write *true* or *false* on each line.

false 1. Flan is a kind of Spanish soup.

true 2. Ensalada is a salad.

true 3. The ingredients in guacamole include avocado, onion, and tomato.

false 4. You can order a cheeseburger and French fries at Taco Joe's restaurant.

true 5. Five of the entrées are prepared with tortillas.

false 6. Taco Joe's is closed on Sundays.

true 7. By reading the menu, you can learn that the Spanish word for chicken is *pollo*.

false 8. If you have $10.00 to spend at Taco Joe's, you have enough money to order burritos, a vegetable, and a mango.

true 9. If you have $10.00 to spend at Taco Joe's, you have enough money to order pollo a la Mexicana and milk.

false 10. Natilla is served with rice and beans.

false 11. Burritos are folded flour tortillas filled with ground beef.

false 12. If you order Joe's Combination, you have your choice of one of the three items offered.

true 13. An order of enchiladas comes with three enchiladas. You can figure out that each enchilada costs about $1.80.

UNIT 6

Neighbors to the South

Lesson 50

Plot

Reading a Literature Selection

Background Information

There are many kinds of tales. A tale that tells about the customs, traditions, beliefs, and lives of a group of people is called a **folktale.** The folktale you will read comes from Colombia.

Skill Focus

The plan of action or the series of events in a story is called **plot**. The plot in most stories follows a basic pattern consisting of five parts.

1. **Beginning**: The events at the beginning of the story build your interest.
2. **Development of Conflict**: A conflict develops within a character, between two characters, or between a character and an outside force.
3. **Climax**: An event occurs that is the most exciting part of the story. It marks the story's turning point. After the climax, you can begin to predict how the story will end.
4. **Resolution of Conflict:** The events after the climax resolve the conflict.
5. **Conclusion**: A final event ends the story.

Sometimes the events in a story are not in chronological order. Understanding plot pattern will help you see the sequence of story events.

If you were to draw the plot of a story, it might look like this. The diagram and the questions below will help you follow the plot.

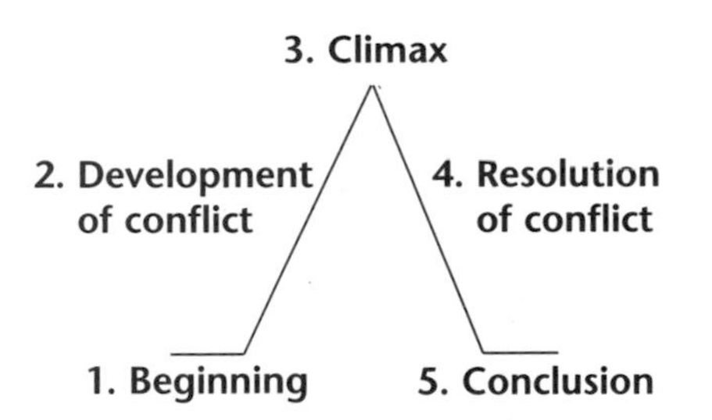

1. What is the conflict the characters face at the beginning of the story?
2. How does the conflict develop?
3. What is the climax?
4. What is the resolution?
5. Is the story's conclusion appropriate?

Word Clues

When you read a selection, you may find words that you don't know. Read the following sentence.

> To his horror, he saw an anaconda, the longest snake in the jungle.

You can tell from the context clues that an anaconda is a snake. However, there are no context clues that tell you more about the anaconda.

When you come across a word you don't know and you can't find context clues, use a dictionary to find the word's meaning. You may find it more convenient to finish what you are reading before you look up the word.

Use a **dictionary** to find the meaning of the three underlined words in the selection.

Strategy Tip

As you read the selection, use the diagram and the five questions to help you follow the plot. When the tale reaches its climax, try to predict how the story will end. Is the ending appropriate? Why or why not?

THE GIANT SNAKE THAT SWALLOWED A GIRL

Long, long ago, an Indian named Magu spent the night far out in the jungle of South American land now known as Colombia. He made himself a soft bed of leaves on the bank of a stream. He slept soundly.

When he awoke in the morning, he felt something move against his side. To his horror, he saw an anaconda, the longest snake in the jungle. Magu could see its spots clearly as it crawled away and slipped into the river.

"I have had a narrow escape," Magu said to himself. "For while the anaconda does not bite, its strong coils could easily have crushed me while I slept."

Magu stood up, and he looked all around to make sure that no other serpent was near. In his search, he discovered that the giant snake had left an egg in the leaves. It was a soft, leathery egg, almost as big as a gourd.

"Ho, this will amuse my wife and my daughter, Mina." Magu picked up the egg and carried it home.

There he told his strange tale. When his wife and child had examined the egg, they laid it on a warm ledge near the cooking fire. They forgot it until fourteen days had gone by. Then the egg's covering broke, and a young anaconda crawled out.

"Kill the snake! Kill it, my husband!" Magu's wife cried.

"No," said Magu. "Why should we kill such a pretty young creature? See its handsome markings! Look how big it is! An anaconda has no teeth and no poison. I shall keep it for a pet."

"Ah, but an anaconda can squeeze, Magu," the man's wife still objected. "An anaconda can swallow a pig or a goat. I do not like having a giant snake live in our hut."

"I will give my snake animals out of my traps in the jungle. I will feed it fish from the river. I will keep its stomach filled at all times. Then it will be content. It will harm no one," said the Indian.

Curiously, Magu was able to tame the anaconda quickly. It lived happily inside the Indian's hut. The man brought it plenty of small animals and fish, which it greatly liked. When Magu called "Boya! Boya!" the snake

would crawl out of its corner and swallow its meal in one mighty gulp. It ate and ate. It grew and it grew. It was truly much bigger than any other anaconda in the jungle.

Magu's pet snake was so long it would reach from the ridge of his roof to the ground. Its body was thicker than a man's thigh. And it was tame, just as tame as Mina's pet parrot.

The snake seemed to love its Indian master. Sometimes it followed him into the forest and looped itself around a tree branch nearby while the man fished or shot turtles with his flying arrows. Always it came back with him to the hut when night fell.

Magu's wife and daughter did not like the serpent. The woman shook her head and said over and over, "This is not good, my husband. One day you will be sorry." Mina was afraid of the giant snake.

Now Magu loved his small daughter Mina more than anything else in the world. But the tame anaconda was jealous of her. Whenever the man played with Mina, the brown snake would coil itself up in a corner and sulk. It would not come out again until Magu had called it and called it. Yet the strange pet never tried to do the child harm.

One day, a feast was to be held in a neighboring village. For weeks, Magu's family had thought about the eating and talking, the singing and dancing that there would be.

As bad luck would have it, Mina fell ill a short time before the feast. Though she was almost well enough on the day of the feast, she did not want to go.

"I shall not be lonely while you are gone, Papita, Mamita. I shall have Papagayo here to talk to." She held her finger out to her parrot, which she loved well. She begged them to go. They went off down the river in their canoe.

All would have been well if the Indian had not forgotten to feed his snake that day. That day the giant snake was hungry. It crawled out of its dark corner, looking for food. Possibly it was hunger. Or perhaps it was jealousy of Mina, who took up so much of the master's attention. Whatever the reason, the giant jaws

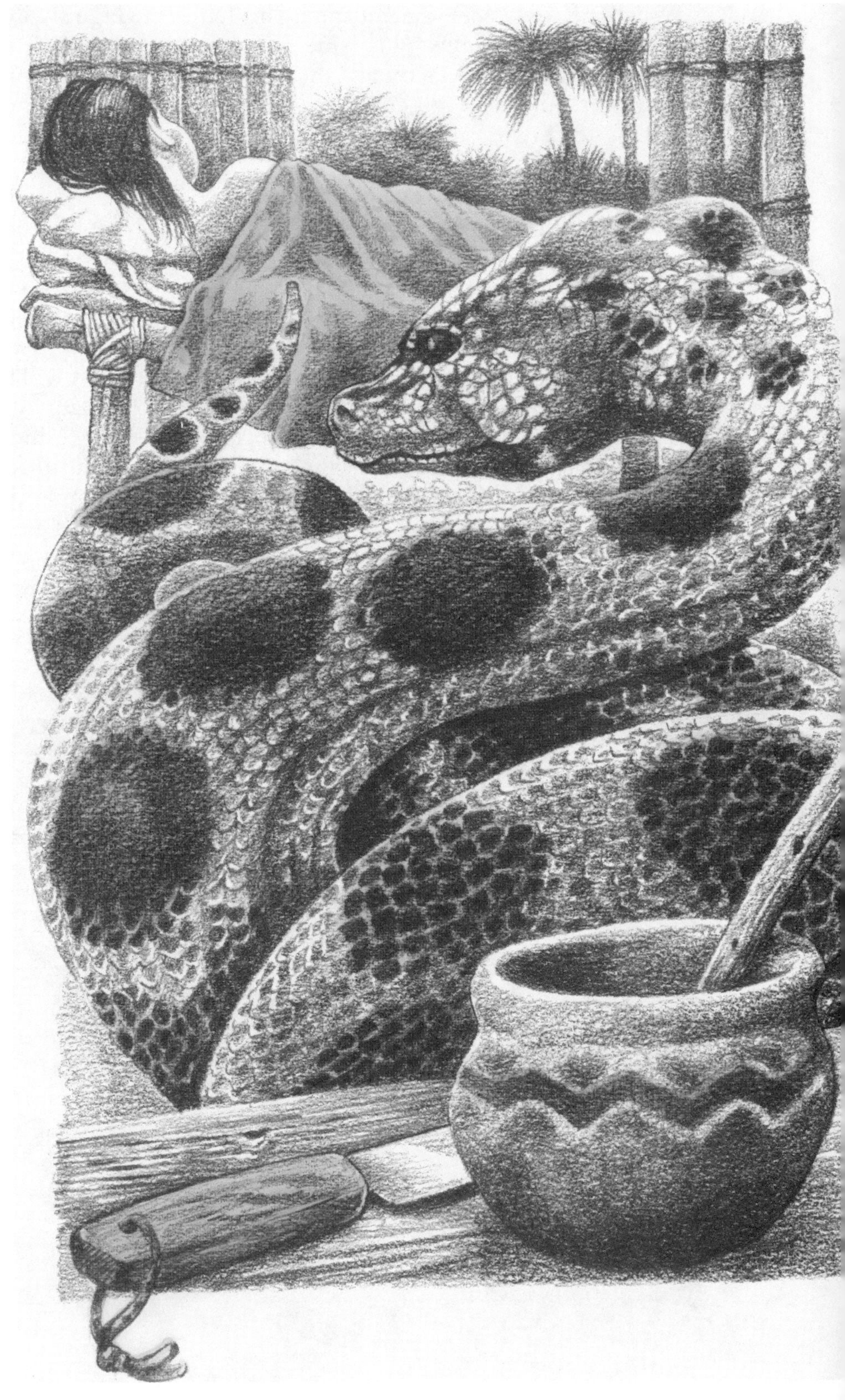

opened wide. With one mighty gulp, the anaconda swallowed the girl.

Papagayo, the parrot, screamed when it saw what had taken place. It flapped its wings wildly and darted out of the hut door. Across the forest to the neighboring village it flew. There it circled among the merrymakers until it found Magu.

In those times, parrots could say many, many more words than such birds today, which only repeat what they have been taught.

"Master! Master!" the parrot squawked into the ear of the surprised Magu. "Master, come quickly! The snake has eaten poor Mina. It has swallowed her whole."

Magu lost no time in getting back to his hut. Beside the cooking fire, he found the anaconda asleep. The Indian could see his child's slim form under the scaly skin of the big snake. Having no teeth, anacondas swallow their food whole. When their stomachs are full, they straightaway go to sleep.

"Boya! Boya!" The father shouted the name by which he called his pet. "Wake, Boya! Give me back my daughter!"

Once more the man called while the parrot screamed. But the snake would not wake up.

Then Magu made a plan. He brought in a freshly killed paca from his traps and laid it on the ground close to the snake. He then heated a small stone until it was red hot and put it down nearby.

The smell of the freshly killed paca, which the snake liked so well, made the sluggish creature lift up its head and open its eyes. The greedy serpent spread its jaws wide to swallow the paca. At that moment, Magu threw the hot stone far down its open throat.

How the snake choked and coughed! It opened its burned throat so wide that it brought up the stone, and with it Magu's daughter. When her father picked her up off the ground, Mina was unhurt.

What became of the giant snake, Boya? The Indian father did not risk his child's life a second time. He told the anaconda to go away and never come back. No doubt the scar left in the snake's throat reminded it that its former master would have no pity upon it if it did.

Travelers tell fabulous tales about the giant snakes, like Magu's Boya, that live in the jungles along the equator. Some say that these serpents are not long enough to swallow a child. Others remind them that this story happened long, long ago. Perhaps it was in prehistoric times when mammoths and giant snakes may have been on the earth.

The Indians of this part of Colombia say that the winding streams are the tracks left by such enormous serpents. They believe that when a lake is dried up, its serpent has gone away and will not come back again.

Recalling Facts

Identifying setting

1. When and where does this story take place?

It takes place long ago, in Colombia.

Recognizing sequence of events

2. What happened to the egg after Magu carried it home?

The egg was forgotten. Fourteen days later, its shell broke and a young anaconda crawled out.

Comparing and contrasting

3. How did Magu and his wife feel about keeping the snake after it hatched?

Magu wanted to keep it for a pet. His wife wanted to kill it.

Recalling details

4. Describe Boya, Magu's pet anaconda.

The snake was larger than any other anaconda in the jungle. It was very long. Its body was very thick.

Identifying cause and effect

5. Why did Mina not go to the feast in a neighboring village?

Mina was ill.

Recalling details

6. Which did Mina prefer to have as a pet—Boya the snake or Papagayo the parrot?

She preferred Papagayo.

Identifying cause and effect

7. What are two possible reasons for Boya's swallowing Mina?

Boya was jealous of Mina; Boya was hungry.

Identifying conflict and resolution

8. a. With whom did the anaconda come into conflict?

The anaconda came into conflict with Magu, Mina's father.

b. How was this conflict resolved?

Magu used a hot stone to trick Boya into coughing up his daughter.

Using context clues

9. Circle the correct meaning of the underlined word(s) in each sentence.

a. A snake could be a dangerous pet.

serpent (circled) **gerbil**

b. Hairy elephants cannot be seen at the zoo because they are no longer living.

hippopotamus **mammoths** (circled)

c. A snake would enjoy a tailless rodent with spotted fur for lunch.

pizza **paca** (circled)

INTERPRETING FACTS

Understanding character

1. Why was Magu unwise for keeping the giant anaconda for a pet?

Answers may vary. A giant snake does not belong in a hut; it should be free and wild in the jungle.

Making inferences

2. Why do you think the snake crawled out of the egg?

Answers may vary. The heat from the cooking fire hatched it.

Making inferences about character

3. What do you think Magu learned from his experience?

Answers may vary. He learned to think of his family's safety first.

Predicting outcomes

4. What do you think became of the giant anaconda?

Answers will vary. The giant snake probably lived in the jungle where it had a steady supply of food.

Making judgments

5. Do you think that the events in the story really happened? Explain.

Answers may vary. The story is fantasy. Birds can't talk, nor can snakes understand humans. It is also unlikely that the little girl could have survived her ordeal unharmed.

SKILL FOCUS

Below are some of the events in the folk tale about the anaconda that swallowed a girl. Starting where it says **Beginning**, fill in the appropriate events on the lines of the diagram below.

> Magu decides to keep as a pet the anaconda that hatched from an egg he brought home.
>
> Magu tells Boya to go away and never return.
>
> The snake swallows Mina.
>
> The snake, although tame and fond of Magu, grows jealous of Mina.
>
> Magu uses a paca and a hot stone to trick Boya into coughing up his daughter.

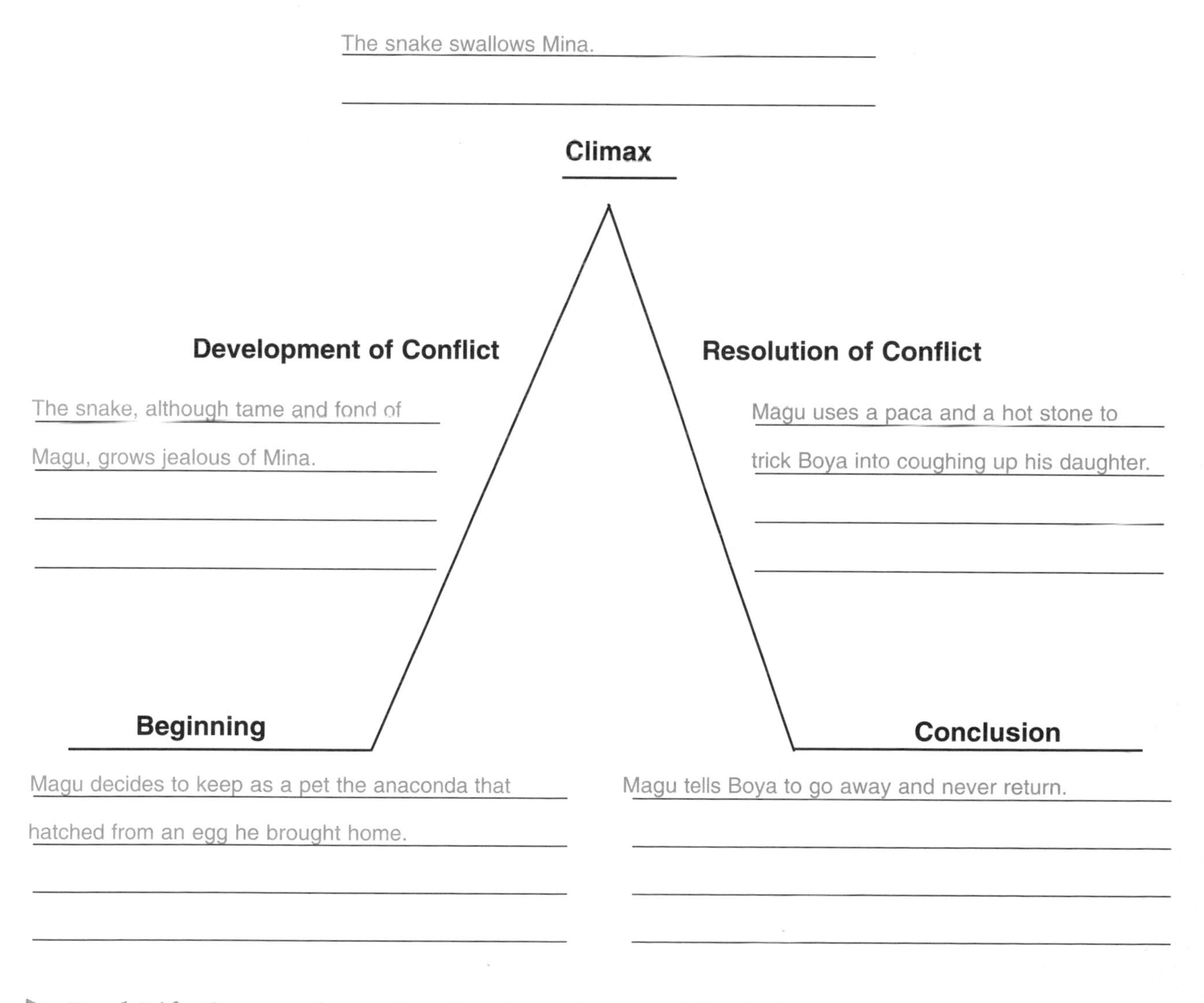

Real Life Connections Retell either a favorite folktale from your native culture or another tale that you know well.

Lesson 51

Comparing and Contrasting

Reading a Social Studies Selection

Background Information

The following selection describes the features of the Humid Subtropic regions in North and South America. Use the maps to locate these regions.

Skill Focus

When a writer tells how two or more things are alike, the writer is **comparing** them. When a writer tells how things are different, the writer is **contrasting** them.

A writer can organize information to show comparison and contrast in several ways. The following two paragraphs show one of them.

> The Northeast has warm summers and cold, snowy winters. The average January temperature varies from 15° to 30° Fahrenheit (-9.4° to -1° Celsius), while the average July temperature varies from 60° to 75° Fahrenheit (15.5° to 23.8° Celsius). The average yearly rainfall varies between 40 and 60 inches (100 and 150 centimeters). The winters are ideal for people who like skiing and other winter sports.

> Unlike the Northeast, the Southeast has hot, humid summers and mild winters. This region has little snow. The average January temperature ranges from 40° to over 65° Fahrenheit (4.4° to 18.3° Celsius), warm enough for sunbathing. The average yearly rainfall is greater than that in the Northeast. It varies from 60 inches (150 centimeters) to more than 80 inches (200 centimeters), causing much humidity during the summer, which is why this region is called the Humid Subtropics.

The first paragraph gives specific information and examples about the temperature and rainfall in the Northeast.

The second paragraph gives specific information about the climate in the Southeast. The details help you see the similarities and differences in climate between the two regions.

You should use the way in which paragraphs are organized to help you make comparisons and contrasts. Look for words and phrases that signal comparisons, such as *like* and *similar to,* and contrasts, such as *unlike* and *in contrast.*

Word Clues

Read the sentences below. Look for context clues that explain the underlined word.

> Major crops are grown in the pampas. The pampas is the large, fertile, grassy plain of Argentina.

If you do not know the meaning of the word *pampas* in the first sentence, read on. The second sentence tells you what the word *pampas* means. A word meaning that is stated directly can often be found before or after the unknown word.

Use **definition** context clues to find the meaning of the three underlined words in the selection.

Strategy Tip

As you read "Humid Subtropics," look for comparisons and contrasts. Use signal words and the way in which the paragraphs are organized to help you make comparisons and contrasts.

Humid Subtropics

The Humid Subtropic regions of the Western Hemisphere lie in the eastern parts of North and South America between latitudes 25° and 38°. In North America, this region is called the United States South. It includes the southeastern part of the United States from the southeastern coast westward to Oklahoma and Texas. In South America, the region is located in the south central part of the continent. It includes northeastern Argentina, all of Uruguay, most of southern Brazil, and the southern part of Paraguay.

The shaded areas show the Humid Subtropics in North and South America.

Climate

The Humid Subtropics have hot, wet summers and mild winters. High humidity and temperatures often above 90° Fahrenheit (32.2° Celsius) make summer weather uncomfortable. Winters, however, are not as extreme as summers.

Snow is not uncommon in the United States South. The reason for this is simple. The North American continent touches the Arctic region. There are no mountain barriers to block cold Arctic air masses from moving south. The cold air masses often bring below-freezing weather and sometimes snow to the southern part of the United States.

In contrast, snow is rare in the South American Humid Subtropics. This region is separated from the Antarctic region by water. By the time a cold air mass crosses the South Atlantic Ocean and reaches the continent, the air mass is no longer very cold. In fact, the air mass is too warm for snow or below-freezing temperatures.

Agriculture

Plenty of rainfall, warmth, and a long growing season combine in the Humid Subtropic regions to produce excellent conditions for farming. Growing a variety of crops is possible, including fruits, vegetables, and grains.

Cotton, once the chief crop of the United States South, now is grown along with other crops. These crops include corn, peanuts, tobacco, and soybeans. Fruits are also an important crop. The oranges and grapefruits of Florida and the peaches of the Carolinas and Georgia are shipped to all parts of the United States. Sugarcane, a traditional crop in the Mississippi delta, is now grown in the Florida Everglades. Rice is grown in Louisiana and Texas. Tobacco is another major crop of this region, as is the livestock and beef cattle industry.

Like the North American Humid Subtropics, the South American Humid Subtropics have excellent conditions for farming. Major crops are grown in the pampas. The pampas is the large, fertile, grassy plain of Argentina. Wheat, corn, sunflowers, and flax for seed are the leading crops. Millions of acres of alfalfa are grown to feed local cattle. In many parts of this region, livestock grazing is more important than farming. Today much of the world's supply of fresh beef is produced in this region.

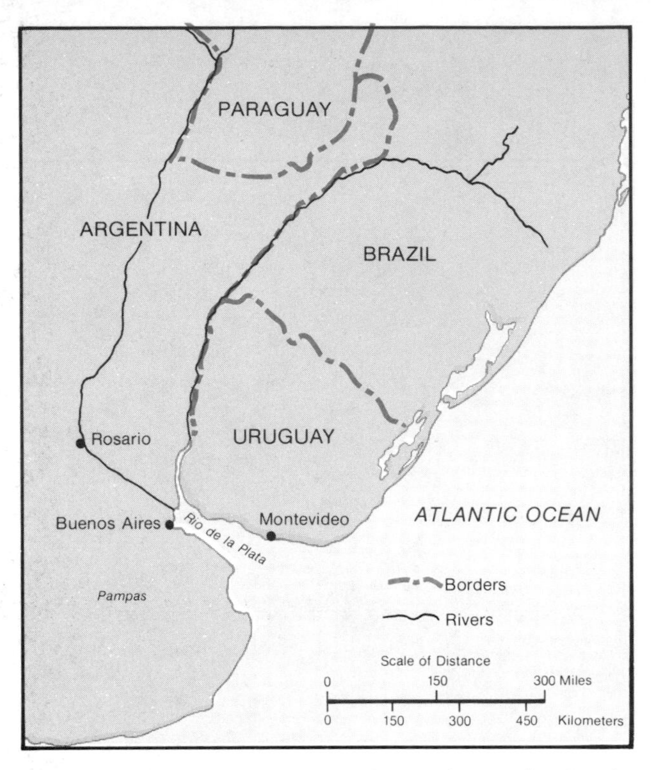

This map shows the countries that make up the South American Humid Subtropics.

Mining

Mining activities vary greatly in the Humid Subtropic regions. The kinds of deposits and their size influence the growth of the mining industry in both regions.

The United States South is the outstanding mining region of the Humid Subtropics. The largest oil and gas supply in the United States is situated in the western half of the region, mainly in the states of Texas, Oklahoma, Louisiana, and Arkansas. Coal is found in Oklahoma, Alabama, Mississippi, and Texas. Iron reserves are being worked in Alabama. Reserves are materials stored up for later use. Bauxite is mined in Arkansas. The major sulfur production of the world is centered on the Gulf Coast of Texas and Louisiana. Most of the nation's phosphate comes from Florida and Tennessee.

In contrast, the South American Humid Subtropic region does not have significant mineral deposits. Brazil's coalfields are modest. They are in the southern states of Santa Catarina and Rio Grande do Sul.

Manufacturing

✘ Several conditions are necessary for a manufacturing economy. Mines, forests, fields, and the sea are needed to provide many kinds of raw materials. Coal, petroleum, natural gas, and water are necessary to produce power. Labor and money must be available. Good transportation systems are necessary so that goods can be transported to markets.

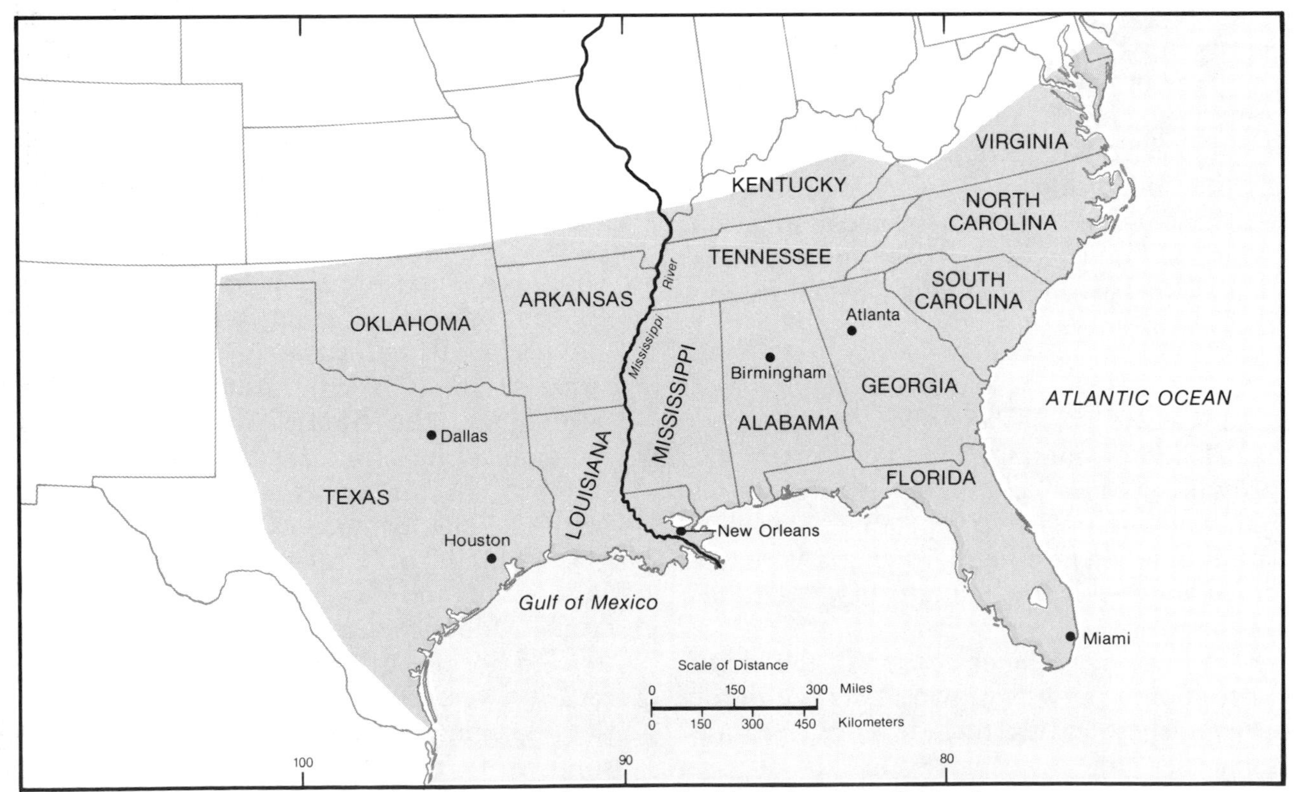

This map shows the areas in the United States that make up the North American Subtropics.

The United States South has all these conditions. As a result, the economy in this region depends on manufacturing. The textile mills of this region lead the nation in the production of cotton goods. The region is also a leader in the manufacture of rayon. Pulp and paper industries are significant. Located here are also numerous hosiery mills, furniture factories, and iron and steel plants.

✔ In contrast, not all the conditions necessary for manufacturing exist in the South American Humid Subtropics. As a result, this region is principally concerned with producing raw materials that are processed in other countries. Industry is limited to processing wheat and meat for export and textiles for local markets.

Some of the largest cities in the world have developed in the Humid Subtropic regions.

Urban Centers

Some of the largest cities of the world have developed in the Humid Subtropic regions. Industrialization has promoted this urban growth.

When the United States South was mainly an agricultural region, with cotton the major crop, most cities were small and few in number. In the last few decades, urban areas have increased in size. The largest cities of the region are Houston, Dallas, Atlanta, New Orleans, Miami, and Birmingham.

Like the North American Humid Subtropics, the South American Humid Subtropics include major cities. In contrast, however, the region has fewer urban centers. Buenos Aires has close to 12 million people and is the largest city in Argentina. A good harbor, rich soil, and land and water transportation that connects it with the rest of Argentina and the world have made it the major port and the commercial, industrial, and governmental center of Argentina. Montevideo, with over 1.4 million people, is the leading city in Uruguay. It is the center of the nation's commerce as well as the capital. Rosario, Argentina, 200 miles (320 kilometers) upstream from Buenos Aires, is the third largest city of the region, with a population of 1 million.

Tourism

Tourism is an important industry in the Humid Subtropic regions. Tourism can be described as the guiding of travelers as a business or governmental function. It is an important source of revenue. Revenue is money collected by a government.

These cypress trees in North Carolina are one of many scenes that you can see in the North American Humid Subtropics.

Each winter, thousands of people are drawn to the United States South, especially the coastal areas. Florida has become the recreation center of the region. Its tourist business brings in billions of dollars yearly. In addition to mild winters, numerous beach resorts, and sport fishing, the region's attractions include many interesting cities and historical sites.

Leading tourist and recreational centers in the South American Humid Subtropics include Buenos Aires and the beaches of Uruguay near Montevideo. Improvements in overseas transportation to this area have helped to attract tourists from around the world.

While the climate of the Humid Subtropics continues to encourage a thriving agriculture, formerly untapped raw materials and energy resources are being used to develop new industries in both regions as well. This growth has resulted in large urban centers and a flourishing tourist trade. Nevertheless, differences as well as similarities between the North and South American Humid Subtropics continue to emerge.

Recalling Facts

Reading a map/recalling details

1. Where is the North American Humid Subtropic region located?

It is located in the southeastern part of the United States.

Reading a map/recalling details

2. Where is the South American Humid Subtropic region located?

It is located in the south central part of South America.

Identifying the main idea

3. Read the paragraphs with an X next to them. Underline the sentence that tells what each paragraph is about.

Identifying cause and effect

4. Why is it too warm for snow and below-freezing temperatures in the South American Humid Subtropics?

By the time a cold air mass from the Antarctic crosses the South Atlantic and reaches the coast of South America, it is no longer very cold.

Using context clues

5. Write the letter of the correct meaning next to each word.

c	reserves	a. the guiding of travelers
a	tourism	b. money collected by a government
b	revenue	c. things stored up for later use

Interpreting Facts

Making inferences

1. Why are there fewer urban centers in the South American Humid Subtropics than in the North American Humid Subtropics?

Answers may vary. The South American Humid Subtropics offer little industry and manufacturing that would attract many people.

Inferring main idea

2. Reread the paragraph with a check mark next to it. Circle the letter of the statement that states what the paragraph is about.

a. Raw materials can easily be sent to South American markets.

(b.) In the South American Humid Subtropics, manufacturing is relatively minor.

c. In the South American Humid Subtropics, there are good transportation systems.

Skill focus

1. Complete the following chart to show the features of the North and South American Humid Subtropic regions that are alike. Skim each section of the selection to find one important similarity. Then write one sentence briefly describing it. The first one is done for you.

Comparisons

Features	North and South American Humid Subtropics
Climate	Both regions have hot, wet summers and mild winters.
Agriculture	Both regions have excellent conditions for farming and produce a variety of crops.
Urban Centers	Both regions have large cities.
Tourism	Both regions value tourism as an important industry.

2. Use the same procedure to complete the chart below to show the differences. The first one is done for you.

Contrasts

Features	North American Humid Subtropics	South American Humid Subtropics
Climate	This region has snow because of its exposure to Arctic air masses.	This region has no snow because Antarctic air masses are warmed when they cross the ocean.
Mining	Mining is a major industry in this region.	Mineral resources are limited, making mining less important in this region.
Manufacturing	This region has all the conditions necessary for heavy manufacturing.	In this region, manufacturing is not as important as exporting raw materials.
Urban Centers	This region has many large cities.	This region has only a few large cities.

▶ **Real Life Connections** Compare and contrast the climate in your area with that of the Humid Subtropics described in this lesson.

Lesson 52

Problem-Solving Pattern

Reading a Science Selection

Background Information

Yellow fever is a virus disease that was once found throughout Central America, parts of South America, Africa, and some tropical islands. It is carried by certain mosquitoes, generally from one person to another. The virus enters an infected person or animal through the mosquito bite. Then yellow fever develops after 9 to 12 days. Once a mosquito becomes infected with the virus, it can continue to transmit the disease for the rest of its life.

Although yellow fever sometimes occurs in jungle areas, especially in South America, it is now under control in most urban areas. Conquering yellow fever was one of the great achievements of modern medicine.

The following selection describes the work of several scientists involved in solving the complex problem of eliminating yellow fever. This problem-solving process took almost 60 years.

Skill Focus

You will sometimes read material in a textbook that describes how scientists solved a problem. Often, one scientist solves one part of a problem, and another scientist goes on to solve another part of the problem. In this way, scientists build on one another's work. Finally, the entire problem is solved.

When reading material that describes problem solving, think about the following questions:

1. What was the problem?
2. Who was the first scientist to work on this problem?
3. What did the first scientist find out about it?
4. What did the next scientist find out?
5. How did this information help the next scientist come closer to solving the problem?

Word Clues

Read the sentences below. Look for context clues that explain the underlined word.

> In his experiments, Pasteur <u>injected</u> half of the animals with microbes. He had first weakened these germs in his laboratory and then forced them into the animals' bodies through a hollow needle.

The word *injected* in the first sentence is explained in the sentence following it. This sentence gives details to help you understand the meaning of the word *injected.*

Detail context clues are often found in the sentence that comes before or after the unknown word. Use **detail** context clues to find the meaning of the three underlined words in the selection.

Strategy Tip

Before you read the selection, preview it. The headings identify seven scientists whose work contributed to wiping out yellow fever. Keep track of how each scientist built on the work of another. As you read, think about the five questions in the Skill Focus. These questions will help you understand the problem-solving process.

How Scientists Solved the Problem of Yellow Fever

Yellow fever is a disease caused by a germ. Yellow fever can damage the liver and cause the sick person's skin to take on a yellow color. The disease usually begins with fever, dizziness, headache, and muscle aches. The sick person sometimes falls into a coma and dies.

In the past, yellow fever killed many people in Central America, South America, Africa, and on tropical islands. The discoveries of several scientists who worked separately helped wipe out yellow fever.

Louis Pasteur

Louis Pasteur

Louis Pasteur was the first scientist who did a great deal of work with **microbes** (MY krohbz). Microbes are living things that cannot be seen without a microscope. Pasteur had two problems to solve. He wanted to find out if microbes cause disease. He also wanted to see if microbes could be used to prevent disease. He experimented with cattle, chickens, and other disease-carrying animals.

In his experiments, Pasteur injected half of the animals with microbes. He had first weakened the microbes in his laboratory and then forced them into the animals' bodies through a hollow needle. The microbes were too weak to make the injected animals very sick. The other half of the group of animals was not injected.

The animals that were not injected usually caught the disease and died. The animals that were injected did not catch the disease. Pasteur believed that the injected animals had developed an **immunity** (i MYOON ə tee) to the disease. This means that their bodies were able to fight it off.

By this experiment, Pasteur proved two things. He proved that microbes cause some diseases. He also proved that weakened microbes injected into animals prevented the animals from getting these diseases. He called this method of fighting off disease *vaccination.*

Charles A. Laveran

Charles A. Laveran

Fifteen years passed after Pasteur's discovery, and still no one knew what caused yellow fever. In 1880, Charles A. Laveran, a French army doctor, studied the blood of people who had yellow fever. He discovered the yellow fever microbe in their blood. This was proof that yellow fever was caused by a microbe. The problem that remained was to find out where the microbe came from and how it got into the blood.

Carlos Finlay

Carlos Finlay

Carlos Finlay, a Cuban doctor, had the idea that a mosquito carried the yellow fever microbe. Dr. Finlay reported this idea in 1881. However, he did not prove it.

Ronald Ross

Ronald Ross

Ronald Ross, a British doctor, began researching the cause of malaria in 1894. After two years, he found traces of the disease in the stomach of the mosquito that had fed on the blood of a person who had malaria. By identifying these tiny amounts of malaria microbes, Dr. Ross had proved that one kind of mosquito carries the germ that causes malaria.

Walter Reed

Walter Reed

In 1900, the United States Army chose a group of men to study yellow fever in Cuba. This disease had recently swept across the island, causing hundreds of deaths. Dr. Walter Reed headed the group of three doctors who made the study.

Dr. Reed's first problem was to find out if the disease was carried in the bedding and clothing of a person who had yellow fever. He watched and questioned people who had the disease. He looked at their bedding and clothing under a microscope. He observed hundreds of cases. His conclusion was that yellow fever microbes were not carried in this way.

Dr. Reed then tried to find out if certain mosquitoes carried yellow fever. To solve this problem, Dr. Reed had mosquitoes bite people who had yellow fever. He then let these same mosquitoes bite some of his fellow doctors and several soldiers who had volunteered for the experiment. All of his coworkers who had been bitten by these mosquitoes caught yellow fever. Two of them died as a result of this daring experiment. The experiment established proof that certain mosquitoes carry yellow fever.

William Gorgas

William Gorgas

The next step was to find out how to control mosquitoes that carried yellow fever. William Gorgas, an army doctor, knew that mosquitoes breed in filth, trash heaps, garbage dumps, unused wells, old tin cans, barnyard puddles, ponds, and swamps. With this information, he began a program to clean up Cuba. This helped stop the **epidemic** (ep ə DEM ik) of yellow fever on this island. An epidemic is widespread disease. Gorgas then went on to Panama and wiped out yellow fever there.

Max Theiler

Max Theiler

In 1937, Max Theiler, a South African doctor, tried to find a way to prevent yellow fever even if mosquitoes remain that carry the microbe. He developed a vaccine that prevents yellow fever.

Today yellow fever is under control in most areas of the world. Although the disease cannot be treated, better sanitary conditions and a vaccination can help prevent its spread.

RECALLING FACTS

Recalling details

1. In what areas did yellow fever occur?

Yellow fever occurred in Central America, South America, Africa, and on tropical islands.

Recalling details

2. What are microbes?

Microbes are living things that cannot be seen without a microscope.

Recalling details

3. How much time passed between Pasteur's work and Laveran's work?

Fifteen years had passed.

Recalling details

4. Where did Dr. Reed study yellow fever?

He studied it in Cuba.

Recalling details

5. What does it mean if you have immunity to a disease?

It means that your body can fight it off.

Using context clues

6. Fill in the circle next to the word that correctly completes each sentence.

a. Some ________ of poison were found in the dead woman's coffee cup.

○ microbes
○ germs
● traces

b. Winning every game of the season ________ the Blue Stars as the best soccer team.

● established
○ injected
○ experimented

c. The new teacher ________ the students in the classroom, in the lunchroom, and on the playground.

○ injected
● observed
○ established

INTERPRETING FACTS

Making inferences

1. In his experiment, why did Louis Pasteur need a group of animals that were not injected with weakened microbes?

Answers may vary. He wanted to prove that the injected animals could fight off the disease, while the other animals could not.

Making inferences

2. Why are vaccinations an important method to fight the spread of diseases?

Answers may vary. Doctors could use vaccinations to prevent people from catching a disease by making them immune to it. As a result, they cannot spread the disease.

Making inferences

3. Where do you think Carlos Finlay got the idea that mosquitoes might carry the yellow fever microbe?

Answers may vary. He probably knew about the work of Pasteur and Laveran

Making inferences

4. Where do you think Walter Reed got the idea that mosquitoes might spread yellow fever?

Answers may vary. He had probably learned about Carlos Finlay's conclusions that identified mosquitoes as the primary carrier of the yellow fever microbe. This was reported in 1881.

Skill Focus

Use the information in the selection to complete the following chart.

Name	Problem(s)	Findings
Louis Pasteur	Can microbes cause disease? Can they prevent disease?	Microbes cause some diseases. Weakened microbes can be used to prevent animals from getting some diseases.
Charles A. Laveran	What causes yellow fever?	Yellow fever is caused by a microbe.
Carlos Finlay	Does a mosquito carry the yellow fever microbe?	The conclusion was not proved.
Ronald Ross	Do mosquitoes carry microbes that cause disease?	One kind of mosquito carried microbes that cause malaria.
Walter Reed	Is yellow fever carried in the bedding and clothing of a person who has yellow fever? Do certain mosquitoes carry yellow fever?	Yellow fever microbes are not carried in this way. Certain mosquitoes carry yellow fever.
William Gorgas	How can mosquitoes be controlled?	Mosquitoes can be controlled by cleaning up trash heaps, swamps, and so on. This can help stop yellow fever.
Max Theiler	Can a vaccine be developed to prevent yellow fever?	He developed a vaccine that prevents yellow fever.

▶ Real Life Connections Discuss how a problem affecting life in your school or your community was solved.

Lesson 53

Graphs

Reading a Mathematics Selection

Background Information

Imagine that you are collecting quarters, dimes, nickels, and pennies in a jar for a year. After the year is up, you will probably want to find out how much money you have saved.

Well, it would be very difficult to tell how much you have by looking at the coins in the jar. You will probably want to separate the coins into piles of quarters, dimes, nickels, and pennies, and then stack the coins one on top of the other.

Now that you have neat stacks, it will be easier to count how much money you have. You will also be able to make comparisons about how many quarters you have as compared to the number of dimes that you have, for example. What you have done is taken steps to organize your coins. In a way, this is what graphs do. They take a large amount of information, organize it, and present it. Graphs allow people to look at a lot of information in a quick and easy way.

There are several different types of graphs, including circle graphs, picture graphs, line graphs, and bar graphs. You would choose one type of graph over the others, depending on the type of information that you have.

You will see these different types of graphs in a variety of places. For this reason, it is important to learn how to read and interpret the information that is presented in graphs.

In this selection, you will read about several types of graphs.

Skill Focus

Graphs can show information very clearly. You can read a graph much more quickly than you can read a paragraph that gives the same information. Graphs also make it easier for you to compare information. For example, by reading certain population graphs, you can easily see how the number of people living in a country changes from year to year.

Different kinds of graphs are used for different purposes. Bar graphs and line graphs show numbers or amounts. Bar graphs are useful for comparing facts. Line graphs are useful for showing facts that change over a period of time.

Before you can use the details in a graph, you need to know the purpose of the graph. You also need to understand the kinds of information that are given in the graph. Then you will be able to use the information in a variety of ways.

Word Clues

When reading the following selection, look for these important words: *data, horizontal, vertical, axis, label.*

These words will help you understand more about graphs.

Strategy Tip

In this selection, you will read about three types of bar graphs and one type of line graph. Read the title of each graph before you read the graph itself. Also, take time to understand what the label on each axis stands for.

Reading Graphs

Graphs give a picture of information, or **data.** They help you to understand information by presenting it visually.

Horizontal Bar Graphs

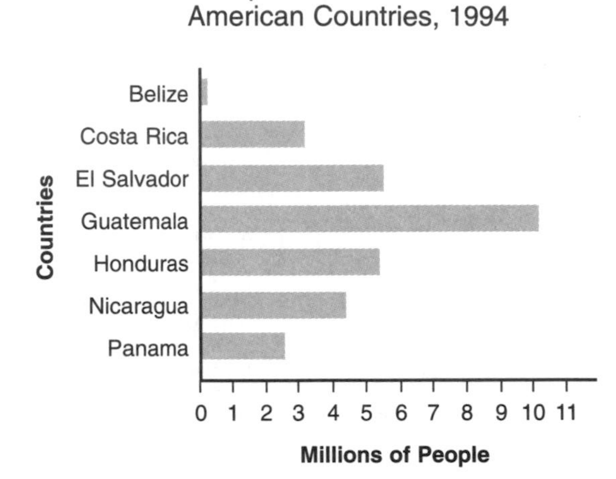

This is a **horizontal bar graph.** The bars that show data run across the graph from left to right.

The first thing that you should read is the title. The title tells what kind of information is shown in the graph. The title of this graph is *Population of Central American Countries, 1994.*

The two sides of the graph that give information are called the **vertical axis** and the **horizontal axis.** The vertical axis runs up and down.

It is important to read the labels for each axis before you read the rest of the graph. In this graph, the vertical axis is labeled *Countries.* It lists the countries whose populations are given. The horizontal axis is labeled *Millions of People.* It has the numbers 0 through 11. Each number stands for millions. The number 2 stands for 2 million people. The number 7 stands for 7 million people.

When you read a bar graph, look at each bar. In this graph, the length of each bar shows the population of one country. For example, one bar shows that Honduras has a population of just over 5 million people. Another bar shows that Guatemala's population is over 10 million people.

This bar graph is more useful than a list of numbers because you can quickly compare the populations of the countries. It is easy to see that Belize has the smallest population. Guatemala has the largest population. You can also see that there are three countries whose populations are greater than 5 million people. Because the bars for Honduras and El Salvador are the same length, you know that they have populations that are about the same.

Vertical Bar Graphs

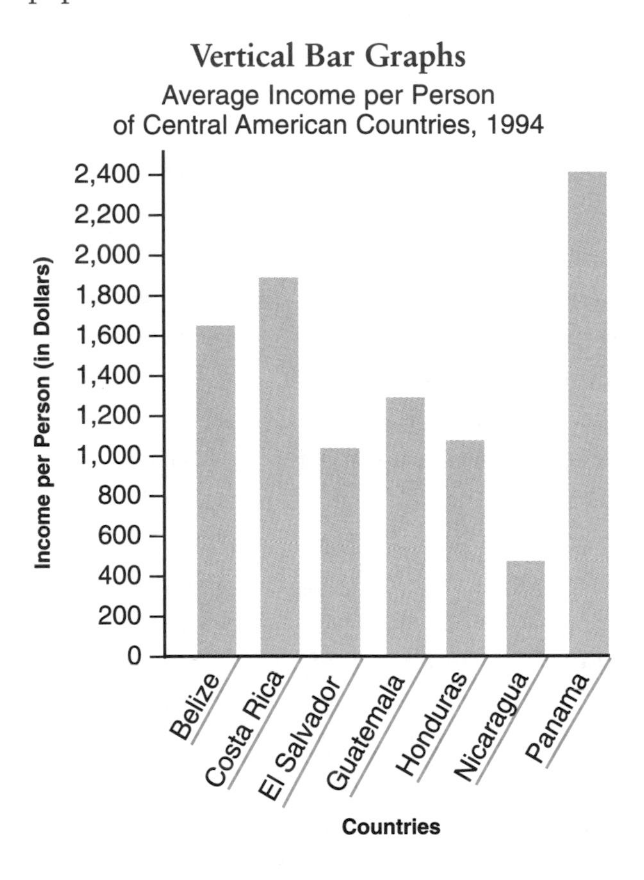

This is a **vertical bar graph.** The bars that show data are vertical. They run up and down the graph, like columns.

The title tells that this graph shows the 1994 average income per person in Central American countries. Average income is figured by dividing each country's total income for the year 1994 by the number of people living in the country. The vertical axis is labeled *Income per Person.* This is the amount of income in dollars. The horizontal axis is labeled *Countries.* Each bar shows the average income per person of a country. The graph shows that Panama has the greatest average income per person. Honduras and El Salvador have average incomes per person that are about the same. Nicaragua has the smallest average income per person.

Double Bar Graphs

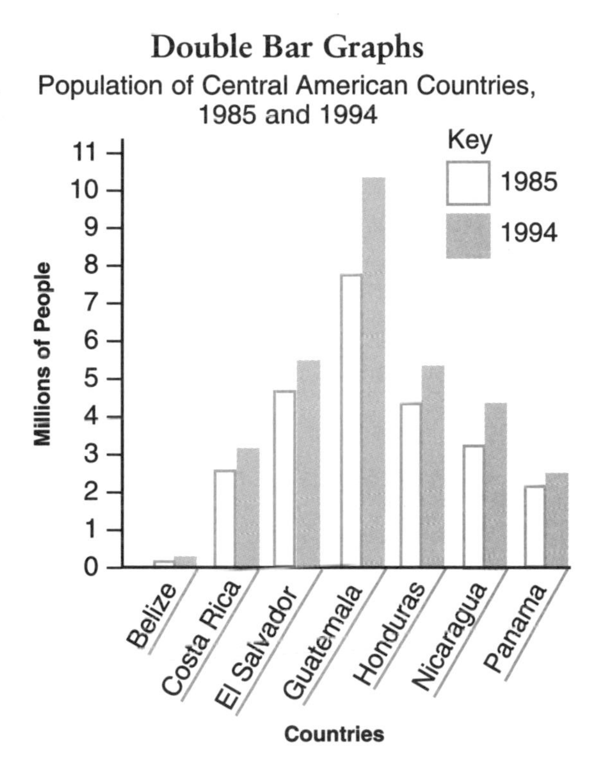

The graph above is a **double bar graph.** It has two bars for each country shown. A double bar graph shows a comparison. This graph compares the populations of each country at two different periods of time.

Read the title of the graph. Then read the labels on the vertical axis and the horizontal axis. There is also a key on this graph. The key tells what the bars stand for. The white bars stand for the 1985 populations of the countries. The green bars stand for the 1994 populations of the countries.

A double bar graph can show a great deal of information. This one shows the population of seven countries in both 1985 and 1994. It also shows that the population of each country has increased from 1985 to 1994 and which countries had the greatest increases. Guatemala had the greatest increase in its population.

Line Graphs

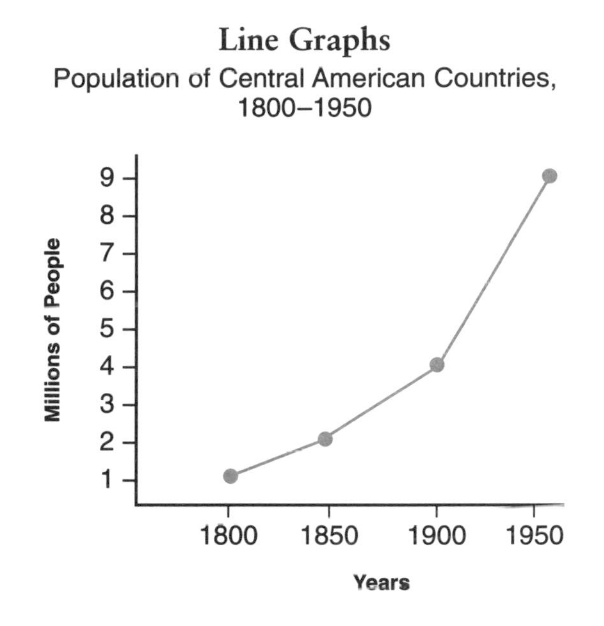

This is a **line graph.** Dots are used to show the population of all Central American countries at certain times. The dots are connected with straight lines. By connecting the dots, it is easy to tell the pattern of population change over a period of time. Line graphs are used to show change.

The title of this line graph is *Population of Central American Countries, 1800–1950.* Like the bar graphs, it has a vertical axis and a horizontal axis. Both are labeled. Using this graph, you can easily see that the population of Central America steadily increased between 1800 and 1950. You can also see that the increase between 1800 and 1850 was much smaller than the increase between 1900 and 1950. You can find that the population passed the 3 million mark sometime between 1850 and 1900.

Recalling Facts

Recalling details
1. What does the title of a graph tell?
It tells what information is shown in the graph.

Recalling details
2. What are the three types of bar graphs discussed in this selection?
horizontal, vertical, double

Recalling details
3. Why is a key necessary in a double bar graph?
It tells what the two kinds of bars mean.

Recalling details
4. What does a double bar graph show?
comparisons

Reading graphs

5. Titles of two graphs are listed below. Underline the title of the graph that is probably a line graph.

Population of European Countries

Daily High Temperature in Central America

Reading graphs

6. Using the line graph in the selection, would you say that the population of Central America will probably increase or decrease in the next 50 years?

increase

Interpreting Facts

Making inferences

1. In a line graph, why do the numbers on the vertical axis and the horizontal axis have to be equally spaced?

Answers may vary. Each space represents a number of equal value.

Making inferences

2. What are some reasons that bar graphs are more useful than a list of numbers?

Answers may vary. Comparisons are easier to make. Differences are easier to see. Changes are easier to see.

Skill Focus

A. Use the graphs in the selection to answer the following questions.

1. Which three countries have an average income per person that is greater than $1,500?

Belize, Costa Rica, and Panama

2. About how many people lived in Honduras in 1994?

5 million

3. What is the title of the double bar graph?

Population of Central American Countries, 1985 and 1994

4. Is the double bar graph horizontal or vertical?

vertical

B. Use the graph below to answer the questions that follow.

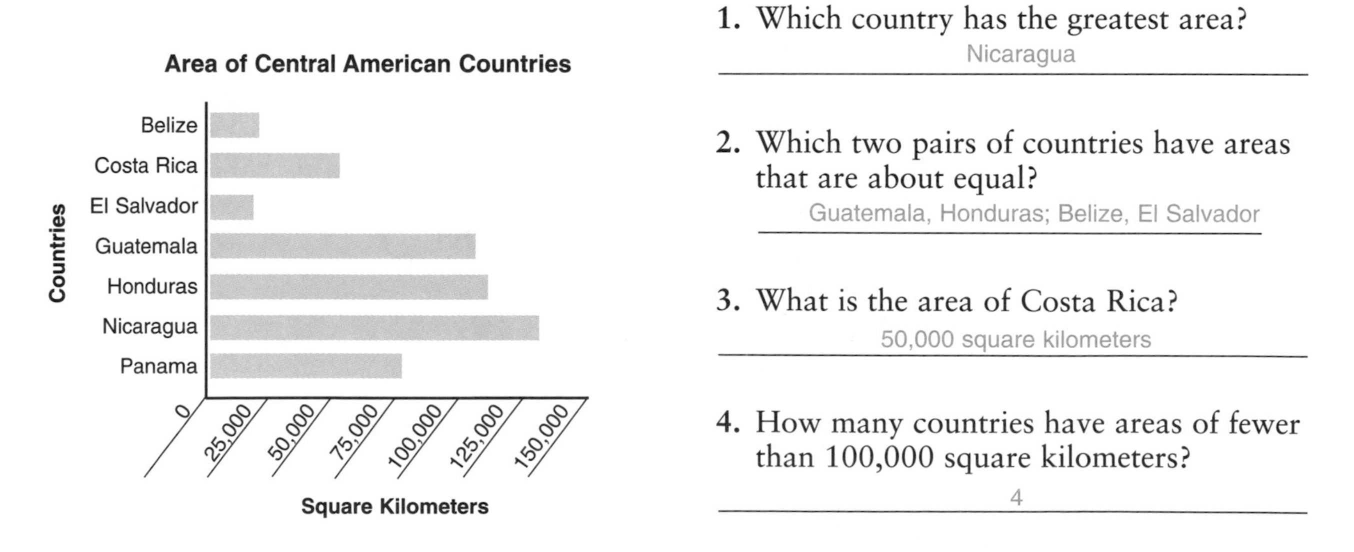

1. Which country has the greatest area?

Nicaragua

2. Which two pairs of countries have areas that are about equal?

Guatemala, Honduras; Belize, El Salvador

3. What is the area of Costa Rica?

50,000 square kilometers

4. How many countries have areas of fewer than 100,000 square kilometers?

4

▶ **Real Life Connections** Name two instances for which a graph would be useful at home or in school.

Lesson 54

Accented Syllable and Schwa

When words contain two syllables, usually one of the syllables is stressed, or accented, more than the other when you pronounce it. For example, the first syllable in the word *picnic* is said with more stress than the second syllable. In most dictionaries, the **accent mark** (') is placed at the end of the syllable that is said with more stress.

Words that have three syllables usually are accented on one of the first two syllables. When you are trying to pronounce a word with three syllables, say the word with more stress on the first syllable. If the word does not sound right, say it again, giving the most stress to the second syllable. This will help you in deciding how to pronounce the word.

Say each of the following words to yourself. Write an accent mark after the syllable that should be stressed.

thun' der	syl' la ble	sat' in
moc' ca sin	top' ic	con tin' ue
sol' dier	ter' ri ble	ru' by
prac' tice	am' ber	va' por
Co lum' bus	ex am' ple	con di' tion
in form'	trop' i cal	dis com' fort
dif' fi cult	ma chine'	re mem' ber

The vowels *a, e, i, o,* and *u* can all have the same sound. This is a soft sound like a short *u* pronounced lightly.

Pronounce *around.* Did the *a* sound like a soft, short *u*? yes

Pronounce *harden.* Did the *e* sound like a soft, short *u*? yes

Pronounce *animal.* Did the *i* sound like a soft, short *u*? yes

Pronounce *collect.* Did the *o* sound like a soft, short *u*? yes

Pronounce *circus.* Did the *u* sound like a soft, short *u*? yes

This short, soft *u* sound is called the **schwa** sound. In dictionary respellings, the symbol ə stands for the schwa sound. If you look up the word *lament* in the dictionary, you will find it respelled this way: lə ment'.

Say each of the words below to yourself. Write an accent mark after the syllable that is accented. Then circle the letter that stands for the schwa sound.

(a) cross'	cor' (a)l	fall' (e)n
c(o)m pel'	(a) light'	com' m(o)n
but' t(o)n	pan' d(a)	li' (o)n
car' (a) van	prob' (a) bly	car' r(o)t

Look at the words in the list above. Does the schwa sound come in the accented or unaccented syllable? Write the correct word in the sentence below.

The schwa sound always falls in an unaccented syllable of a word.

Lesson 55

Unstated Main Idea

When you read for information, you often find the main idea of each paragraph stated in a sentence. The supporting details, which give more information about the main idea, are found in the rest of the paragraph.

Sometimes, the main idea of the paragraph is not stated. You may need to figure out, or infer, the main idea yourself. To do this, think about the supporting details. Then think of a sentence that summarizes them.

Read the following selection. Think about whether the main idea of each paragraph is stated or unstated.

Horses

1. There are more than 150 breeds and types of horses and ponies. The breeds vary greatly in size, strength, and speed. The smallest breed is the Fallabella, which grows only 30 inches (75 centimeters) high. The largest breed is the Shire, which may measure more then 68 inches (170 centimeters) high.

2. Percherons, a kind of draft horse, once pulled heavy plows on farms. Other draft horses, such as Belgians, were used to haul freight wagons from town to town. Suffolk, a smaller draft horse, was a favorite for pulling milk wagons.

3. Southern plantation owners developed the American Saddle Horse and the Tennessee Walking Horse for pleasure riding. The owners wanted mounts that were comfortable to ride. Tennessee Walking Horses are especially noted for their comfortable running walk and smooth and easy pace. Morgans were originally used as harness horses for pulling carriages. After the automobile became popular, breeders developed the Morgan into an excellent pleasure riding horse.

4. Horses that roam freely in parts of the western United States are called wild horses. At one time, they were actually tame horses. Spanish explorers, American Indians, and cowhands of the Old West rode these horses. The horses escaped from their owners and eventually formed bands. In the early 1900s, more than 2 million of these horses roamed the West. But people rounded up many of them to make room for farms and ranches. Only about 20,000 wild horses roam the West today.

For each paragraph in the selection, if the main idea is stated, write the word *stated* on the lines provided. If the main idea is unstated, choose a sentence from the list below that gives the main idea of the paragraph and write its letter on the lines provided.

a. Draft horses are the tallest and heaviest group of horses.
b. Draft horses once supplied much of the power needed for jobs that trucks and tractors do today.
c. Federal laws now prohibit the killing of wild horses.
d. Fallabella were originally bred in Argentina and are kept as pets.
e. The most popular breeds used for pleasure riding include the American Saddle Horse, Tennessee Walking Horse, and Morgan.
f. Morgan horses were also used in harness racing.

Paragraph 1. stated

Paragraph 2. b

Paragraph 3. e

Paragraph 4. stated

Now go back to the paragraphs that have a stated main idea and circle the sentence in each paragraph that states the main idea.

Lesson 56

Making Inferences

To answer the questions following the selection, you will have to **infer**, or figure out, the answers. To infer the correct answers, you need to put together what you read in the selection with what you already know. Then you can figure out more information about the selection.

Emma Lazarus

Emma Lazarus was born in 1849. As a child, she was different from her six sisters and brothers. She was not interested in sports and games. She was serious and frail. More than anything, she wanted to write great poetry. She read the work of famous poets and dreamed that someday her poetry would be like theirs.

When Emma was older, she went to Ward's Island. There she worked tirelessly to help the refugees who were streaming into New York City. Many of these people had been persecuted in their own countries. Now they came to the United States seeking freedom. Emma felt sorry for them and started a group to aid them.

Emma continued to write poetry. She became famous, as more and more people read and loved her work. One day, she was asked to help raise money for the pedestal for the Statue of Liberty that was to be placed on Bedloe's Island in New York Harbor. Famous writers were asked to contribute pieces from their writings to be sold at auction. Emma agreed to help with the project. She decided to write a sonnet about the statue itself.

Emma Lazarus's poem, "The New Colossus," became famous the world over. In 1903, her words were engraved on the pedestal of the statue. Millions of immigrants coming to America in search of a new life read the stirring words. For the immigrants, the poem became as much of a symbol as the statue of a new land waiting for them, a land full of promise for a new beginning.

Give me your tired, your poor,
Your huddled masses yearning to breathe free,
The wretched refuse of your teeming shore.
Send these, the homeless, tempest-tossed to me,
I lift my lamp beside the golden door!

1. Why was Emma Lazarus sometimes called the "Champion of Immigrants"?

   She wrote the words carved on the pedestal of the Statue of Liberty. She also worked on Ward's Island to help the refugees.

2. Why was it so appropriate that Emma Lazarus's poem was chosen to be engraved on the pedestal of the Statue of Liberty?

   Besides being a famous poet, she had worked with the immigrants and knew their problems.

3. Why was New York Harbor chosen as the site for the statue?

   It was the first place in the United States that most immigrants saw.

4. When do you think Emma Lazarus wrote her poem? How can you tell?

   The poem was engraved on the pedestal in 1903, so Emma wrote it before that date.

Lesson 57

Propaganda

A statement of fact can be checked and proven to be true. This is a statement of fact: The Cupcakes' newest album has sold 10,000 copies. A statement of opinion tells what someone thinks is true. Here is a statement of opinion: The Cupcakes' newest album is the best album ever made.

If people believe that their opinions are important enough, they may try to persuade others to agree with them. When people try to persuade others to believe something, do something, or buy something, they are using **propaganda**. Most advertisements use some kind of propaganda to convince people to buy a certain product. Propaganda is also used by political candidates to convince people to vote for them.

The different types of propaganda have names. As you read the examples of three types, ask yourself, "Is this statement supported by facts?"

1. **Name Calling:** This device gives a bad name to people or products so that other people will avoid them.
Example: If you don't mind wrinkled shirts, buy Miller's Wash-'n'-Wear Shirts.

2. **Glad Names:** This device states good things about the listeners or readers so that they will agree with what they hear or read.
Example: A smart person like you knows that Oatsies are good for you.

3. **Testimonial:** This device uses the name of a well-known person so that people will do a certain thing because the person they admire says that it is a good thing to do.
Example: Use Bubble-Glo Shampoo. Famous movie star Lulu Cleo says it is terrific.

Read the following statements. On the first line after each, write the type of propaganda used. On the second line, write the word or words from the statement that make it that type of propaganda.

1. Stan Waters, Rookie of the Year, eats a bowl of Strackles every morning. You, too, can be a superstar! Switch to Strackles.
Testimonial
Rookie of the Year

2. I am convinced that you, as intelligent, thoughtful, patriotic people, will vote for me in the coming election.
Glad Names
intelligent, thoughtful, patriotic

3. You can buy that one if you like, but it's a real gas-burner. The body is about as strong as a tin can. Come over here, and I'll show you a really good car.
Name Calling
gas-burner, strong as a tin can

4. If you want Lou Power to be class president, that's your business. But I think you should know that Lou is a born liar.
Name Calling
born liar

5. Our survey shows that you are highly successful in your business. Join other famous people who subscribe to our weekly newsletter *Facts of Finance*.
Glad Names
highly successful, famous

6. What is the secret of Tina Tappler's unique voice? She gargles three times a day with Phizzmore. Try it!
Testimonial
unique voice

Lesson 58

Skimming for Information

When you are looking for specific information in a selection that you have already read, it is not necessary to reread every word. You can save a lot of time by **skimming** for the facts that you need.

If you have to answer factual questions, find the key words in the question. The key words will tell you what information or facts to look for. Use the headings in the selection to help organize your search. Because you have already read the selection, you know what information is covered in the paragraphs that follow each heading. When you find the section that has the information that you are looking for, stop and reread that material. Look for the key words in your question. Remember to reread only as much as necessary to get the information that is needed.

Read the following selection.

America's Favorite City

On the northern Pacific coast of California is one of the world's most interesting cities, San Francisco. It lies directly south of the Golden Gate Strait at the entrance to San Francisco Bay. San Francisco has a charm that makes it different from any other city. It is this special charm that attracts millions of tourists to the city each year.

Location and Climate

San Francisco is on a hilly peninsula that stretches 30 miles southward along San Francisco Bay. The city covers an area of 46 square miles (119 square kilometers). San Francisco also includes several islands in the Pacific Ocean and in San Francisco Bay. Alcatraz, an island in the bay, was once the site of a federal prison. It is now a tourist attraction.

San Francisco has a moderate climate. It is relatively mild in winter and cool in summer. The temperature rarely rises to 70° Fahrenheit (21° Celsius) or drops to 30° Fahrenheit (-1° Celsius). The sun shines in San Francisco an average of 66 of every 100 daylight hours. Nevertheless, San Francisco has become well known for its fog.

History

The Costanoan Indians lived in what is now the San Francisco area long before Europeans arrived. In 1542, Juan Cabrillo sailed past San Francisco Bay without noticing it, and, in 1602, Sebastian Vizcaino did the same. The fog that often lies along the Pacific Coast probably prevented early European navigators from finding the entrance to the bay. In 1579, the English

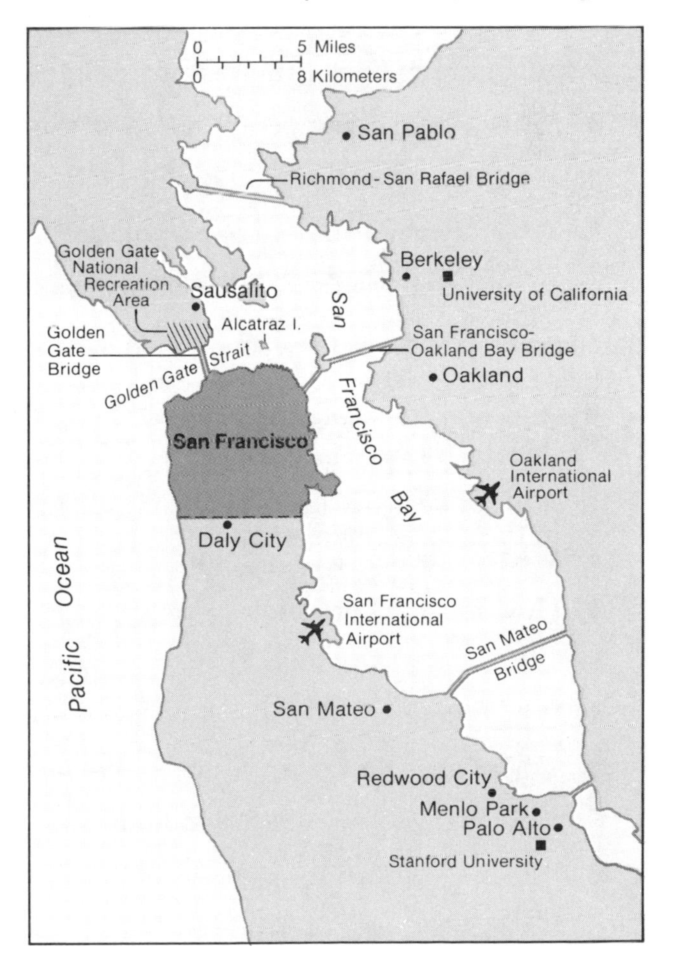

explorer Sir Francis Drake also sailed by the bay.

In 1769, members of a Spanish expedition led by Gaspar de Portola traveled up the coast overland and became the first white people to climb the hills and see the bay. It was not until the late eighteenth century that Spaniards started a settlement there.

Government

San Francisco was incorporated as a city in 1850. The legislative branch of the government has an 11-member board of supervisors. The mayor and the chief administrative officer, who is appointed by the mayor, head the administrative branch. The voters elect the mayor and the members of the board of supervisors to four-year terms.

The city government gets most of its income from real estate taxes. The remaining funds that the city needs come from state and federal grants and from city bond sales.

Economy

Industry is a major source of income in San Francisco. Food processing is the chief industrial activity. Among the other important industries are shipbuilding and the manufacture of clothing and other textile products. The city is one of the leading printing and publishing centers in the United States.

About a fifth of San Francisco's workers are employed in retail and wholesale trade. The biggest group are the workers who run the restaurants, hotels, and other businesses that serve the tourist trade. Several million tourists visit San Francisco yearly. They contribute close to a half billion dollars to the city's annual income.

A. Read the following questions. Underline the key words that tell the information you should look for. Then skim the headings in the selection. On the line provided, write the heading under which you would find the answer to each question.

1. Who led the first European expedition to San Francisco Bay? History
2. What are two important industries in San Francisco? Economy
3. Who were the first people to live in the San Francisco area? History
4. How many members are on the board of supervisors? Government
5. Which explorer missed San Francisco Bay? History
6. What is the weather like in San Francisco? Location and Climate

B. Skim the paragraphs in each section to locate the facts that answer the following questions. Underline the key words in each question, and then use the headings to locate the information. Write the answer to each question on the line provided.

1. In what year did Europeans first see San Francisco Bay? 1769
2. What is the city's chief industrial activity? food processing
3. How much money do tourists spend in San Francisco each year? close to a half billion dollars
4. Which famous island lies in San Francisco Bay? Alcatraz
5. Where does the city government get most of its income? real estate taxes
6. How many tourists visit San Francisco yearly? several million
7. Which American Indian tribe lived in San Francisco? Costanoan
8. What is the area of San Francisco? 46 square miles

Lesson 59

Choosing the Correct Meaning

When you look up the meaning of an unfamiliar word in a dictionary, you may find that the word has several definitions. Read all of the definitions. Then find the meaning that fits the context of what you are reading. Always read all the definitions of a word before you decide on the correct meaning.

Read each entry word and its definitions below. Following the definitions are three sentences, each with an underlined word. Find the correct meaning for the underlined word. Write the number of this meaning on the line provided. The first one has been started for you.

bank 1 a business place where money is held, exchanged, or loaned. **2** the land along the sides of a river. **3** a shallow place in a sea.

a. Ms. Lorca put her money in the bank for safekeeping. ___1___

b. Kevin enjoyed sitting on the bank of the river and watching the ships go by. ___2___

c. The ship ran aground on the sand bank. ___3___

cane 1 the slender stem of some plants. **2** a walking stick. **3** thin strips of rattan used for the seats of chairs.

a. Mr. Pappas sprained his ankle. He had to use a cane. ___2___

b. Mrs. Howe took her chairs to a shop to be mended. The cane seats had worn out. ___3___

c. Sara picked the ripe berries from the raspberry cane. ___1___

crop 1 any farm product grown in the soil, such as cotton, corn, or fruit. **2** a pouch in the neck of some birds where food is first digested. **3** hair cut very short.

a. Mrs. Robinson, a farmer, had a fine crop of wheat this year. ___1___

b. Insects and worms may be found in the crop of a robin. ___2___

c. You will feel cooler in the summer if you have a close crop. ___3___

mine 1 a pit from which precious stones, coal, or other minerals are taken by digging. **2** a large supply or store of something. **3** an explosive hidden in water or ground to destroy enemy ships or troops.

a. Mr. Putnam had a mine of rare, old paintings. ___2___

b. Our battleships watched closely for mines during World War II. ___3___

c. Three people were shut in a coal mine without food for several days. ___1___

plain 1 easy to understand. **2** without beauty; homely. **3** not fancy; not much decorated.

a. Mr. Morse was a very plain man. ___2___

b. The teacher explained the problem until it was quite plain to the class. ___1___

c. Bob served a plain cake for dessert. ___3___

yard 1 a measure of length. **2** a small space in front or back of a house or barn. **3** a place in the open where work or business is carried on.

a. Marina planted some roses in the yard of her home. ___2___

b. Mr. Sampson works in a railroad yard. ___3___

c. It took five yards of cloth to make Rosa's new dress. ___1___

Lesson 60

Using the Yellow Pages

What can you do if you need the phone number of a certain business in your town? You look up the business's number in the yellow pages of the phone book. Businesses are grouped together under headings. All of the same kinds of businesses are listed under the same heading. Every heading in the yellow pages is listed in alphabetical order. You can find the right heading using the guide words at the top of each page. Businesses are listed alphabetically under the headings. After the business's name, its address and phone number are given. Some businesses advertise in the yellow pages to provide information other than their address and phone number.

Look at the sample yellow page on page 175.

A. Using the yellow page, answer each question on the line provided.

1. Which travel agency is located on North Country Road in Baldwin? Sun and Fun Vacations
2. What phone number can you call to get a trailer to transport a pony? 555-3730
3. Which travel agency has offices in two different towns? Friendly Travel Service
4. What is Janet Plummer's phone number? 555-2000
5. Which travel agency is open until 9:00 P.M. six days a week? Go-Away Tours

B. Circle the letter of the phrase that completes each sentence.

1. Using the Travel Bug advertisement, you can learn the following information:
   a. its address, its phone number, the kinds of trips it specializes in, and the length of the trips
   (b.) its address, its phone number, the kinds of trips it specializes in, and the year it was started
   c. its address, its phone number, the countries it specializes in, and the year it was started

2. You want a travel brochure about Mexico. You plan to be on Jericho Turnpike this afternoon. You can use the yellow pages to find out that
   a. the only travel agency on Jericho Turnpike is Go-Away Tours.
   b. you can call the Foreign Travel Association to ask if it has any information.
   (c.) two travel agencies are located on Jericho Turnpike.

3. To get some information about ski trips, you can call
   (a.) Adventures in Travel at 555–2000 and Travel Bug at 555–1111.
   b. South American Adventures at 555–6265 and Travel Bug at 555–1111.
   c. Adventures in Travel at 555–2000 and Lake Grove Travel Center at 555–8199.

4. If you have two broken legs and have to travel somewhere, you might want to contact Lake Grove Travel Center because
   a. it used to be the Lilly Morgan Travel Agency.
   (b.) it can hire an aide to travel with you.
   c. it can rent an automobile for you so that you can travel first class.

5. The three travel agencies that can help you plan a trip to South America are
   (a.) Go-Away Tours, South American Adventures, and Travel Bureau of South America.
   b. Inter Country Tours, Sayville Travel, and South American Adventures.
   c. Adventures in Travel, Foreign Travel Association, and South American Adventures.

Trailer Renting & Leasing (3) (cont'd)

Riverhead Campers
3922 Jessup La Baldwin 555–0112
Trailer City
903 Ketchum St Oakton 555–4438
U-Haul-It Trailer Rentals
644 Hampton Bay Rd Hampton 555–8428
2000 Bellport Av Sayville 555–6347

Trailers-Horse

Long Island Horse Trailers
404 Farmhouse Rd Hampton 555–3730

Travel Agencies & Bureaus

ADVENTURES IN TRAVEL
See Our Ad
243 Deer Park Av Baldwin 555–2000
Asian Travel Agency
142 E Broadway Sayville 555–6628
Budget Travel
921 Norwalk Av Baldwin 555–8312

Foreign Travel Association
1653 Jericho Trnpk Oakton 555–8316

FRIENDLY TRAVEL SERVICE
Complete Travel Planning
Vacations or Business Trips
2 Convenient Locations
Hampton
555–1400
201 E. Main St.
Oakton
555–3300
In the Oakton Mall

Ginger Peachy Tours & Travel
43 Scottsdale Av Sayville 555–3322
GO-AWAY TOURS, INC.
See Our Ad
1709 Jericho Trnpk Oakton 555–0044
Inter Country Tours
Individual or Group Travel Experts
1888 Bellport Av Sayville 555–1289
LAKE GROVE TRAVEL CENTER
See Our Ad
2400 Lake Grove Rd Hampton 555–8199
Sayville Travel
Central Shopping Plaza Sayville 555–0606
SOUTH AMERICAN ADVENTURES
See Our Ad
41 Brookhaven St Hampton 555–6265
Sun and Fun Vacations
819 N Country Rd Baldwin 555–8133
Travel Associates
945 Wheeler St Oakton 555–8477
TRAVEL BUG
See Our Ad
724 W Broadway Sayville 555–1111
Travel Bureau of South America
6406 Wellwood Av Oakton................. 555–7000

For a trip to remember, call

Context Clue Words

The following words are treated as context clue words in the lessons indicated. Lessons that provide instruction in a particular context clue type include an activity requiring students to use context clues to derive word meanings. Context clue words appear in the literature, social studies, and science selections and are underlined for ease of location.

Word	Lesson
activist	12
altitude	21
anaconda	50
anthropologist	21
brittle	2
bullfighters	41
catastrophe	43
centavos	41
condors	21
contracting	3
demonstrate	13
descent	21
destructive	43
donated	20
drive	20
economy	42
employ	30
encouraged	30
engrossed	1
established	52
expanding	3
extend	3
fiesta	41
fleeing	1
gash	2
gauze	13
genealogy	12
generators	22
griot	12
hieroglyphics	12
honorable	11
hull	2
injected	52
jagged	43
league	30
luster	32
magnifying	13
makeshift	1
mammoths	50
minerals	42
molten	43
observed	52
on-line	20
paca	50
pampas	51
pierced	11
process	13
properties	32
pulp	42
refugee	1
representatives	31
reserves	51
respiratory	22
revenue	51
scale	32
segregated	30
senators	31
serape	41
serpent	50
slithered	11
sprint	11
strategy	20
suction	3
sufficient	42
tariffs	31
territory	31
texture	32
thermal	22
thrive	22
tourism	51
traces	52
watertight	2

Concept Words

In lessons that feature social studies, science, or mathematics selections, words that are unique to the content and whose meanings are essential to the selection are treated as concept words. Many of these words appear in boldface type and are often followed by a phonetic respelling and a definition.

Word	Lesson
angle	44
Arabic	14
azurite	32
carbon monoxide	22
chlorophyll	13
cinder-cone	43
Coelenterata	3
composite	43
conduit	43
crater	43
data	53
decimal places	4
decimal point	4
double bar graph	53
Echinodermata	3
end point	44
environment	22
epidemic	52
eruption	43
flagellum	3
flourite	32
horizontal axis	53
horizontal bar graph	53
immunity	52
lava	43
line	44
line graph	53
line segment	44
magma	43
malachite	32
microbes	52
photosynthesis	13
point	44
pollutants	22
Porifera	3
precious	32
primates	18
quartz	32
ray	44
regenerate	3
semiprecious	32
shield volcanoes	43
side	44
stomates	13
symbol	14
tentacles	3
vent	43
vertex	44
vertical axis	53
vertical bar graph	53

Read the following selection. Then choose the best answer for each question. Mark your answer on the answer sheet.

The Biggest Hurdle

1. I watched the helicopter as it flew over the hills of my dad's ranch. Dad was flying the helicopter looking for lost calves. There I was, standing by the pickup truck, unable to do anything but watch. Sitting in the truck was Will Torrance, the ranch foreman. He's worked for my dad for many years.

2. I leaned against the truck, wanting desperately to help. The sky was blue with tiny puffs of cloud. Sunlight reflected off the hills, and there was a gentle breeze.

3. Suddenly, I heard my dad's voice crackling over the radio mike. Will picked up the mike.

4. "This is Will," he said. "Go ahead, Floyd."

5. "Just as we suspected, Will. Rustlers in Buzzard Canyon," said Dad. His voice sounded excited. "I just spotted them. They're herding some of our cattle into a trailer truck."

6."I'm on my way," said Will. "I'll have to ride. The canyon is too rough to catch up to them in the pickup."

7. "Right," said Dad. "I'll follow them as long as I can. I'm running low on fuel."

8. Will jumped out of the truck. I ran after him. "Wait for me!" I shouted.

9. "You can't come," Will said over his shoulder. "You stay right here, Sue. You hear?"

10. I glared at Will as he rode off. How was I ever going to learn about ranching? When were Will and Dad going to realize that I was thirteen years old? Oh well, maybe there was nothing I could do to help. Even so, I couldn't just wait at the ranch. I headed for the barn and saddled my horse, Rainbow.

11. As I rode along the north trail, I thought about Dad. I knew he was worried. In the past few years, rustlers had made off with hundreds of Dad's cattle. Each time the rustlers had gotten away. Each time I watched Dad become more anxious about losing the ranch. Even so, Dad had a lot of confidence. He was not one to give up easily.

12. I looked up and saw Dad's helicopter circling the north end of the canyon. That meant the rustlers were coming to the end of the canyon. They were nearing a highway where they could make a fast getaway.

13. I nudged Rainbow into a gallop, grateful that I was a good rider. As I reached the top of a rise in the trail, I spotted Will's horse. It was peacefully grazing. Will was sitting on the grass holding his leg.

14. "The horse stumbled, and I went head over heels," he said. "Think he stepped into a prairie-dog hole. Anyway, I pulled a leg muscle, but I'll be all right in a while. You ride back to the ranch, Sue, and call the state troopers at Hooper Falls."

15. "But it will be too late by the time the state troopers get here. The rustlers will get away again," I said.

16. Will stared as I rode past him. "Hey!" he shouted. "Where do you think you're going?"

17. I continued on the trail toward the end of the canyon. I wasn't sure there was anything I could do to help Dad. As a matter of fact, I hadn't the faintest idea what I would do. Maybe Will and Dad are right. This is a job for adults. What can a teenager do? Still, with all my doubts, I wasn't going to leave Dad on his own to deal with the rustlers.

18. In a few minutes, I reached the end of the canyon. I stood up in the stirrups and saw a cloud of dust coming in my direction. It was the rustlers' truck!

19. As I jumped off Rainbow, I spotted Dad's helicopter circling overhead. Then I heard the roar of the truck coming down the canyon. Somehow, I had to stop it. But how?

20. I had given up, when suddenly I had an idea. I eyed the Winchester rifle on the side of my saddle. Whenever we went out on a trail, we usually kept a Winchester within reach to shoot wolves that drifted through the ranch looking for calves.

21. I took the Winchester and headed toward some boulders. The truck roared closer. I dismounted and knelt atop a boulder, rifle ready. I felt my hands getting sweaty. Dad, and even Will, had told me that I was a good shot. But even after all those hours of practicing, I wasn't sure that I could do it. Suddenly, I remembered what Dad had told me. "The biggest hurdle is self-doubt," he had said. "You can't do anything without confidence in yourself."

22. The truck roared by. I took a deep breath. Then I brought up the rifle. I sighted at the truck tires. My finger tightened on the trigger. "Now, Sue. Now. You can stop them," I told myself. I squeezed off the first round and the next.

23. The truck kept on going. Then it lurched like a wounded animal and slammed into the side of the canyon.

24. For a moment, it was quiet. Then I heard the *whish-whish* of the helicopter blades. The helicopter settled down, and Dad stepped out.

25. I smiled as Dad waved toward me. I gave him my rifle. Together we headed toward the two rustlers, who were staggering out of the truck. Walking lightly, I don't remember ever feeling so good about myself.

1. Who is the main character in this story?
- **a.** Will
- **b.** Sue
- **c.** Dad

2. Choose the words that best describe the main character at the beginning of the story.
- **a.** very shy
- **b.** overly self-confident
- **c.** not very self-confident

3. The main character
- **a.** wants to help but doesn't know how.
- **b.** rides cattle trails.
- **c.** trips in a prairie-dog hole.

4. By the end of the story, the main character
- **a.** achieves a goal.
- **b.** does not achieve a goal.
- **c.** has a new goal to achieve.

5. The main character's conflict is with
- **a.** himself or herself.
- **b.** another character.
- **c.** an outside force.

6. Which sentence best describes this conflict?
- **a.** The main character is struggling against a fear of heights.
- **b.** The main character is struggling against a lack of self-confidence.
- **c.** The main character is struggling against overconfidence.

7. Sue's father faces a conflict with
- **a.** Sue.
- **b.** Will.
- **c.** the rustlers.

8. How is the conflict resolved?
- **a.** Will orders Sue back to the ranch.
- **b.** Sue shoots the truck tires and stops the cattle rustlers.
- **c.** Dad lands the helicopter safely.

9. The first important event in the story occurs when
- **a.** Will refuses to let Sue go with him.
- **b.** Dad spots the cattle rustlers' truck.
- **c.** Sue leans against the pickup.

10. Which event causes Sue to become involved in resolving the problem?
- **a.** Sue's watching the helicopter
- **b.** Dad's radio message to Will
- **c.** Will's fall from his horse

11. The most exciting part of the story occurs when
- **a.** Dad says the helicopter is running low on fuel.
- **b.** Sue decides to put her idea into action.
- **c.** the rustlers' truck slams into the side of the canyon.

12. The story ends with
- **a.** Sue feeling very good about herself.
- **b.** Dad landing his helicopter.
- **c.** Will finding his horse.

13. Where does the main action of the story take place?
- **a.** near a ranch house
- **b.** in a canyon
- **c.** on a highway

14. Where does the first scene take place?
- **a.** in the helicopter
- **b.** by the pickup truck
- **c.** atop a boulder

15. Where does the scene described in paragraph 12 take place?
- **a.** by the pickup truck
- **b.** on the north trail
- **c.** near the highway

16. Where does Will fall off his horse?
- **a.** at the end of the canyon
- **b.** by the ranch house
- **c.** on the north trail

17. To what does the story's title refer?
- **a.** self-doubt
- **b.** self-confidence
- **c.** self-consciousness

18. What is the author's message?
- **a.** Individuals should learn to fly helicopters.
- **b.** Individuals should be brave.
- **c.** Individuals should have confidence in themselves.

19. By the end of the story, Sue has learned that she
- **a.** should learn about ranching.
- **b.** should not chase after cattle rustlers.
- **c.** should not let self-doubt stand in her way.

20. Which of the following titles would also be appropriate for this story?
- **a.** "Cattle Rustling"
- **b.** "With the Aid of a Helicopter"
- **c.** "Think Positively"

21. What is the unstated main idea of paragraph 10?
- **a.** Will and Sue had an argument.
- **b.** Sue didn't like being treated as a child.
- **c.** It's great being thirteen years old.

22. What is the unstated main idea of paragraph 11?
- **a.** Dad was a successful rancher.
- **b.** Dad was having problems because of the cattle rustlers.
- **c.** Dad had little to worry about.

23. What is the unstated main idea of paragraph 25?
- **a.** Sue was tired but relieved.
- **b.** Sue was glad her dad had arrived.
- **c.** Sue had made it over the biggest hurdle.

24. Who is the narrator of the story?
- **a.** Sue
- **b.** Will
- **c.** Dad

25. Why is first-person point of view a good way of telling this story?
- **a.** The narrator saw most of the events happen.
- **b.** The narrator has a good sense of humor.
- **c.** The narrator describes how the rustlers feel.

26. Which of these events did the narrator *not* witness?
- **a.** the helicopter circling the canyon
- **b.** the truck slamming into the side of the canyon
- **c.** the rustlers herding cattle into the trailer truck

27. Who first spotted the rustlers?
- **a.** Will
- **b.** Dad
- **c.** Sue

28. The word *lurched* in paragraph 23 means

a. "rolled over."
b. "came to a sudden stop."
c. "swayed suddenly to one side."

29. Choose the correct definition of the word *rise* as it is used in paragraph 13.

a. standing position
b. hill
c. advance in importance

30. Choose the correct definition of the word *round* as it is used in paragraph 22.

a. a single outburst
b. a complete game
c. a charge of ammunition

Read the following selection. Then choose the best answer for each question. Mark your answer on the answer sheet.

A Way of Life

1. "Roll out!" the chuck wagon boss shouts. It is four o'clock in the morning. In the darkness, the cowhands stumble out of their tents. They head for the cook tent, their boots swishing through the high grass. The cowhands line up for breakfast—bacon and eggs, biscuits with honey, hot cakes covered with syrup, and steaming coffee. They need a good breakfast because they have a long morning of hard work ahead of them. As the sun rises, they ride out of camp to begin their special kind of work. Some people still call them *cowboys,* but they prefer to be called *cowhands.* That is a better name because they are hired *hands,* or workers, who look after cows.

Cowhands Help Feed People

2. The work that cowhands do is important. They help feed Americans and people in other countries. Many people like to eat beef. Beef is a valuable food because it contains proteins and vitamins, which are important to our health. We eat beef in such popular forms as steaks, roasts, frankfurters, and hamburgers. Each year, Americans eat an average of 90 pounds (40.5 kilograms) of beef per person. Cowhands tend the cattle that are raised for beef. They take care of more than 100 million beef cattle on ranches in Wyoming, Montana, and other western states.

Learning to Be a Cowhand

3. Some people think that all a cowhand needs to know is how to ride a horse. A cowhand has to have many skills. Handling a rope on horseback, a cowhand must be able to lasso a running cow. A cowhand must also know how to tend newborn calves, round up and herd cattle, mend fences, wrestle calves for branding, and break in wild horses. It takes a cowhand about three years to learn the basic skills of the job.

4. Cowhands usually work in crews of five or six. In an average crew, about half of the cowhands are forty or more years old and have many years of experience behind them. The others are in their late teens or early twenties and are still learning cowhand skills. In this way, the young cowhands are like apprentices.

Why People Work as Cowhands

5. Cowhands work long hours. For weeks at a time, they work as many as fourteen hours a day without a day off. No matter what the weather, the work has to be done. Cowhands often have to work in rain, snow, and freezing cold. Their work is dangerous. Many cowhands have been thrown by a horse or struck by the flying hooves of a frightened calf at branding time. For the long hours and the dangers they endure, cowhands receive low wages. Why, then, do people follow this way of life?

6. Cowhands enjoy the independence of their work. They know what has to be done, and—without having to be told—they do it. They also enjoy the variety in their job. One day, a cowhand is roping steers. Another day, a cowhand may be checking fences, pitching hay, or herding cattle. Also, like cowhands of the past, they take great pride in their work. They enjoy working in clean air and beautiful country—rolling grassland, gentle streams, and graceful pines.

How Cowhand Work Has Changed

7. Cowhands call food *chuck.* Years ago, cowhands lined up beside a chuck wagon for their meals. In contrast, most ranches today use special trucks to bring hot food to cowhands. In the past, the only way to look for stray cattle was on horseback. Now pickup trucks or helicopters are used to search for wandering cattle. Digging holes for fence posts was a regular chore for cowhands, but now this unpleasant task is done by machines.

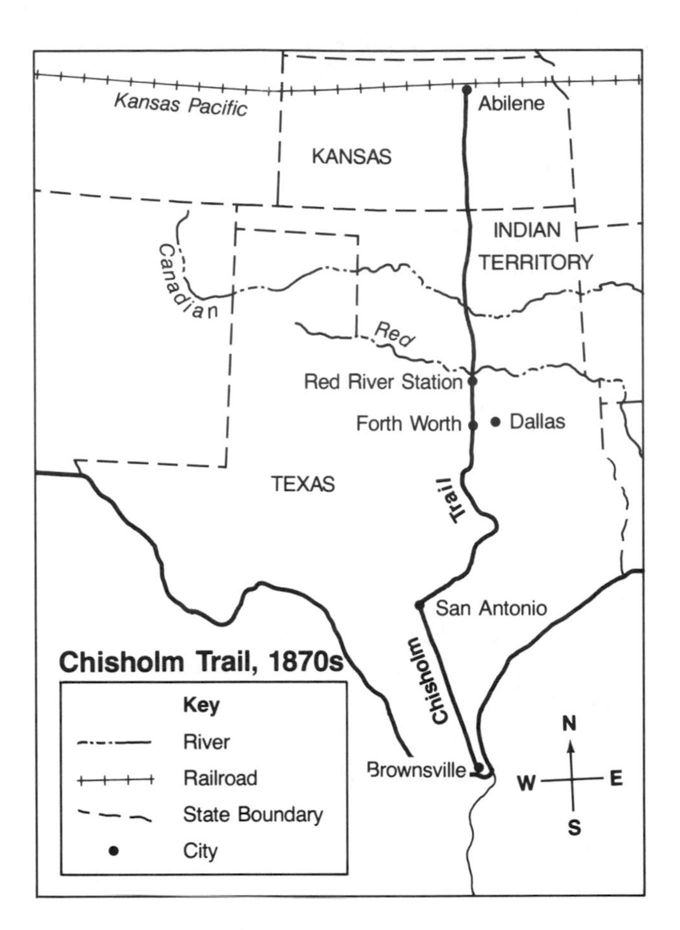

Chisholm Trail, 1870s

8. One of the most tiring jobs for cowhands of the nineteenth century was getting a herd to railroad towns. Cowhands herded cattle for hundreds of miles along trails. One of the most famous of these was the 1,200-mile (1,920-kilometer) Chisholm Trail. The journey along these trails took several months. When the herds reached the railroad towns, the cattle were shipped to Chicago and other meat-packing centers.

9. In many ways a cowhand's way of life has not changed. Although cowhands now take cattle to shipping pens that are not more than a day's travel away, a cowhand still works long hours for little pay and has to withstand heat, cold, and loneliness. Like cowhands of the past, today's cowhands must be skilled in handling a rope, herding cattle, and riding a horse. They must want to live a simple but rugged life. "It's a way of life," said one cowhand, "that I wouldn't want to trade for anything."

31. Choose the main idea of paragraph 2.
- **a.** The work that cowhands do is important.
- **b.** Each year, Americans eat an average of 90 pounds (40.5 kilograms) of beef per person.
- **c.** Many people like to eat beef.

32. Choose the main idea of paragraph 3.
- **a.** Some people think that all a cowhand needs to know is how to ride a horse.
- **b.** A cowhand has to have many skills.
- **c.** It takes a cowhand about three years to learn the basic skills of the job.

33. Choose the main idea of paragraph 9.
- **a.** In many ways a cowhand's way of life has not changed.
- **b.** A cowhand still works long hours for little pay and has to withstand heat, cold, and loneliness.
- **c.** Like cowhands of the past, today's cowhands must be skilled in handling a rope, herding cattle, and riding a horse.

34. What is the unstated main idea of paragraph 5?
- **a.** A cowhand's work is exciting.
- **b.** A cowhand's job is sometimes dangerous.
- **c.** A cowhand's job is sometimes difficult.

35. What is the unstated main idea of paragraph 6?
- **a.** People become cowhands because they like outdoor work.
- **b.** People become cowhands for a number of reasons.
- **c.** People become cowhands because of the job's variety.

36. What is the unstated main idea of paragraph 7?
- **a.** Machines have brought changes to the lives of cowhands.
- **b.** Cowhands have more time for relaxation today.
- **c.** Cowhands of today prefer to use trucks when herding cattle.

37. The unstated main idea of paragraph 4 is that cowhands vary greatly in age and skill. Which detail supports this main idea?

a. Cowhands usually work in crews.
b. There are five or six people in a crew.
c. About half the cowhands in a crew are experienced, and the others are learners.

38. Find the main idea of paragraph 8. Then choose the detail that supports the main idea.

a. The Chisholm was the most famous trail for herding cattle.
b. The journey to railroad towns took several months.
c. From the railroad towns, the cattle were shipped to meat-packing centers.

39. Cowhands need a good breakfast because they have

a. only two meals a day.
b. to conserve energy.
c. a long morning of hard work ahead of them.

40. Cowhands work even in bad weather because

a. they dislike working indoors.
b. the work has to be done.
c. cattle can be herded more easily when it rains or snows.

41. One reason people become cowhands is that they

a. enjoy independence.
b. receive good wages.
c. lead an exciting life.

42. In contrast to the past, most ranches today use

a. special trucks to bring hot food to cowhands.
b. helicopters to herd cattle to shipping pens.
c. pickup trucks to deliver cattle to market.

43. Like cowhands of the past, today's cowhands must be skilled in

a. chopping wood, finding water, and cooking.
b. handling a rope, herding cattle, and riding a horse.
c. digging holds for fence posts and setting up a tent.

44. As in the past, cowhands today

a. work long hours but earn high wages.
b. live a simple but rugged life.
c. work only in the morning.

45. What is the meaning of the word *hands* in paragraph 1?

a. workers
b. part of the arm below the wrist
c. people who look after cows

46. What is the meaning of *apprentices* in paragraph 4?

a. young cowhands
b. learners or beginners
c. experienced workers

47. In paragraph 7, a *chuck wagon* is a ________ wagon.

a. store
b. supply
c. food

48. A word that has the same meaning as *stray* in paragraph 7 is

a. wandering.
b. searching.
c. digging.

49. Which of the following statements is a fact?

a. Beef cattle are raised in western states.
b. Herding cattle is the best part of a cowhand's job.
c. Most cows are ugly and mean.

50. Which of the following statements is an opinion?

a. A cowhand works long hours.
b. Cowhands lead a simple but rugged life.
c. The best cowhands come from Montana.

51. *Cowhands in the past were better riders than cowhands of today.* This statement is
 a. a fact.
 b. an opinion.
 c. neither of the above.

52. *A cowhand has to learn many skills.* This statement is
 a. an opinion.
 b. a fact.
 c. both of the above.

53. Some American beef is
 a. important to cattle trails.
 b. low in proteins and vitamins.
 c. shipped to other countries.

54. Young cowhands learn most of their skills by
 a. attending special schools.
 b. working with experienced cowhands.
 c. studying books about ranch life.

55. Today, finding stray cattle is
 a. easier than in the past.
 b. more difficult than in the past.
 c. about as difficult as in the past.

56. Choose the correct definition for the word *handling* as it is used in paragraph 3.
 a. holding
 b. managing or controlling
 c. touching with the hand

Use the map on page AT6 to answer questions 57 through 60.

57. Which city was at the end of the Chisholm Trail?
 a. San Antonio
 b. Abilene
 c. Brownsville

58. In which direction did the Kansas Pacific Railroad go?
 a. west and east
 b. north and south
 c. neither of the above

59. Which village on the trail was northwest of Dallas?
 a. San Antonio
 b. Fort Worth
 c. Red River Station

60. What was the first river the trail crossed?
 a. Canadian
 b. Red
 c. Kansas Pacific

Read the following selection. Then choose the best answer for each question. Mark your answer on the answer sheet.

Prairie Dogs

1. Prairie dogs are ground squirrels. Other animals that belong to this group are chipmunks and ground hogs. Prairie dogs live in the prairies of the western United States, and they bark like a dog. That is why they are called prairie dogs.

Kinds of Prairie Dogs

2. The prairie dog is a short-tailed animal with small eyes, rounded ears, and short legs. Its fur is grayish brown in color.

3. There are two major groups of prairie dogs: black-tailed and white-tailed. The black-tailed prairie dog is about 1 foot (30 centimeters) long and weighs about 3 pounds (1.4 kilograms). The white-tailed prairie dog is smaller in size and has a white tip on its tail. Black-tailed prairie dogs live in western states, including Texas, Oklahoma, Kansas, Nebraska, and Montana. White-tailed prairie dogs are fewer in number. Unlike the black-tailed prairie dog, the white-tailed **hibernates** (HI bər nayts) in the winter.

4. The main food of prairie dogs is grass. During **droughts** (droutz), when there is little or no rain, prairie dogs eat the roots of plants. By late summer, prairie dogs spend much of their time eating. They must store up fat within their bodies for the winter. In one month, a prairie dog eats more than twice its own weight.

Dog Towns

5. Like chipmunks and other ground squirrels, prairie dogs live in underground burrows. A prairie dog builds its burrow by digging a shaft about 12 feet (about 4 meters) deep. Along the length of the shaft, the prairie dog digs several side tunnels called turning bays. Prairie dogs use the turning bays to hide from their enemies. At the bottom of the burrow, the animals dig a nesting chamber. In this chamber, prairie dogs sleep and raise their young. At the entrance and exit of the burrows, they build up a mound of earth. The mounds keep the burrows from being flooded during heavy rains. The entrance and exit mounds are of different heights to allow for a steady supply of oxygen.

6. Prairie dogs are very sociable animals. They live together in communities that are called dog towns. A town may have many burrows. Years ago, some dog towns extended

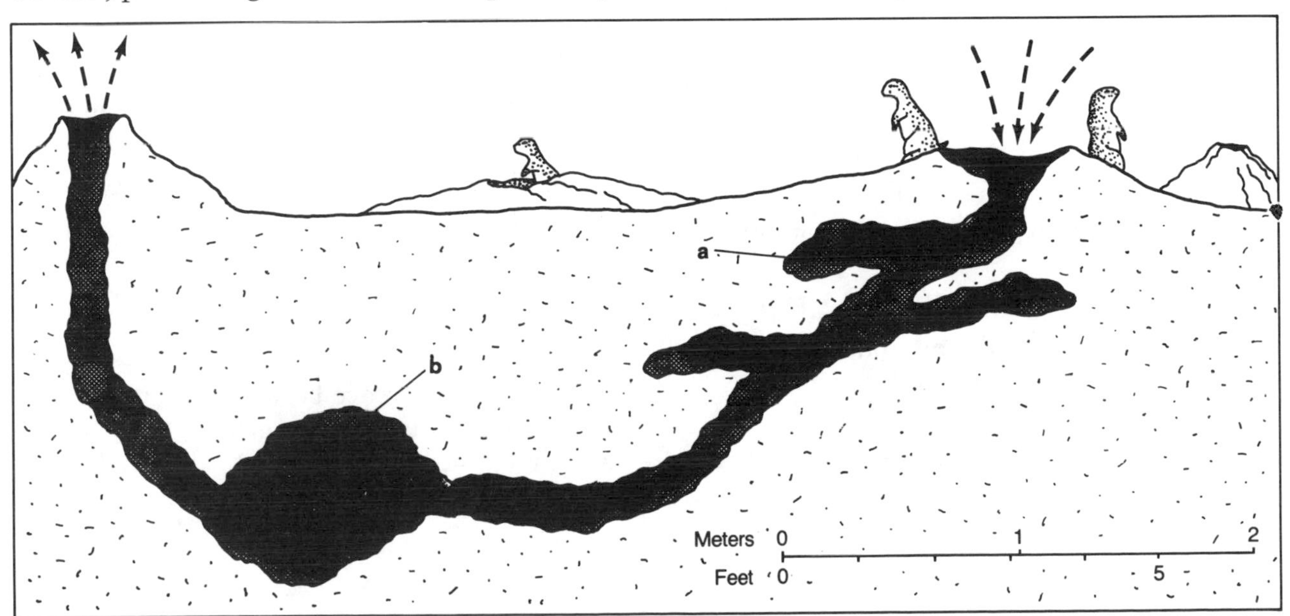

for miles and housed millions of prairie dogs. One of the largest dog towns, in northern Texas, was 155 miles (250 kilometers) long and 62 miles (100 kilometers) wide. More than 300 million prairie dogs lived in this dog town.

How Prairie Dogs Protect Themselves

7. Prairie dogs have enemies all around them. Some of their enemies, such as eagles and hawks, are in the air. Other enemies are on the ground. They include coyotes, foxes, and bobcats. Even in burrows, prairie dogs are not safe. Their homes are invaded by rattlesnakes, burrowing owls, and black-footed ferrets.

8. Prairie dogs have different ways of protecting themselves. They often sit upright, which helps them to see an approaching enemy. They also keep the grass that is growing around burrows nibbled close to the ground. This makes it difficult for enemies to approach without being seen. But the prairie dog's best protection is barking. When a prairie dog spots an enemy, it gives a warning bark. Instantly all the prairie dogs dive into their burrows. When the danger has passed, a prairie dog gives an all-clear bark. The prairie dogs then cautiously come out of their burrows.

Prairie Dogs Cause Problems

9. Prairie dogs are pests to farmers and ranchers. In addition to grass and roots, the animals eat grains, **alfalfa** (al FAL fə), and other crops. Precious irrigation water for crops often drains into burrows. Sometimes a running horse or cow breaks a leg by stepping into these holes.

10. Large numbers of prairie dogs have been killed by poisoning, shooting, and drowning. Since about 1900, their population has been reduced by more than 90 percent. Today certain kinds of prairie dogs, such a the Utah white-tail, are in danger of being wiped out. Laws are being passed to prevent them from becoming extinct.

61. In which group does the prairie dog belong?

- **a.** ground squirrel
- **b.** ground hog
- **c.** western dog

62. Which animal belongs to the same group as prairie dogs?

- **a.** chicken
- **b.** snake
- **c.** chipmunk

63. What are the two major groups of prairie dogs?

- **a.** white-tipped and black-tipped
- **b.** black-tailed and white-tailed
- **c.** hibernating and nonhibernating

64. How do the two groups differ?

- **a.** length of tail
- **b.** size
- **c.** location

65. What effect do the mounds of earth at the entrance and exit have on the burrow?

- **a.** They keep the burrows from being flooded.
- **b.** They protect the burrows from caveins.
- **c.** They hide the burrows from enemies.

66. Prairie dogs keep the grass that is growing around burrows nibbled close to the ground. What effect does this have?

- **a.** It makes the grass grow thicker.
- **b.** It makes for more attractive surroundings.
- **c.** It makes it easier to see enemies approaching.

67. Another difference between the two groups of prairie dogs is that one group __________, while the other does not.

- **a.** hibernates
- **b.** eats grass and roots
- **c.** lives in burrows

68. The number of prairie dogs
- **a.** will probably decrease.
- **b.** will probably increase.
- **c.** will probably not change.

69. Choose the main idea of paragraph 6.
- **a.** Prairie dogs are very sociable animals.
- **b.** They live together in communities that are called dog towns.
- **c.** A town may have many burrows.

70. The main idea of paragraph 8 is that prairie dogs have different ways of protecting themselves. Which detail best supports this main idea?
- **a.** Grass grows around burrows.
- **b.** Prairie dogs dig long burrows.
- **c.** The prairie dog gives a warning bark.

71. Find the main idea of paragraph 9. Then choose the detail that supports the main idea.
- **a.** Prairie dogs eat grass and roots.
- **b.** Prairie dogs eat crops.
- **c.** Prairie dogs are pests to farmers and ranchers.

72. Choose the correct definition of *bays* as it is used in paragraph 5.
- **a.** small bodies of water
- **b.** long, deep barking sounds
- **c.** sections or compartments

Use the diagram on page AT9 to answer questions 73–76.

73. In the diagram, which is taller, the entrance mound or the exit mound?
- **a.** the exit mound
- **b.** the entrance mound
- **c.** neither

74. The burrow in the diagram has a depth of approximately
- **a.** 3 feet (1 meter).
- **b.** 5 feet (1.6 meters).
- **c.** 2 feet (6 meters).

75. The section marked *a* is
- **a.** an entrance.
- **b.** a turning bay.
- **c.** a nesting chamber.

76. The section marked *b* is
- **a.** an exit.
- **b.** a turning bay.
- **c.** a nesting chamber.

Questions 77 through 80 are word problems. Use the space below each one for your calculations.

77. The largest prairie-dog town, in northern Texas, was 250 kilometers long. Two smaller prairie-dog towns were 68 kilometers long and 89 kilometers long. How much longer is the largest prairie-dog town than the two smaller towns together?
- **a.** 193 km
- **b.** 93 km
- **c.** 107 km

78. If all three prairie-dog towns in question 77 were placed end to end, how many kilometers long would they be?
- **a.** 407 km
- **b.** 417 km
- **c.** 370 km

79. Assume that the prairie-dog population of dog town *A* in 1900 was about 500,000. Since that year, the population has been reduced by about 430,000. Assume that the prairie-dog population of dog town *B* in 1900 was about 350,000. Its population has decreased about 140,000. How many more prairie dogs are left in town *B* than in town *A*?

a. 70,000
b. 140,000
c. 210,000

80. The average black-tailed prairie dog weighs 1.4 kilograms. The average white-tailed prairie dog weighs 1 kilogram. In a month, each kind of prairie dog eats about twice its own weight. How much more does the black-tailed prairie dog eat than the white-tailed prairie dog?

a. 0.8 kg
b. 1.4 kg
c. 2.4 kg

A. Use the following dictionary entry to answer questions 81 through 85.

> **piece** (pēs) ***n.*** **1** a part broken or separated from a whole thing [The glass shattered and I swept up the *pieces*.] **2** a part or section of a whole, thought of as complete by itself [a *piece* of meat; a *piece* of land]. **3** any one of a set or group of things [a dinner set of 52 *pieces;* a chess *piece*]. **4** a work of music, writing, or art [a *piece* for the piano]. **5** a firearm, as a rifle [an old shooting *piece*]. **6** a coin [a fifty-cent *piece*]. **7** a single item or example [a *piece* of information]. **8** a thing or the amount of a thing made up as a unit [to sell cloth by the *piece*]. ◆***v.*** **1** to add a piece or pieces to, as in making larger or repairing [to *piece* a pair of trousers]. **2** to join the pieces of, as in mending [to *piece* together a broken jug]. **3** to eat a snack between meals: *used only in everyday talk.* —**pieced, piec′ing** —**go to pieces, 1** to fall apart. **2** to lose control of oneself, as in crying. —**of a piece** or **of one piece,** of the same sort; alike. —☆**speak one's piece,** to say what one really thinks about something.

81. How many noun meanings of the entry word are given?
- **a.** 3
- **b.** 8
- **c.** 13

82. How many verb meanings of the entry word are given?
- **a.** 8
- **b.** 2
- **c.** 3

83. Which of the following is the respelling of the entry word?
- **a.** pēs
- **b.** —pieced, piec′ing
- **c.** [The glass shattered and I swept up the *pieces.*]

84. Which of the following is a verb meaning of the entry word?
- **a.** to join the pieces of, as in mending
- **b.** speak one's piece
- **c.** a part broken or separated from a whole thing

85. The expression "go to pieces" is
- **a.** used only in everyday talk.
- **b.** a definition.
- **c.** an idiom.

86. To change the meaning of *understood* to "wrongly understood," you would add the prefix
- **a.** *dis-.*
- **b.** *pre-.*
- **c.** *mis-.*

87. To change the meaning of *agree* to the opposite of *agree*, you would add the prefix
- **a.** *pre-.*
- **b.** *dis-.*
- **c.** *trans-.*

88. To change the meaning of *eat* to "eat too much," you would add the prefix
- **a.** *mis-.*
- **b.** *under-.*
- **c.** *over-.*

89. To change the meaning of *set* to "set ahead," you would add the prefix
- **a.** *dis-.*
- **b.** *mis-.*
- **c.** *pre-.*

90. To change the meaning of *end* to "without end," you would add the suffix
- **a.** *-en.*
- **b.** *-less.*
- **c.** *-ly.*

91. To change the meaning of *sorrow* to "full of sorrow," you would add the suffix
- **a.** *-ment.*
- **b.** *-ing.*
- **c.** *-ful.*

92. To change the meaning of *haste* to "make haste," you would add the suffix
- **a.** *-ly.*
- **b.** *-ful.*
- **c.** *-en.*

93. Choose the correct way to divide the word *silky* into syllables.
- **a.** silk y
- **b.** sil ky
- **c.** si lk y

94. Choose the correct way to divide the word *wagon* into syllables.
- **a.** wa gon
- **b.** wag on
- **c.** wa g on

95. Choose the correct way to divide the word *burrow* into syllables.
    - a. burr ow
    - b. bur row
    - c. bu rrow

96. Choose the correct way to divide the word *mellow* into syllables.
    - a. me llow
    - b. mel low
    - c. mell ow

97. What is the root word in *peacefully*?
    - a. fully
    - b. peace
    - c. peaceful

98. What is the root word in *disappearing*?
    - a. dis
    - b. appearing
    - c. appear

99. What is the root word in *underdeveloped*?
    - a. under
    - b. develop
    - c. developed

100. What is the root in the word *portable*?
    - a. port
    - b. able
    - c. table

Name ______________________________

Student Answer Sheet

Test 1

	a	b	c
1	○	○	○
2	○	○	○
3	○	○	○
4	○	○	○
5	○	○	○
6	○	○	○
7	○	○	○
8	○	○	○
9	○	○	○
10	○	○	○
11	○	○	○
12	○	○	○
13	○	○	○
14	○	○	○
15	○	○	○
16	○	○	○
17	○	○	○
18	○	○	○
19	○	○	○
20	○	○	○
21	○	○	○
22	○	○	○
23	○	○	○
24	○	○	○
25	○	○	○
26	○	○	○
27	○	○	○
28	○	○	○
29	○	○	○
30	○	○	○

Test 2

	a	b	c
31	○	○	○
32	○	○	○
33	○	○	○
34	○	○	○
35	○	○	○
36	○	○	○
37	○	○	○
38	○	○	○
39	○	○	○
40	○	○	○
41	○	○	○
42	○	○	○
43	○	○	○
44	○	○	○
45	○	○	○
46	○	○	○
47	○	○	○
48	○	○	○
49	○	○	○
50	○	○	○
51	○	○	○
52	○	○	○
53	○	○	○
54	○	○	○
55	○	○	○
56	○	○	○
57	○	○	○
58	○	○	○
59	○	○	○
60	○	○	○

Test 3

	a	b	c
61	○	○	○
62	○	○	○
63	○	○	○
64	○	○	○
65	○	○	○
66	○	○	○
67	○	○	○
68	○	○	○
69	○	○	○
70	○	○	○
71	○	○	○
72	○	○	○
73	○	○	○
74	○	○	○
75	○	○	○
76	○	○	○
77	○	○	○
78	○	○	○
79	○	○	○
80	○	○	○

Test 4

	a	b	c
81	○	○	○
82	○	○	○
83	○	○	○
84	○	○	○
85	○	○	○
86	○	○	○
87	○	○	○
88	○	○	○
89	○	○	○
90	○	○	○
91	○	○	○
92	○	○	○
93	○	○	○
94	○	○	○
95	○	○	○
96	○	○	○
97	○	○	○
98	○	○	○
99	○	○	○
100	○	○	○

	Test 1	Test 2	Test 3	Test 4		
Number Possible	30	30	20	20	Total	100
Number Incorrect					Total	
Score					Total	

Class Record–Keeping Chart

Test Item	Skill	Name									
1–4	Understanding character										
5–8	Identifying conflict and resolution										
9–12	Identifying plot										
13–16	Identifying setting										
17–20	Inferring theme										
21–23, 34-36	Identifying/Inferring the unstated main idea										
24–27	Identifying point of view										
28, 45–48,	Using context clues										
29–30, 56, 72	Recognizing multiple meanings of words										
31–33, 69	Identifying the main idea										
37–38, 70–71	Identifying the main idea and supporting details										
39–41, 65–66	Identifying cause and effect										
42–44, 67	Comparing and contrasting										
49–52	Distinguishing fact from opinion										
53–55, 68	Making inferences										
57–60	Reading a map										
61–64	Classifying										
73–76	Reading text with diagrams										
77–80	Solving word problems										
81–85	Using a dictionary entry										
86-100	Recognizing root words, roots, prefixes, suffixes, and syllables										
	Total Incorrect										
	Score (subtract total incorrect from 100)										